The Psychobiology of
Bulimia

The
PROGRESS IN PSYCHIATRY
Series

David Spiegel, M.D.,
Series Editor

The Psychobiology of Bulimia

Edited by
James I. Hudson, M.D.
Harrison G. Pope, Jr., M.D.

American
Psychiatric
Press, Inc.

1400 K Street, N.W.
Washington, DC 20005

Copyright © 1987 American Psychiatric Press, Inc.
ALL RIGHTS RESERVED
Manufactured in the United States of America
First Edition

The paper used in this publication meets the minimum requirements of American National Standard for Information Sciences—Permanence of Paper for Printed Library Materials, ANSI Z39.48-1984.

Library of Congress Cataloging-in-Publication Data

The Psychobiology of bulimia.

(The Progress in psychiatry series)
Based on a symposium held at the 139th Annual Meeting of the American Psychiatric Association in Washington, D.C., May 1986.
Includes bibliographies.
1. Bulimia—Physiological aspects—Congresses.
2. Psychobiology—Congresses.   I. Hudson, James I., 1953-   .   II. Pope, Harrison.   III. American Psychiatric Association.   Meeting (139th : 1986 : Washington, D.C.)   IV. Series.   [DNLM: 1. Bulimia—pscyhology—congresses.   2. Neurobiology—congresses. WM 175 P9744 1986]

RC552.B84P89   1987   616.85'2   87-14431
ISBN 0-88048-139-0

Contents

Relationship of Bulimia to Other Disorders

Contributors

Timothy Brewerton, M.D.
Medical Staff Fellow, Section of Biomedical Psychiatry, National
Institute of Mental Health, Bethesda, Maryland

Gregory M. Brown, M.D., Ph.D., F.R.C.P.(C)
Professor and Chairman, Department of Neurosciences, McMaster
University, Hamilton, Ontario, Canada

Paul M. Copeland, M.D.
Endocrine Unit, Massachusetts General Hospital; Co-Director,
Eating Disorders Program, Salem Hospital, Salem, Massachusetts;
Clinical Instructor in Medicine, Harvard Medical School, Boston,
Massachusetts

Daniel Costa, M.D.
Resident in Psychiatry, University of Toronto, Ontario, Canada

Michael H. Ebert, M.D.
Professor and Chairman, Department of Psychiatry, Vanderbilt
University School of Medicine, Nashville, Tennessee

Manfred M. Fichter, M.D.
Psychosomatic Hospital, Roseneck Psychiatric Hospital of the
University of Munich, Munich, Federal Republic of Germany

Michael Genhart, B.S.
Medical Staff Fellow, Clinical Psychobiology Branch, National
Institute of Mental Health, Bethesda, Maryland

David T. George, M.D.
Senior Staff Fellow, National Institute of Mental Health Laboratory
of Clinical Science, Bethesda, Maryland

Madeline Gladis, M.A.
Medical Staff Fellow, Section of Biomedical Psychiatry, National
Institute of Mental Health, Bethesda, Maryland

Alexander H. Glassman, M.D.
Chief, Clinical Psychopharmacology, New York State Psychiatric Institute; Professor of Clinical Psychiatry, College of Physicians and Surgeons, Columbia University, New York, New York

Mark S. Gold, M.D.
Director of Research, Fair Oaks Hospital, Summit, New Jersey

David S. Goldstein, M.D., Ph.D.
Senior Investigator, Hypertension-Endocrine Branch, National Heart, Lung, and Blood Institute, Bethesda, Maryland

Harry E. Gwirtsman, M.D.
Director of Adult In-patient and Day Treatment Program, Neuropsychiatric Institute and Hospital Center for the Health Services, Los Angeles, California; Assistant Professor of Psychiatry, University of California at Los Angeles Medical School

David B. Herzog, M.D.
Director, Eating Disorders Unit, Massachusetts General Hospital; Assistant Professor of Psychiatry, Harvard Medical School, Boston, Massachusetts

James I. Hudson, M.D.
Associate Chief, Epidemiology Laboratory, Laboratories for Psychiatric Research, McLean Hospital, Belmont, Massachusetts; Assistant Professor of Psychiatry, Harvard Medical School, Boston, Massachusetts

David C. Jimerson, M.D.
Chief, Section on Biomedical Psychiatry, National Institute of Mental Health Laboratory of Clinical Science, Bethesda, Maryland

Jeffrey M. Jonas, M.D.
Director, Eating Disorders Program, Fair Oaks Hospital, Summit, New Jersey

Allan S. Kaplan, M.D., F.R.C.P.(C)
Director, Eating Disorders Center, Toronto General Hospital; Assistant Professor of Psychiatry, University of Toronto, Toronto, Ontario, Canada

Walter H. Kaye, M.D.
Director, Inpatient Eating Disorders Program, Western Psychiatric Institute and Clinic; Associate Professor of Psychiatry, University of Pittsburgh School of Medicine, Pittsburgh, Pennsylvania

Sidney Kennedy, M.B., F.R.C.P.(C)
Head, Nutritional and Affective Disorders Unit, Toronto General Hospital; Assistant Professor of Psychiatry, University of Toronto, Toronto, Ontario, Canada

David J. Kupfer, M.D.
Professor and Chairman, Department of Psychiatry, Western
Psychiatric Institute and Clinic, University of Pittsburgh School of
Medicine, Pittsburgh, Pennsylvania

Reinhold Laessle, Ph.D.
Division of Psychoneuroendocrinology, Max-Planck-Institute for
Psychiatry, Munich, Federal Republic of Germany

David C. Lindy, M.D.
Research Fellow, New York State Psychiatric Institute, College of
Physicians and Surgeons, Columbia University, New York, New
York

Joseph F. Lipinski, M.D.
Chief, Clinical Research Section, and Director, Mental Health
Research Center, Laboratories for Psychiatric Research, McLean
Hospital, Belmont, Massachusetts; Associate Professor of Psychiatry,
Harvard Medical School, Boston, Massachusetts

James E. Mitchell, M.D.
Eating Disorders Program, Associate Professor of Psychiatry,
University of Minnesota School of Medicine, Minneapolis,
Minnesota

John E. Morley, M.B., B.Ch.
Director, Geriatric Research, Education and Clinical Center,
Sepulveda V.A. Medical Center, Sepulveda, California; Professor of
Medicine, University of California at Los Angeles Medical School,
Los Angeles, California

Victor Parienti, M.D.
Clinical Fellow, Department of Psychiatry, University of Toronto,
Toronto, Ontario, Canada

Karl-M. Pirke, M.D.
Chief, Division of Psychoneuroendocrinology, Max-Planck-Institute
for Psychiatry, Munich, Federal Republic of Germany

Harrison G. Pope, Jr., M.D.
Chief, Epidemiology Laboratory, Laboratories for Psychiatric
Research, McLean Hospital, Belmont, Massachusetts; Associate
Professor of Psychiatry, Harvard Medical School, Boston,
Massachusetts

Steven P. Roose, M.D.
Research Psychiatrist, New York State Psychiatric Institute; Assistant
Professor of Clinical Psychiatry, College of Physicians and Surgeons,
Columbia University, New York, New York

Norman E. Rosenthal, M.D.
Chief, Outpatient Research Unit, Clinical Psychobiology Branch, National Institute of Mental Health, Bethesda, Maryland

David A. Sack, M.D.
Chief, Inpatient Research Unit, Clinical Psychobiology Branch, National Institute of Mental Health, Bethesda, Maryland

Ulrich Schweiger, M.D.
Division of Psychoneuroendocrinology, Max-Planck-Institute for Psychiatry, Munich, Federal Republic of Germany

Robert G. Skwerer, M.D.
Medical Staff Fellow, Clinical Psychobiology Branch, National Institute of Mental Health, Bethesda, Maryland

B. Timothy Walsh, M.D.
Research Psychiatrist, New York State Psychiatric Institute; Associate Professor of Clinical Psychiatry, College of Physicians and Surgeons, Columbia University, New York, New York

Thomas A. Wehr, M.D.
Chief, Clinical Psychobiology Branch, National Institute of Mental Health, Bethesda, Maryland

Guenther Wolfram, M.D.
Technical University of Munich, Munich, Federal Republic of Germany

Judith J. Wurtman, Ph.D.
Laboratory of Neuroendocrine Regulation, Massachusetts Institute of Technology, Cambridge, Massachusetts

Introduction to the Progress in Psychiatry Series

T he *Progress in Psychiatry* Series is designed to capture in print the excitement that comes from assembling a diverse group of experts from various locations to examine in detail the newest information about a developing aspect of psychiatry. This series emerged as a collaboration between the American Psychiatric Association's Scientific Program Committee and the American Psychiatric Press, Inc. Great interest was generated by a number of the symposia presented each year at the APA Annual Meeting, and we realize that much of the information presented there, carefully assembled by people who are deeply immersed in a given area, would unfortunately not appear together in print. The symposia sessions at the Annual Meetings provide an unusual opportunity for experts who otherwise might not meet on the same platform to share their diverse viewpoints for a period of three hours. Some new themes are repeatedly reinforced and gain credence, while in other instances disagreements emerge, enabling the audience and now the reader to reach informed decisions about new directions in the field. The *Progress in Psychiatry* Series allows us to publish and capture some of the best of the symposia and thus provide an in-depth treatment of specific areas which might not otherwise be presented in broader review formats.

Psychiatry is by nature an interface discipline, combining the study of mind and brain, of individual and social environments, of the humane and the scientific. Therefore, progress in the field is rarely linear—it often comes from unexpected sources. Further, new developments emerge from an array of viewpoints that do not necessarily provide immediate agreement but rather expert examination of the issues. We intend to present innovative ideas and data that will enable you, the reader, to participate in this process.

We believe the *Progress in Psychiatry* Series will provide you with an opportunity to review timely new information in specific fields of interest as they are developing. We hope you find that the excitement of the presentations is captured in the written word and that this book proves to be informative and enjoyable reading.

David Spiegel, M.D.
Series Editor
Progress in Psychiatry Series

Acknowledgments

Two individuals, more than any others involved in this project, were instrumental in the production of this monograph. David Spiegel, editor of the American Psychiatric Press's Progress in Psychiatry monograph series and a member of the symposium selection subcommittee of the American Psychiatric Association's Scientific Program Committee, recognized from our proposal for a symposium on the psychobiology of bulimia that this subject would be worthy of a monograph. Since approaching us about the possibility of editing such a volume, he has guided our efforts to put it together and has provided valuable editorial comments on each of the chapters.

Evelyn Stone, at McLean Hospital, encouraged us initially to propose the symposium on the psychobiology of bulimia and had suggested for some time that we write or edit a book on bulimia for the American Psychiatric Press. When David Spiegel presented us with the offer to do so, she was quick to point out the advantages of such a monograph and has assisted us subsequently in keeping the project on track.

James I. Hudson, M.D.
Harrison G. Pope, Jr., M.D.

Introduction

This monograph grew out of a symposium on the psychobiology of bulimia held at the Annual Meeting of the American Psychiatric Association in Washington, D.C., in May 1986. The original 6 symposium presentations have been supplemented by 8 additional contributions to form this volume. The resulting monograph, containing chapters from 12 major research groups in North America and Europe, represents something of a coming of age in this field, in that it is the first volume ever devoted to biological studies of bulimia. In contrast to the number of biological studies on the closely related eating disorder anorexia nervosa, which have yielded a voluminous literature over the past 60 years, bulimia has been the focus of scientific attention only in the last 8 years, since the first description of its existence in normal-weight individuals by Gerald Russell in 1979 and its inclusion as a separate diagnostic entity in the *Diagnostic and Statistical Manual of Mental Disorders (Third Edition)* in 1980. However, since 1982, biological research in bulimia has proceeded at a rapid pace, and the time is ripe to attempt a comprehensive review of this young and exciting field.

The volume reviews the current status of three areas: endocrine and metabolic function, neurotransmitter function, and the psychobiological relationship of bulimia to other disorders. The sections on endocrine, metabolic, and neurotransmitter function address two major questions. First, do bulimic patients exhibit specific disturbances in the systems under study? Second, if such disturbances exist, are they due to the effects of abnormal eating behavior per se, or are they attributable to a primary central nervous system disturbance that might, in turn, lead to the development of compulsive binge eating? The chapters in the section on the relationship between bulimia and other disorders use two approaches to this issue. First, two chapters review the use of biological tests that have been associated with characteristic abnormalities in other disorders (lactate infusion in panic disorder and electroencephalographic sleep in depression) to evaluate patients with bulimia for the presence of similar abnormalities. Second, a pair of chapters examine individuals with other syndromes in which there is abnormal eating behavior—seasonal affective disorder and carbohydrate craving—for clinical similarities to patients with bulimia.

As Michael Ebert discusses in his concluding commentary, the jury is still out on all of these issues. Thus, despite the impressive number of investigations reviewed in this monograph, we are at a preliminary stage in the evolution of our understanding of the psychobiology of bulimia, and it is not possible, as of yet, to either confirm or reject the various proposed unifying hypotheses under study in this area. Nevertheless, this monograph, presenting the state of the art of this rapidly expanding field, documents the encouraging start that has been made toward this end.

James I. Hudson, M.D.
Harrison G. Pope, Jr., M.D.

Chapter 1

Hypothalamic-Pituitary-Adrenal Axis in Bulimia

B. Timothy Walsh, M.D.
Steven P. Roose, M.D.
David C. Lindy, M.D.
Madeline Gladis, M.A.
Alexander H. Glassman, M.D.

Chapter 1

Hypothalamic-Pituitary-Adrenal Axis in Bulimia

The clinical features of patients with bulimia overlap, to a considerable degree, those of patients with anorexia nervosa and those of patients with major depressive illness. Research studies conducted in the last 25 years have demonstrated conclusively that many patients with these latter two syndromes have abnormalities of adrenal activity. Therefore, the study of the hypothalamic–pituitary–adrenal (HPA) axis in patients of normal weight who have bulimia is of interest, both for what it may reveal about bulimia, and for what it may tell us about the biological similarities of bulimia and anorexia nervosa and major depressive illness. Before proceeding to the data on HPA activity in bulimia, it may be useful to review briefly the disturbances of the HPA axis in anorexia nervosa and depression.

HYPOTHALAMIC–PITUITARY–ADRENAL AXIS ACTIVITY IN ANOREXIA NERVOSA

The adrenal gland in anorexia nervosa has been studied for decades. Thirty years ago, when the methods of measuring adrenal activity were crude by today's standards, adrenal activity was felt to be diminished in anorexia nervosa, and this assessment contributed to the idea that anorexia nervosa was a form of panhypopituitarism. As techniques to assess adrenal activity became more sophisticated and were applied to anorexia nervosa, it became clear that adrenal activity in anorexia nervosa was not diminished. In fact, most patients with anorexia nervosa were discovered to have increased levels of plasma cortisol (Bliss and Migeon 1957; Bethge et al. 1970; Boyar et al. 1977).

This increase in plasma cortisol in anorexia nervosa appears to be the result of two factors. First, it is clear that the rate of metabolism of cortisol in anorexia nervosa is slower than normal (Boyar et al. 1977). Second, reasonably convincing evidence has now accumulated indicating that the rate of production of cortisol, at least relative to body size, is elevated in anorexia nervosa (Walsh et al. 1978; Doerr et al. 1980). Thus, the level of cortisol is high because of both increased production and slowed metabolism. Although the nature of the cortisol abnormalities is better understood, their significance is still enigmatic. Patients with nonpsychiatric forms of malnutrition also have elevated levels of plasma cortisol, slowed rates of cortisol metabolism, and inadequate suppression of plasma cortisol by dexamethasone, suggestive of increased adrenal activity. Thus, it seems clear that the malnutrition of serious anorexia nervosa is at least one factor that contributes to the abnormalities of HPA activity. But it is less clear whether malnutrition entirely explains the HPA disturbances characteristic of underweight patients with anorexia nervosa. Is the adrenal activity of patients with anorexia nervosa consistent with their degree of malnutrition? Or do other factors, such as major depression, contribute to the HPA disturbances of anorexia nervosa?

The study of bulimic patients who are of normal body weight may be helpful in this regard. There are prominent psychological and behavioral similarities between underweight patients with anorexia nervosa and normal weight patients with bulimia. Both groups show similar preoccupations with weight and body shape, about half of patients with anorexia nervosa also engage in bulimic behavior, and about one-third of bulimic patients of normal body weight have past histories of anorexia nervosa. If the psychological and behavioral characteristics common to both syndromes play a major role in disturbing the HPA activity of anorexia nervosa, then one would predict that patients with bulimia would show abnormalities of HPA activity even at normal weight.

HYPOTHALAMUS–PITUITARY–ADRENAL ACTIVITY IN DEPRESSION

A second reason to be interested in HPA activity in bulimia is the association between eating disorders and major depressive illness. In the last 25 years it has been established that about half of patients with endogenous major depressive illness show increases of HPA activity. Recently, a number of groups have reported a high frequency of depression among normal weight patients with bulimia, though it is unclear to what degree the mood disturbance seen in these patients resembles classic forms of major depressive illness. Nonetheless, if patients with bulimia have a form of major depressive illness, one might expect to see an increase in their adrenal activity.

Therefore, the study of HPA activity in normal weight patients with bulimia is of interest both because it might help clarify which factors are responsible for the HPA disturbances of anorexia nervosa and because it might shed some light on the relationship between bulimia and typical major depressive illness.

THE DEXAMETHASONE SUPPRESSION TEST IN BULIMIA

One of the most convenient ways to assess HPA activity is use of the dexamethasone suppression test (DST). In this test, dexamethasone, usually 1 mg, is taken at 11:00 P.M. and blood is obtained the following day at one or more times, most frequently at 4:00 P.M. In normal individuals, the plasma level of cortisol usually remains less than 5 μg/dl during the following day. Individuals with increased HPA activity typically have elevated plasma levels of cortisol on the following day and it is generally assumed that an individual with a plasma cortisol level greater than 5 μg/dl following a DST (an abnomal DST) has increased HPA activity.

At least five studies have examined the DST in normal weight patients with bulimia (Gwirtsman et al. 1983; Hudson et al. 1983; Mitchell et al. 1984; Musisi and Garfinkel 1985; Lindy et al. 1985). Four of the five reports have noted a higher-than-expected frequency of abnormal DSTs. Although there have been hints of a link between a specific clinical feature of bulimia, such as the amount of weight loss or the presence of major depression, and the abnormal DST, no consistent relationship has been established between a positive DST in bulimia and severity or chronicity of illness, presence of major depression, history of anorexia nervosa, current body weight, or recent weight change. Therefore, although the elevated frequency of abnormal DSTs in bulimia is intriguing and suggests a potential link between bulimia and typical major affective illness, it has been disturbing that the likelihood of an abnormal DST could not be related to any specific clinical feature of bulimia, including the degree of mood disturbance.

PLASMA CORTISOL LEVELS IN BULIMIA

Another method of assessing HPA activity is more direct than the DST but is more time consuming. About 20 years ago techniques were developed to permit blood samples to be drawn several times an hour over 24-hour periods. In this way it was possible to document the circadian variation of plasma cortisol levels in normal individuals and also to demonstrate that in patients with major depressive illness and in underweight patients with anorexia nervosa, the plasma level of cortisol was elevated both during the day and at night.

We used this technique to assess HPA activity in 8 underweight women with anorexia nervosa, 11 women of normal weight with bulimia and 9 control subjects (Walsh et al. 1987). The results are shown in Figure 1. The plasma cortisol level for the anorexia nervosa group was found to be above normal for most of the 24-hour period. This result is consistent with previous reports of increased plasma levels of cortisol in underweight patients with anorexia nervosa. What is surprising, particularly in view of the multiple reports of abnormal DSTs in normal weight bulimic patients, is that the 24-hour pattern of cortisol secretion in the 11 bulimic women was virtually identical to that of the controls. Thus, at least by this measure, the HPA activity in this small group of normal weight bulimics seems normal.

PLASMA DEXAMETHASONE LEVELS IN BULIMIA

The results described thus far appear paradoxical. On one hand, the 24-hour pattern of cortisol secretion in normal weight bulimic patients was found to be normal and therefore significantly different

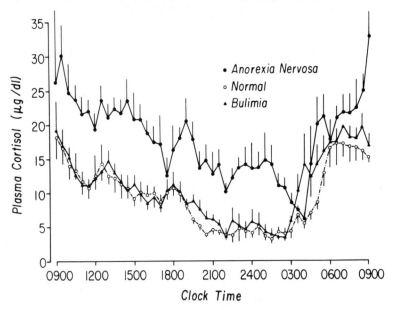

Figure 1.   Mean (± SEM) 24-hour patterns of plasma cortisol secretion in anorexia nervosa ($n = 8$), bulimia ($n = 11$), and control subjects ($n = 9$). Reprinted with permission from Walsh BT, Roose SP, Katz JL, et al: Hypothalamic–pituitary–adrenal–cortical activity in anorexia nervosa and bulimia. Psychoneuroendrocrinology 12:131-140, 1987

from that of patients with anorexia nervosa. On the other hand, patients with bulimia also have an increased frequency of positive DSTs, which is usually interpreted as a sign of increased HPA activity. Is there any way to reconcile these two observations?

Several recent studies of the DST in psychiatric patients without eating disorders have suggested that there is a marked variability among patients in the plasma levels of dexamethasone achieved following the DST. Furthermore, patients with lower plasma dexamethasone levels appear more likely to have positive DSTs (Holsboer et al. 1984; Arana et al. 1984; Johnson et al. 1984; Berger et al. 1984; Morris et al. 1986). Thus, it seems conceivable that part of the explanation for the increased frequency of abnormal DSTs in bulimia might be low levels of plasma dexamethasone.

Our colleagues Ee Sung Lo and Thomas Cooper at the New York State Psychiatric Institute have recently developed a sensitive and specific assay for plasma dexamethasone. Using this assay, they determined the concentration of dexamethasone in the plasma of 66 normal weight bulimic patients on whom we had conducted 1 mg DSTs. We therefore had available both the concentration of dexamethasone and that of cortisol in the 4:00 P.M. sample. We also carried out standard 1 mg DSTs in 26 age- and sex-matched controls and determined the plasma levels of dexamethasone and cortisol in 4:00 P.M. samples from these subjects (Walsh et al. 1986).

The plasma levels of dexamethasone varied substantially, and the mean plasma level of dexamethasone was significantly lower in the bulimic group than in the control group ($p < .002$). Furthermore, when both groups were combined, we found a highly significant relationship between the plasma level of cortisol and that of dexamethasone (Figure 2). That is, patients with low levels of dexamethasone were more likely to have positive DSTs than were patients with high levels of dexamethasone. Nineteen (83 percent) of the 23 positive DSTs occurred in subjects whose plasma dexamethasone levels were below the median plasma dexamethasone level, compared with 27 (37 percent) of the 72 negative DSTs ($p < .001$). Thirty-nine (59 percent) of the 66 bulimic patients had plasma dexamethasone levels less than the median, compared with only 7 (27 percent) of the 26 controls ($p < .02$). Thus, a low plasma dexamethasone level was statistically associated with both having a positive DST and being bulimic.

The significance of the low level of plasma dexamethasone remains unclear at this point. We examined the relationship between plasma dexamethasone level and clinical variables but found no significant association between the plasma level and age, duration of illness, binges per week, percent of ideal weight, or presence of major depression. The lower level of dexamethasone may simply reflect some patients' vomiting part of the dexamethasone dose after it had been ingested. Or, conceivably, it could reflect differences between bulimic patients and controls in the absorption and metabolism of drug. Holsboer et al. (1986) recently presented preliminary data suggesting that depressed patients with positive DSTs may metabolize dexamethasone more rapidly than do depressed patients with negative DSTs. Additional studies of the absorption and metabolism of dexamethasone in bulimia are required to determine if disturbances in such characteristics account for the low plasma level of dexamethasone in this syndrome.

We feel that the results concerning the plasma dexamethasone levels may be useful in explaining the paradoxical results of the 1 mg DST and the 24-hour monitoring of plasma cortisol. It appears that in at

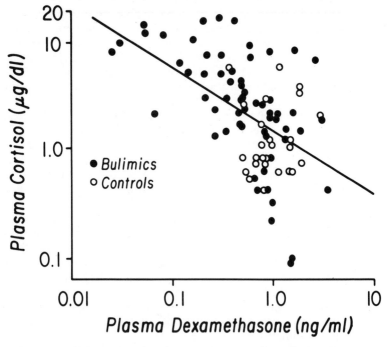

Figure 2. Plasma cortisol versus plasma dexamethasone levels at 4:00 P.M. following 1 mg dexamethasone in 62 women with bulimia and 26 controls. The regression line is log (cortisol) = 0.16 − 0.60 log (dexamethasone).

least patients with bulimia, an abnormal 1 mg DST result does not necessarily imply the presence of increased HPA activity. In some patients, it may reflect an unusually low level of plasma dexamethasone.

CONCLUSIONS

The results of our studies of normal weight patients with bulimia suggest that in general, such individuals do not show elevated HPA activity. In this way, most normal weight bulimic patients appear to differ from patients with anorexia nervosa who do show elevated plasma cortisol levels. As noted earlier, normal weight patients with bulimia resemble patients with anorexia nervosa in many ways. Both groups are mostly composed of young women who are preoccupied with body weight, have abnormal attitudes about food, and engage in abnormal patterns of eating. The fact that the 24-hour pattern of cortisol secretion is normal in normal-weight patients with bulimia implies that these psychological and behavioral characteristics in the absence of significant weight loss are insufficient to account for the abnormalities of HPA activity seen in anorexia nervosa. Similarly, it appears that HPA activity in normal weight bulimic patients is different from that of patients with endogenous major depressive illness.

It should be noted that these conclusions apply to patients of normal weight with bulimia *in general*. It would not be surprising to find individual patients who do show increased adrenal activity. For example, in Figure 2, it can be noted that several bulimic patients have high plasma cortisol levels even though their plasma dexamethasone levels are similiar to those of the controls, suggesting that some of these patients may have increased HPA activity. However, in general, it appears that patients of normal weight who have bulimia have relatively normal levels of HPA activity.

One additional caveat should be noted about the use of measures of HPA activity to examine the relationship between bulimia and typical major depressive illness. Several studies have indicated that increases in HPA activity are more likely to be observed in older patients with major depression, compared with younger patients (Feinberg and Carroll 1984; Greden et al. 1986). In other words, the presence of increased HPA activity may not be a very good marker for the presence of major depression in younger patients. Since most patients with bulimia are in their 20s, the absence of an increase in HPA activity may not be as revealing as it might seem at first glance.

REFERENCES

Arana GW, Workman RJ, Baldessarini RJ: Association between low plasma levels of dexamethasone and elevated levels of cortisol in psychiatric patients given dexamethasone. Am J Psychiatry 141:1619-1620, 1984

Berger M, Pirke K-M, Doerr P, et al: The limited utility of the dexamethasone suppression test for the diagnostic process in psychiatry. Br J Psychiatry 145:372-382, 1984

Bethge H, Nagel AM, Solbach HG, et al: Zentrale Regulationsstorung der Nebennierenrindenfunktion bei der Anorexia nervosa [Central disturbance of adrenal function in anorexia nervosa]. Materia Medica Nordmark 22:204-214, 1970

Bliss EL, Migeon CJ: Endocrinology of anorexia nervosa. J Clin Endocrinol Metab 17:766-776, 1957

Boyar RM, Hellman LD, Roffwarg HP, et al: Cortisol secretion and metabolism in anorexia nervosa. N Engl J Med 296:190-193, 1977

Doerr P, Fichter M, Pirke KM, et al: Relationship between weight gain and hypothalamic pituitary adrenal function in patients with anorexia nervosa. J Steroid Biochem 13:529-573, 1980

Feinberg M, Carroll BJ: Biological 'markers' for endogenous depression. Effect of age, severity of illness, weight loss, and polarity. Arch Gen Psychiatry 41:1080-1085, 1984

Greden JF, Tiongeo D, Haskett RF, et al: Aging increases HPA dysregulation in depressives [NR 99]. Presented at the 139th Annual Meeting of the American Psychiatric Association, Washington, DC, May 1986

Gwirtsman HE, Roy-Byrne P, Yager J, et al: Neuroendocrine abnormalities in bulimia. Am J Psychiatry 140:559-563, 1983

Holsboer F, Haack D, Gerken D, et al: Plasma dexamethasone concentrations and differential suppression response of cortisol and corticosterone in depressives and controls. Biol Psychiatry 19:281-291, 1984

Holsboer F, Wiedemann K, Boll E: Shortened dexamethasone half-life in depressed dexamethasone non-suppressors. Arch Gen Psychiatry 43:813-815, 1986

Hudson JI, Pope HG, Jonas JM, et al: Hypothalamic-pituitary-adrenal axis hyperactivity in bulimia. Psychiatry Research 8:111-117, 1983

Johnson GF, Hunt G, Kerr K, Caterson I: Dexamethasone suppression test (DST) and plasma dexamethasone levels in depressed patients. Psychiatry Res 13:305-313, 1984

Lindy DC, Walsh BT, Roose SP, et al: The dexamethasone suppression test in bulimia. Am J Psychiatry 142:1375-1496, 1985

Mitchell JE, Pyle RL, Hatsukami D, et al: The dexamethasone suppression test in patients with bulimia. J Clin Psychiatry 45:508-511, 1984

Morris H, Carr V, Gilliland J, et al: Dexamethasone concentrations and the dexamethasone suppression test in psychiatric disorders. Br J Psychiatry 148:66-69, 1986

Musisi S, Garfinkel P: Comparative dexamethasone suppression test measurements in bulimia, depression, and normal controls. Can J Psychiatry 30:190-194, 1985

Walsh BT, Katz JL, Levin J, et al: Adrenal activity in anorexia nervosa. Psychosom Med 40:499-506, 1978

Walsh BT, Roose SP, Katz JL, et al: Hypothalamic-pituitary-adrenal-cortical activity in anorexia nervosa and bulimia. Psychoneuroendocrinology 12:131-140, 1987

Walsh BT, Lindy DC, Lo ES, et al: Plasma dexamethasone levels and the DST in bulimia [NR 29]. Presented at the 139th Annual Meeting of the American Psychiatric Association, Washington, DC, May 1986

Chapter 2

Hypothalamic-Pituitary-Ovarian Axis in Bulimia

Karl-M. Pirke, M.D.
Ulrich Schweiger, M.D.
Manfred M. Fichter, M.D.

Chapter 2

Hypothalamic-Pituitary-Ovarian Axis in Bulimia

Amenorrhea is an obligatory symptom in patients with anorexia nervosa, who have a serious weight deficit. Several authors have emphasized the importance of weight limits that must be reached during weight gain in anorectic patients before the gonadotropin-releasing hormone stimulation test (Beumont et al. 1976), the 24-hour sleep–wake pattern of luteinizing hormone (Pirke et al. 1979), and the cyclic activity of the gonads (Frisch 1977) return to normal. The importance of weight deficit for the disturbance of the hypothalamic–pituitary–gonadal axis in anorexia nervosa is further emphasized by the observation that weight deficit not caused by anorexia nervosa also brings about amenorrhea (for a review see Keys et al. 1950) and disturbances of the secretion pattern of luteinizing hormone (Vigersky et al. 1977). Patients with bulimia do not have a serious weight deficit (if so, they would be classified as having anorexia nervosa, according to the criteria in the *Diagnostic and Statistical Manual of Mental Disorders [Third Edition]* [DSM-III; American Psychiatric Association 1980]). Despite this fact, amenorrhea is reported in about half of the patients suffering from bulimia nervosa (Russell 1979; Pirke et al. 1985; see also Chapter 3).

To evaluate menstrual function in bulimic patients, we conducted two studies. In the first, we followed bulimic patients for one menstrual cycle or, in the event of amenorrhea or oligomenorrhea, for six weeks. In the second study we followed bulimic patients during the early follicular phase.

STUDY 1

Fifteen patients diagnosed as having bulimia by *DSM-III* criteria, aged 20 to 36 years (mean ± SD = 23.7 ± 2.4 years), were studied. Their body weight ranged from 77 to 121 percent (99.5 ± 6.2 percent) of ideal body weight (IBW) according to Metropolitan Life Insurance Company (1959) criteria. The duration of illness ranged from 2 to 14 years (6.1 ± 3.2 years). Seven patients had a history of anorexia nervosa. No drugs other than small doses of laxatives were used by any of the patients. The control group consisted of 10 healthy women aged 20 to 30 years (mean = 26.2 years) whose menstrual cycles were normal. Body weight ranged from 95 to 118 percent (106.9 ± 6.3 percent) of IBW.

Design

Blood sampling commenced with the beginning of the menstrual cycle. Five ml of blood were obtained between 7:30 and 10:00 A.M. each Monday, Wednesday, and Friday. Plasma was stored at −20°C until analyzed. Patients and controls were weighed in their underwear.

Hormone Analysis

Luteinizing hormone (LH) and follicle-stimulating hormone (FSH) were analyzed using assay kits purchased from Serono, Freiburg, Germany. Interassay precision was 6.6 percent at an average concentration of 9.2 mU/ml for LH and 7.2 percent at an average concentration of 8.6 mU/ml for FSH. Estradiol was measured by radio-immunoassay including ether extraction using assay material provided by Travenol, Munich, West Germany. Interassay precision was 8.0 percent at an average concentration of 105 pg/ml. Progesterone was measured by radioimmunoassay (kit by Travenol) after ether extraction. Interassay variability was 7.9 percent at an average concentration of 3.2 ng/ml. All assays were performed under statistical quality control. The Wilcoxon rank sum test, two tailed, was used for comparisons between groups. Spearman's rank correlation test was used to calculate correlation coefficients.

Results

On the basis of the menstrual history of the preceding year, three patients had amenorrhea (fewer than three cycles per year), eight had oligomenorrhea (three to eight cycles per year), and four reported regular cycles. When the amplitude of weight fluctuations during the observation period was calculated, patient values significantly exceeded those of controls (2.7 ± 1.0 versus 1.6 ± 0.4 kg; $p <$ .01).

When the hormonal pattern throughout the observation period was plotted, four different types were discernible. Type 1, in which estradiol values never exceeded 120 pg/ml (the lower normal limit during the preovulatory phase in our laboratory), was found in seven patients; three examples are illustrated in Figure 3.

Type 2, in which estradiol values exceeded 120 pg/ml, indicating normal development of the follicle, was exhibited by five patients; two examples are depicted in Figure 4. During the second half of the cycle, when in normal subjects the corpus luteum produces progesterone plasma values greater than 3 ng/ml, progesterone values of patients corresponding to Type 2 never exceeded 3 ng/ml. This finding can be interpreted as an absent or a grossly defective luteal phase.

Type 3, which was a normal increase of estradiol during the follicular phase (>120 pg/ml) followed by an increase of progesterone values to beyond 3 ng/ml, was demonstrated by only two patients (see Figure 5). The elevated progesterone values (> 3 ng/ml) lasted only about five days, in comparison with the 14.0 ± 2.1 days in our normal control group. Type 4, normal estradiol and progesterone secretion pattern during the menstrual cycle, was displayed by only one patient (see Figure 5).

The body weights of the seven patients with Type 1 hormone

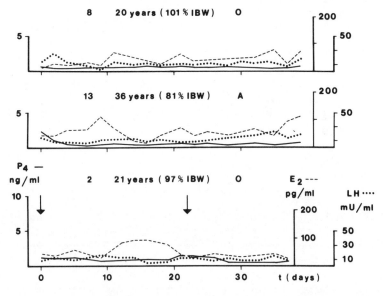

Figure 3. Estradiol (E_2), progesterone (P_4), and luteinizing hormone (LH) levels in three patients with bulimia. O = oligomenorrhea; A = amenorrhea; IBW = ideal body weight per Metropolitan Life Insurance (1959) data. Note that E_2 values are lower than 120 pg/ml, indicating disturbed follicular development.

pattern were significantly lower than those of the eight patients with Types 2, 3, and 4 (mean ± SD percent of IBW = 87 ± 8.8 percent versus 110 ± 11 percent, respectively; $p < .01$). Estradiol and progesterone values during the cycle did not differ in patients with, as compared with patients without, a past history of anorexia nervosa. Gonadotropin concentrations in plasma of bulimic patients were not significantly different from those in normal controls. Since gonadotropin concentrations in plasma show rapid fluctuations, LH and FSH values measured at three points in time during one week must be interpreted with caution. To evaluate further the pattern of gonadotropin secretion in bulimia, we conducted a second study, measuring the secretory pattern of LH and FSH over a 12-hour period during the early follicular phase.

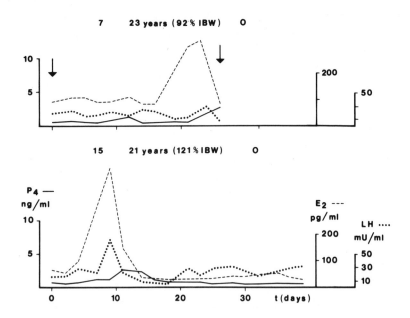

Figure 4. Estradiol (E_2), progesterone (P_4), and luteinizing hormone (LH) levels in two patients with bulimia. O = oligomenorrhea; IBW = ideal body weight per Metropolitan Life Insurance (1959) data. Note that E_2 values exceed 120 pg/ml, indicating a normal follicular development; however, no luteal phase occurred, judging from the low P_4 values.

STUDY 2

Fifteen outpatients diagnosed as having bulimia by *DSM-III* criteria were studied. Age and weight of patients and control subjects are given in Table 1.

Six patients reported a history of anorexia nervosa. Three patients reported amenorrhea, three reported oligomenorrhea, and nine had more or less regular cycles (26 to 35 days). The 12 healthy control subjects all reported regular cycles.

At 6:00 P.M., an indwelling catheter was inserted into a forearm vein. Two ml of blood were drawn at 30-minute intervals over a 12-

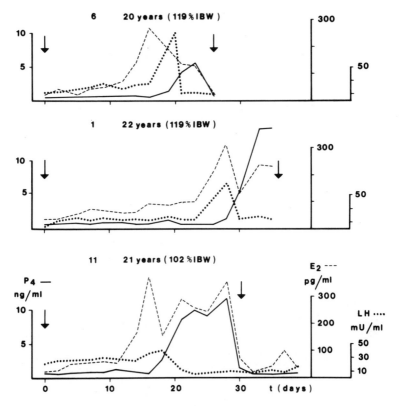

Figure 5.   Estradiol (E₂), progesterone (P₄), and luteinizing hormone (LH) levels in three patients with bulimia. Note that patients 1 and 6 show normal elevation of P₄; however, the luteal phase is abnormally shortened. Only patient 11 shows a normal hormonal pattern during the menstrual cycle.

Table 1. Age; Weight; Duration of Illness; and Levels of Prolactin, Triiodothyronine, and Betahydroxybutyric Acid in Bulimic Patients and Healthy Controls

	Age (years)	Ideal Body Weight[a] (%)	Duration of Illness (years)	Prolactin (ng/ml)	Triiodothyronine (ng/ml)	Betahydroxybutyric acid (μmol/l)
			Bulimic Patients ($n = 15$)			
Mean	25.2	99.3	5.5	6.3	0.76[b]	0.23[c]
SD	4.6	7.0	2.2	2.4	0.2	0.2
Range	21–38	90–116	1–9	3.0–11.4	0.4–1.0	0.003–0.921
			Control Subjects ($n = 12$)			
Mean	24.3	99.3	—	9.4	1.2	0.05
SD	4.2	5.1	—	3.4	0.9	0.01
Range	21–27	90–110	—	3.0–18.0	0.7–1.9	0.0–0.175

[a]Based on Metropolitan Life Insurance (1959) data.
[b]$p < .02$ versus controls.
[c]$p < .01$ versus controls.

hour period. The gonadotropin secretion patterns were obtained during the follicular phase (days 4 to 8). In cases of uncertain information on the cycle or major menstrual irregularities, only those studies are reported in which measurement of estradiol and progesterone revealed values consistent with an early follicular phase pattern (estradiol < 120 pg/ml; progesterone < 1.0 ng/ml). At the end of the 12-hour blood-sampling period, a single blood sample was collected for the measurement of betahydroxybutyric acid (BHBA), triiodothyronine (T_3), and prolactin (PRL), using methods of measurement described earlier (Pirke et al. 1985). An episodic secretion was defined as an increase of more than 2 mU/ml of LH or FSH when the concentration after the increase was still greater than the initial value. The peak size was calculated by subtracting the initial value from the maximum occurring in a given secretory episode.

Results

Table 1 presents the BHBA, T_3, and PRL values for bulimic patients compared with control subjects. Triiodothyronine values were significantly lower ($p < .02$) and BHBA values significantly higher in bulimic patients ($p < .01$). Six patients had BHBA values of greater than 0.175 μmol/l, pointing to an acute dieting period for these patients (Pirke et al. 1985; see also Chapter 8). Seven of 15 patients had abnormally decreased T_3 values (<0.7 ng/ml). Low T_3 values in bulimia represent one of the body's endocrine mechanisms for adapting to intermittent starvation (Pirke et al. 1985; Heufelder et al. 1985; see also Chapter 8). As can be seen in Table 1, plasma concentrations of PRL were not elevated in bulimic patients as compared with controls.

Table 2 summarizes the average 12-hour LH and FSH concentration in patients and control subjects. The number of peaks and the average peak size are also given for both gonadotropins. Comparison of patients and controls revealed significantly ($p < .025$) lower average FSH concentrations in bulimic patients. Peak size and frequency were not significantly decreased, although the average FSH peak size was below normal in five patients. Mean 12-hour LH concentrations, peak size, and frequency did not differ significantly in bulimic patients as compared to control subjects. However, five patients showed decreased average LH values and four of these had average LH peak sizes beneath the range observed in the 12 healthy controls. There was a significant correlation between the average 12-hour FSH values and plasma T_3 ($r_s = 0.58$; $p < .025$).

Table 2. Estradiol (E_2), Progesterone (P_4), 12-Hour Luteinizing Hormone (LH), number of LH peaks, average height of LH peaks, 12-hour follicle-stimulating hormone (FSH), and number and average height of FSH peaks in bulimic patients and controls

	E_2 (pg/ml)	P_4 (ng/ml)	LH (mU/ml)	Number of LH Peaks	Average LH Peak Height	FSH (mU/ml)	Number of FSH Peaks	Average FSH Peak Height (mU/ml)
			Bulimic Patients (n = 15)					
Mean	54.9	0.41	12.37	4.07	5.91	9.69[a]	4.07	5.02
SD	27.28	0.09	5.20	1.16	2.41	3.01	1.22	1.46
Range	25.3–119	0.25–0.58	6.1–23.9	2–6	3.1–9.8	5.0–15.5	2–6	2.8–7.7
			Control Subjects (n = 12)					
Mean	—	—	13.9	3	5.7	14.8	4.6	5.7
SD	—	—	2.2	0.6	1.2	3.9	0.8	0.9
Range	—	—	9.5–17.6	3–5	4.4–8.1	9.4–20.9	4–6	4.3–7.0

[a] $p < .025$.

DISCUSSION

Previous studies have suggested that up to 50 percent of normal-weight bulimic patients have amenorrhea (Russell 1979; Pirke et al. 1985; see also Chapter 3). In the two studies reported here, 6 out of 30 patients had amenorrhea and 11 had oligomenorrhea. Study 1 revealed that the percentage of disturbed menstrual cycles is even higher than 50 percent when the cycle is judged by endocrine parameters. The most severe form of disturbance was observed in seven patients who showed no signs of normal follicular development, as judged from persistently low estradiol values (<120 pg/ml) throughout the observation period. Although this group had no weight deficit, as do patients with anorexia nervosa, their weight was significantly lower than that of the remaining eight patients. This points to an influence of weight deficit on hormone secretion. Alternatively, we may assume that this group experiences more severe and longer periods of dieting, as we shall discuss below. A less severe form of endocrine disturbance during the cycle was observed in seven bulimic patients whose follicular phase appeared to be normal, judging from the normal estradiol increase. These patients, however, had either no luteal phases or only insufficient ones, judging from the progesterone values during the second half of the cycle. Only one out of 15 bulimic patients had a normal cycle.

What are the endocrine mechanisms responsible for the disturbances of the menstrual cycle in bulimia? As shown in Study 2, PRL values are not elevated in bulimic patients. This makes it quite unlikely that hyperprolactinaemia is responsible for the menstrual cycle disturbances reported here. Whether hypercortisolism plays a role in suppressing gonadal hormone secretion in bulimic patients cannot be decided on the basis of our data. Several authors have reported nonsuppressed responses to the dexamethasone suppression test in bulimic patients (see Chapter 1). We observed normal morning cortisol values in bulimic patients in an earlier study (Heufelder et al. 1985) and also in the patients described here (Fichter et al. unpublished data). Since we observed nonsuppressed responses to the dexamethasone suppression test in only 25 percent of 28 bulimic patients (Fichter et al. unpublished data), it is unlikely that hypercortisolism plays a significant role in the menstrual disturbances found in bulimia.

Study 2 sheds some light on the endocrine mechanisms behind menstrual disturbances. The average 12-hour FSH values were significantly lower in bulimic patients than in healthy, age-matched controls. Since FSH stimulates follicular growth during the first half of the cycle, the decreased FSH values may well be responsible for the impaired estradiol secretion described in Study 1. Disturbed gonadotropin secretion during the early follicular phase may even be responsible for the luteal phase defects (di Zerega and Hodgen 1981). It is remarkable that the frequency of FSH and LH peaks was unaltered in bulimia. Thus, the reduced follicular stimulation is probably caused by a decrease in the average FSH concentration and, possibly, by the reduced peak size of LH and FSH observed in some bulimic patients. Seven out of 15 patients had a reduced average FSH or LH peak size.

Understanding of the menstrual cycle disturbances may be enhanced by evaluating the episodic gonadotropin secretion at different times of the cycle.

What causes disturbances of the menstrual cycle in bulimia? First, we have demonstrated that most bulimic patients experience episodes of dieting or starvation (see Chapter 8). This behavior is responsible

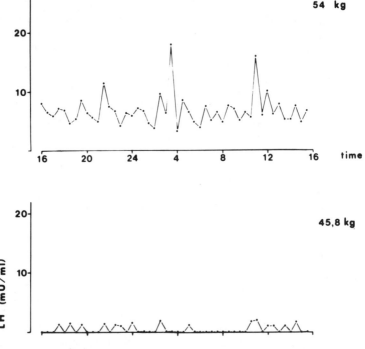

Figure 6.   Luteinizing hormone (LH) secretion is a normal healthy starving subject before and after a weight loss of 8.2 kg, showing almost total suppression of LH secetion.

for the significantly greater fluctuations in body weight of bulimic patients observed in Study 1. Approximately half of the patients in Study 2 showed elevated levels of BHBA, which is associated with acute starvation (see Chapter 8).

In addition to increased BHBA levels, starvation is associated with a reduction of the basal metabolic rate (Landsberg et al. 1982). One of the mechanisms responsible for reduced metabolic rate is decreased conversion of thyroxine to T_3 (Burman et al. 1977). Consistent with a metabolic adaptation to starvation, low T_3 values were observed in about half of the patients in Study 2. Furthermore, T_3 values were significantly correlated with the average 12-hour FSH levels in Study 2.

Second, dieting has been shown to influence the menstrual cycle. When healthy normal weight volunteers starved for two to three weeks, weight did not fall below the critical threshold defined by Frisch and Revelle (1970), but 60 percent showed an impairment of the LH secretion pattern (Fichter and Pirke 1984). Figure 6 shows the total suppression of LH secretion in a healthy starving subject.

Milder forms of weight reduction were studied by Pirke et al. (1985) in healthy subjects of normal weight. No changes in the secretory pattern of LH were observed, but 30 percent of the subjects developed anovulatory cycles, while another 30 percent who had had anovulatory cycles before the dieting phase developed amenorrhea.

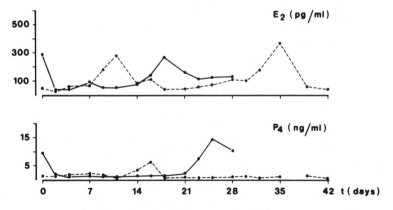

Figure 7. Influence of a weight reduction diet (1 kg per week) on estradiol (E_2) and progesterone (P_4) levels in healthy control subjects. Solid line = control cycle; dotted line = diet period. Note that the preovulatory E_2 increase is maintained, whereas the P_4 increase during the luteal phase is greatly decreased.

In another study (Pirke et al. in press), 18 healthy, normal weight young women voluntarily lost 1 kg body weight per week for six weeks. Fifty percent of the women developed disturbed hormone secretion during the cycle. Two typical examples are provided in Figures 7 and 8. Figure 7 shows that the preovulatory estradiol increase remains unchanged during the dieting period. Progesterone secretion during the luteal phase, however, was depressed. This pattern was also seen in seven bulimic patients (see Figure 4).

Figure 8 shows an even more severe disturbance of hormone secretion during weight loss in healthy, dieting women. The follicular development is greatly impaired, judging from the depressed estradiol values. No luteal phase develops. It should be kept in mind that the suppression of preovulatory estradiol values occurred after only two

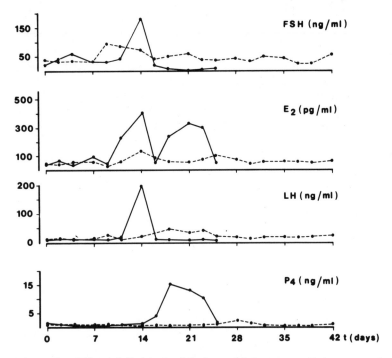

Figure 8. Effect of dieting (weight loss of 1 kg per week) in a normal healthy subject. Solid line = control cycle; dotted line = diet period. Note that both the preovulatory estradiol (E_2) increase and the luteal progesterone (P_4) increase are suppressed. FSH = follicle-stimulating hormone; LH = luteinizing hormone.

weeks of mild dieting (weight loss of 2 kg). Patients with bulimia often show a weight loss of this extent (see Chapter 8). Seven out of 15 bulimic patients exhibited the same type of menstrual disturbance, as a comparison of Figure 3 with Figure 8 shows. Thus, although other factors such as electrolyte disturbances or severe exercise may contribute to the genesis of menstrual disturbances, the fact that dieting and weight loss in healthy young women lead to disturbances in the hypothalamic–pituitary–gonadal axis (Fichter and Pirke 1984; Pirke et al. 1985; Pirke et al. in press) similar to those reported here for bulimic patients supports our hypothesis that intermittent starvation and dieting are the major causes of menstrual disturbances in bulimia.

REFERENCES

American Psychiatric Association: Diagnostic and Statistical Manual of Mental Disorders (Third Edition). Washington, DC, American Psychiatric Association, 1980

Beumont PJV, George GCW, Pimstone BL, et al: Body weight and the pituitary response to hypothalamic-releasing hormones in patients with anorexia nervosa. J Clin Endocrinol Metab 43:487-496, 1976

Burman KD, Vigersky RA, Loriaux DL, et al: Investigations concerning thyroxine diiodinative pathways in patients with anorexia nervosa, in Anorexia Nervosa. Edited by Vigersky RA. New York, Raven Press, 1977

di Zerega GS, Hodgen GD: Luteal phase dysfunction infertility: a sequel to aberrant follicular genesis. Fertil Steril 35:489-501, 1981

Fichter MM, Pirke KM: Hypothalamic pituitary function in starving healthy subjects, in The Psychobiology of Anorexia Nervosa. Edited by Pirke KM, Ploog D. Berlin, Springer Verlag, 1984

Frische RE: Food intake, fatness, and reproductive ability, in Anorexia Nervosa. Edited by Vigersky RA. New York, Raven Press, 1977

Frisch RE, Revelle R: Height and weight at menarche and a hypothesis of critical body weights and adolescent events. Science 169:397-399, 1970

Heufelder A, Warnhoff M, Pirke KM: Platelet 2-adrenoceptor and adenylate cyclase in patients with anorexia nervosa and bulimia. J Clin Endocrinol Metab 61:1053-1060, 1985

Keys A, Brozek J, Henschel A, et al: The Biology of Human Starvation. Minneapolis, MN, University of Minnesota Press, 1950

Landsberg L, Young JB: Effects of nutritional status on autonomic nervous system function. Am J Clin Nutr 35:1234-1240, 1982

Metropolitan Life Insurance Company: New weight standards for men and women. Statistical Bulletin 40:1, 1959

Pirke KM, Fichter MM, Lund R, et al: Twenty-four hour sleep–wake pattern of plasma LH in patients with anorexia nervosa. Acta Endocrinol 92:193-204, 1979

Pirke KM, Pahl J, Schweiger U, et al: Metabolic and endocrine indices of starvation in bulimia: a comparison with anorexia nervosa. Psychiatry Res 15:33-39, 1985

Pirke KM, Schweiger U, Lemmel W, et al: The influence of dieting on the menstrual cycle of healthy young women. J Clin Endocrinol Metab 60:1174-1179, 1985

Pirke KM, Schweiger U, Laessle R, et al: Dieting influences the menstrual cycle. Vegetarian versus non-vegetarian diet. Fertil Steril, in press

Russell GFM: Bulimia nervosa: an ominous variant of anorexia nervosa. Psychol Med 9:429-448, 1979

Vigersky RA, Andersen AE, Thompson RH, et al: Hypothalamic dysfunction in secondary amenorrhea associated with simple weight loss. N Engl J Med 297:1141-1145, 1977

Chapter 3

Menstrual Abnormalities

Paul M. Copeland, M.D.
David B. Herzog, M.D.

Chapter 3

Menstrual Abnormalities

Several of the characteristics that compose the syndrome of bulimia may be provocative factors in causing menstrual disturbances. Among other diagnostic features, bulimia is characterized by 1) rapid eating of large amounts of food in a discrete period of time, 2) compensation for the food ingestion by fasting (or by vomiting, laxative, or diuretic use), 3) accompaniment of the binges by depressed mood and self-deprecating thoughts, and 4) frequent weight fluctuations of greater than 10 pounds. Each of these features can disrupt the hypothalamic–pituitary–gonadal axis and produce menstrual disturbances in bulimic women. In this chapter, we shall explore how these features affect neuroendocrine systems that control the menstrual cycle.

EPIDEMIOLOGY OF MENSTRUAL DISTURBANCES IN BULIMIA

Menstrual disturbances are common in bulimic women. According to various surveys, 40 to 95 percent of normal weight bulimic women have menstrual irregularities. This proportion of menstrual irregularities is much greater than in an aged-matched normal populations or even aged-matched populations of individuals with depression or psychosis. College-aged women, for example, have a 2 to 5 percent prevalence of amenorrhea and approximately an 11 percent incidence of oligomenorrhea (Bachman and Kemmann 1982). The frequency of amenorrhea among psychiatric patients varies widely in different studies (Khuri and Gehi 1981). A recent report noted a prevalence of 27 percent in psychiatric inpatients (Flint and Stewart, 1983).

Pyle et al. (1981) found that 26 of 34 bulimic patients had at least one episode of amenorrhea lasting at least three months. Ten of these patients had a past history of weight loss to less than 15 percent below the minimum acceptable small-frame weight in the Metropolitan Life Insurance (1959) tables. All of their patients' weights were above this level at the time of evaluation. The authors did not report the menstrual status of these patients at their restored weights.

31

Abraham and Beumont (1982) similarly noted that 23 of 30 female bulimics had at least one episode of amenorrhea of three months' duration. An additional three patients had some menstrual irregularity. Nine of these patients were treated for anorexia nervosa in the past.

Johnson et al. (1983) found current menstrual irregularities in 50.7 percent of 361 bulimic women who requested information from the authors' clinic and then responded to a questionnaire. Nineteen of their respondents had a past history of weight loss greater than 25 percent of original weight; an additional three had a current weight below this criterion.

Fairburn and Cooper (1982) identified 499 cases of bulimia among women who completed a questionnaire distributed with the help of an article in a women's magazine. Of the original total of 669 respondents, the investigators excluded 19 who met criteria for current anorexia nervosa; of their final sample, 12.4 percent had a past weight below 75 percent of matched population mean weight. Irregular menses were reported by 39.7 percent and amenorrhea by 6.9 percent. Fairburn and Cooper (1984) also examined a clinic population of 35 bulimics. Patients with a current weight below 80 percent of the matched population mean weight were excluded from the study, but 20 percent of the patients had a past weight below 75 percent of the matched population mean weight. Of the 35 patients, 45.7 percent were taking oral contraceptives. Of the remainder, 21.1 percent reported amenorrhea, 36.8 percent reported irregular menses, and only one patient (5.3 percent) reported regular menstruation.

Other researchers have restricted their population to bulimics who never met weight criteria for anorexia nervosa. In Lacey's (1982) clinic study, 11 of 15 bulimics had amenorrhea (excluding 5 others who took oral contraceptives). Another 3 of these 15 patients had irregular menses. Garner et al. (1985) reported amenorrhea in 40 percent of 59 bulimic women. Weiss and Ebert (1983) found amenorrhea in 11 of 15 bulimic patients. Finally, Pirke and his colleagues note menstrual irregularities in 14 of 15 bulimic women in Chapter 2.

While menstrual disturbances are prevalent among bulimic women, they are not as universal a finding as they are in the related eating disorder anorexia nervosa. Nearly all women with anorexia nervosa are amenorrheic. Amenorrhea was a diagnostic criterion for anorexia nervosa by Feighner et al. (1972). Although the American Psychiatric Association's *Diagnostic and Statistical Manual of Mental Disorders (Third Edition)* (*DSM-III;* 1980) did not require amenorrhea for the diagnosis, this criterion has been reinstated in the revised version, *DSM-III-R*.

The amenorrhea of anorexia nervosa has been more extensively studied than that of bulimia. Bulimic patients manifest many of the physical and psychological abnormalities observed in anorexia nervosa. Both bulimic and anorexic patients have weight phobia and a high prevalence of depression. An analysis of the amenorrhea of anorexia nervosa can serve as a point of departure for understanding the menstrual disturbances of bulimia.

Weight loss itself leads to amenorrhea. In one study, an average weight loss of 12 percent below ideal body weight (average loss of 8 kg) over three weeks produced amenorrhea in four out of five normal volunteers (Fichter and Pirke 1984). In population surveys, a loss of 10 to 15 percent below ideal body weight is associated with amenorrhea (Frisch and McArthur 1974). In "simple" weight loss, the individual does not manifest the unrelenting pursuit of thinness seen in anorexia nervosa. Typically, in cases of simple weight loss, when the excessive weight loss is brought to the patient's attention as the cause of her amenorrhea, she will regain weight and normal menses will be restored.

Weight loss is not the only determinant for the onset of amenorrhea in anorexia nervosa. Up to 25 percent of patients lose menses before weight loss occurs (Hsu 1983; Casper 1984). Restricted food intake, psychological stress, or an unknown specific factor may produce this early loss of menses. In addition, many anorexics fail to regain menses even when body weight is restored (Falk and Halmi 1982).

Weight loss appears to influence menstrual function in bulimic patients as well. The more substantial the weight loss, the more prevalent the menstrual disturbances. In a study of 105 normal weight bulimic patients (patients taking oral contraceptives were excluded), 38 percent of the 26 patients with a history of anorexia nervosa had amenorrhea at the time of presentation despite restoration of normal body weight (Copeland et al. 1984). This prevalence of amenorrhea was significantly greater than the 19 percent of the bulimic women without a diagnosable history of anorexia nervosa. Conversely, other studies have linked abnormal eating patterns with failure to regain menses in weight-recovered anorexic patients. Falk and Halmi (1982) documented that disordered eating attitudes persisted among weight-recovered anorexics who failed to regain menses. A past history of bingeing and purging, however, does not appear to predispose patients to continued amenorrhea. Wakeling and DeSouza (1983) found continued amenorrhea after weight gain among anorexic patients who practiced abstinence or abstinence alternating with bingeing.

Anorexic patients who had primarily binged and purged recovered menses while those who had primarily dieted did not. Among the bingers and purgers, it should be noted that 8 of 13 again ceased menses when they again lost weight.

Even among normal weight bulimic patients in whom weight loss never reached *DSM-III* criteria for anorexia nervosa, lower past weights have been associated with a higher prevalence of amenorrhea. In our study, amenorrheic bulimic patients without a diagnosable history of anorexia nervosa had lower past body weights than those with regular menses (Copeland et al. 1984). A weight loss to less than 92 percent of ideal body weight differentiated those with amenorrhea from those with regular menses: Forty-one percent of normal weight bulimics with regular menses had a nadir below this value, whereas a significantly greater 87 percent of those with amenorrhea had nadirs below this level. Among those amenorrheic patients with weight nadirs greater than 92 percent of ideal body weight, there was a history of excessive exercise or substantial situational stress. Therefore, intermediate low weights, not meeting criteria for anorexia nervosa, predisposed to amenorrhea. These bulimic patients may illustrate what Russell (1979) has termed "cryptic" anorexia nervosa. These patients share the weight phobia and pursuit of thinness seen in patients with anorexia nervosa but do not lose 25 percent of body weight. As in patients with diagnosable anorexia nervosa, there is a delay in the recovery of menses after weight restoration. The same neuroendocrine phenomena that accompany severe weight loss may be activated in these patients with intermediate weight loss.

GONADOTROPINS

The amenorrhea of anorexia nervosa and bulimia reflects a failure of the normal secretion of gonadotropins from the pituitary gland. In anorexia nervosa there is a profound disruption of luteinizing hormone (LH) and, to a lesser extent, follicle-stimulating hormone (FSH) release (Boyar et al. 1974; Warren et al. 1974; Pirke et al. 1983; reviewed in Hudson and Hudson 1984). Rather than normal pulsatile release of LH, the pulsation pattern resembles that seen in prepuberty (absence of pulsations) or early puberty (only sleep-related pulsations). Upon weight recovery, the normal adult pattern reemerges. Bulimic behavior in recovering anorexic patients may delay the restoration of normal gonadotropin pulsations (Katz et al. 1978).

Luteinizing hormone release is stimulated by gonadotropin-releasing hormone (GnRH) secreted by the hypothalamus. The mean LH levels are a consequence of the frequency and amplitude of LH pulses, the former of which is set by the frequency of GnRH pulses from the hypothalamus and the latter of which may be determined both by the amount of GnRH released and by the response of the pituitary to LH. Thus, alterations in LH pulse amplitude may reflect changes at the level of the pituitary.

In normal weight bulimic patients, the disruption of gonadotropin secretion is not as profound as it is in anorexia nervosa. In one study, serum estradiol levels (measured thrice weekly for one menstrual cycle or up to six weeks) exceeded 120 pg/ml in only 8 of 15 normal weight bulimic women (Pirke and Schweiger in press; see also Chapter 2). This estradiol level indicates maturation of an ovarian follicle. Estradiol levels are uniformly lower in anorexia nervosa. Those bulimic patients in whom estradiol levels remained below 120 pg/ml had lower body weights than did those with normal estradiol levels. Among the eight bulimic patients with normal follicular phase estradiol levels, seven had low luteal phase progesterone levels. Gonadotropin release was shown to be disrupted in many of the bulimic women (Pirke and Schweiger in press). Five of 15 bulimic women had decreased mean LH values, and four had subnormal mean LH peak levels. The overall mean FSH level was low, and the peak FSH level was low in 5 of the 15 bulimic women.

The decreased release of gonadotropins in anorexia nervosa reflects a failure of the normal pulsatile release of GnRH from the hypothalamus, and a similar abnormality may exist in bulimia. A hypothalamic abnormality, rather than an intrinsic pituitary disturbance, is demonstrated in anorexia nervosa by the restoration of normal LH and FSH pulsations with the administration of the hypothalamic hormone GnRH (Marshall and Kelch 1979). The pituitary is capable of responding if exogenous GnRH is administered in a pulsatile fashion. A reduction of GnRH secretion is also likely in bulimia; however, reduced LH peak levels, rather than reduced LH pulse frequency, raise the possibility of an alteration at the pituitary level.

The mechanism of the postulated disrupted GnRH release in eating disorders is less clear. Epidemiologically, the factors to be considered are weight loss, nutritional inadequacy, binge eating, psychological stress, or a possible intrinsic abnormality unique to patients with eating disorders. Excess exercise may be an ancillary factor. The neuroendocrine transducers of these epidemiologic factors remain to be determined. Several hormones and neurotransmitters known to influence GnRH release, and GnRH action may mediate the menstrual disturbances in bulimia. We shall consider the possible roles of altered estradiol feedback, elevated serum carotene levels, "euthyroid sick" status, endogenous opioids, norepinephrine, prolactin, serotonin, corticotropin-releasing hormone, and cortisol (see Table 3).

ESTRADIOL FEEDBACK

Gonadotropin secretion in anorexia nervosa can be viewed as a biological regression to the prepubertal pattern. Primarily, this prepubertal pattern is dictated by a lack of secretion of GnRH. During puberty, there is also a change in the feedback response to estradiol. In addition to inhibition of GnRH secretion within the hypothalamus, a separate positive feedback effect of estradiol develops (Kaplan and Grumbach 1982).

In low weight anorexic women there appears to be regression to the exclusively negative feedback effect of estradiol (Halmi and Sherman 1957, Wakeling et al 1977). In normal women, administration of ethinyl estradiol produces a bimodal response of LH (Wakeling et al. 1977). If 200 μg of ethinyl estradiol are administered daily for three days to normal women in the midfollicular phase of the menstrual cycle, there is an initial lowering of LH levels followed by a rise on the last day of estradiol administration or on the day following. In low weight anorexic patients with detectable LH levels, an initial lowering of LH occurred (Wakeling et al. 1977). Thus, the negative feedback of estradiol was present. Four of 11 patients showed a small subsequent rise in LH, but these rises were delayed, and neither timing nor magnitude resembled the normal positive feedback.

Positive feedback of estradiol is essential for the surge in LH levels that triggers ovulation (Nakai et al. 1978). Patients with anorexia nervosa lose this necessary positive feedback. As was noted in the preceding section, pulsatile administration of GnRH is capable of restoring normal ovulation. Therefore, the amenorrhea in anorexia nervosa ultimately reflects a failure of the central nervous system control of reproduction. As noted above, the reduction of gonadotropin pulse amplitude in bulimia allows for the possibility of an effect on the pituitary rather than the hypothalamus. As shall be discussed below, in the section on endogenous opioids, decreased body fat can lower the peripheral production of estrogens. If estrogen levels fall far enough to decrease the positive feedback for gonadotropin release at the level of the pituitary, gonadotropin pulse amplitude may decline. Such a decrease in gonadotropin pulse amplitude could precipitate a further spiraling downward of estrogen levels and result in menstrual disturbance. Further research is needed to test this hypothesis.

Table 3. Hypothesized Mechanisms of Menstrual Disturbances in Bulimic Women

Sites	Precipitating Factors	Mediators	Consequences
Hypothalamus	Stress Exercise Binge eating	↑ CRH ↑ endogenous opioids ↑ serotonin → norepinephrine	→ GnRH
Pituitary	Binge eating → GnRH	↑ prolactin → gonadotropins	→ GnRH Ovarian dysfunction
Periphery	→ Body fat	→ estrogens	→ Gonadotropin pulse amplitude
	Intermittent starvation	↓ T_3 →↑ carotene	→ Gonadotropins
Ovary	→ Gonadotropins	Ovarian dysfunction	Oligoamenorrhea

Note: CRH = corticotropin-releasing hormone; GnRH = gonadotropin-releasing hormone; T_3 = triiodothyronine.

SERUM CAROTENE AND THE "EUTHYROID SICK" SYNDROME

A defect in the normal secretion of GnRH underlies the loss of normal LH pulse frequency in anorexia nervosa. Loss of body weight may create a signal that disrupts GnRH secretion. Peripheral hormones or metabolites may have an important impact on GnRH secretion.

One candidate for a peripheral metabolite that may alter central nervous system GnRH pulsations is carotene (Frumar et al. 1979). Frankly elevated carotene levels are found in 38 to 76 percent of patients with anorexia nervosa (Pops and Schwabe 1968; Warren and Vande Wiele 1973; Silverman 1983). It is possible that other anorexic patients have carotene levels that are relatively high for their normal physiology. Hypercarotenemia has been associated with amenorrhea among vegetarians (Kemmann et al. 1983). Alterations in diet to reduce carotene levels have restored menstrual functioning. The hypercarotenemia of anorexia nervosa is not strictly correlated with carotene intake. Rather, it is likely a consequence of slower carotene metabolism. Hypercarotenemia may be seen in hypothyroidism. While patients with anorexia nervosa do not have true hypothyroidism, they do have a functional hypothyroidism. With low weight there is a decreased peripheral conversion of thyroxine to the more active triiodothyronine (Moshang et al. 1975). In anorexia nervosa, diminished thyroid hormone levels are associated with elevated serum carotene (Curran-Celentano et al. 1985). Patients with elevated serum carotene levels have significantly lower triiodothyronine and thyroxine levels than do anorexics who have normal serum carotene levels.

A similar lowering of triiodothyronine levels is also observed in normal weight bulimics (Pirke et al, 1985a; see also Chapters 4 and 8). The decreased peripheral conversion of thyroxine to triiodothyronine in these bulimic patients may result from the intermittent starvation. Lowered carbohydrate intake rapidly diminishes peripheral conversion of thyroxine to triiodothyronine (Spaulding et al. 1976). It is not known whether intermittent starvation without significant weight loss is an important factor in the menstrual disturbance of bulimics. Consistent with this hypothesis is the finding that low FSH levels are correlated with low triiodothyronine levels in bulimic patients (Pirke and Schweiger in press; Chapter 2).

Carotene may simply be a marker of the functional hypothyroidism, but restoration of menses with lowering of serum carotene in vegetarians suggests a causal relationship for the amenorrhea. How carotene might affect gonadotropin secretion remains to be explored.

ENDOGENOUS OPIOID PEPTIDES

Increased central nervous system opioid activity may contribute to GnRH suppression in a subset of patients with eating disorders. Opioid peptides are synthesized from three distinct known precursors (Yen et al. 1985). Proopiomelanocortin is the source of beta-endorphin, which is synthesized in the pituitary, the brain, and other sites. Proenkephalin A is the precursor for met-enkephalin, leu-enkephalin, and other small opioid peptides. Met-enkephalin and leu-enkephalin are present in brain, posterior pituitary, and other organs. Proenkephalin B is the precursor for the dynorphins, which are potent stimulants of appetite when injected into brain ventricles in rats. Dynorphins are found in the brain as well as in other locations.

Opiate receptor blockade with naloxone has been an important tool in assessing the role of endogenous opioids in the regulation of gonadotropin secretion. Administration of naloxone blocks the opiate mu-receptors and, to a lesser extent, the delta receptors. Naloxone is ineffective in blocking the kappa-receptor. A hormonal response to naloxone implies that endogenous opioids were active in inhibiting hormone secretion via action at mu-receptors, or possibly at delta-receptors.

Naloxone increases GnRH secretion both in vitro from rat mediobasal hypothalamus and in vivo in several physiological states (Leadem et al. 1985; Kuderling et al. 1984). Naloxone increases the frequency of LH pulses during the late follicular and midluteal phases of the menstrual cycle (Yen et al. 1985). It is ineffective in the early follicular phases, and it is ineffective in altering LH pulses in postmenopausal women. These data suggest that ovarian steroids modify the inhibitory effect of endogenous opioids on LH pulsation. In the early follicular phase of the menstrual cycle and after menopause, estrogen and progesterone levels are low. It appears that the effect of naloxone on LH pulsation is dependent on adequate ovarian steroid levels. Starvation in male rats lowered testosterone levels and similarly reduced the stimulatory effect of naloxone on LH release (Kuderling et al. 1984).

Naloxone elicited LH pulsations in only a subset of eating disorder patients (Baranowska et al. 1984). This group may be one in which ovarian steroid secretion is still preserved. Naloxone raised LH levels in 11 of 25 anorexic patients. Amenorrhea preceded the weight loss in 9 of the 11 patients who had LH pulses induced by naloxone. Naloxone did not change LH levels in 14 other anorexic patients in whom weight loss preceded amenorrhea. Weight loss can lower peripheral aromatization of androstenedione to estrone and thus could diminish the estrogen mileu needed for the action of endogenous

opioids (Fishman et al. 1975). Peripheral aromatization of androstenedione normally accounts for 20 to 30 percent of estrone production. In one study of normal women, weight loss lowered estradiol
levels before an effect on LH pulsation could be discerned (Pirke et
al. 1985b). It may be speculated that amenorrheic eating disorder
patients who lose menses before very low weights are reached secrete
excess endogenous opioids.

Using a radioreceptor assay that measures binding of an enkephalin
analogue, Kaye et al. (1982) found anorexic patients at low weights
to have an increase in cerebrospinal fluid endogenous opioid activity.
With weight recovery, the levels returned to normal. When specific
opioid peptides were measured, the increase could not be accounted
for by beta-endorphin, beta-lipotropin, adrenocorticotropic hormone (ACTH), or the N-terminal fragment of proopiomelanocortin
(Kaye et al. 1986a). Cerebrospinal fluid levels of all of these peptides
were reduced in low weight anorexic patients and became normal
after weight restoration. It should be appreciated that the levels of
beta-endorphin accounted for only 1 percent of the total opioid
activity, as measured by the radioreceptor assay. Other endogenous
opioids probably account for the increased activity.

Endogenous opioids may suppress GnRH release by inhibiting
hypothalamic noradrenergic neurons (Kalra 1981). When norepinephrine synthesis was inhibited by diethyl dithiocarbamate, naloxone
implants failed to augment LH release. Noradrenergic pathways appear to be necessary for the effects of hypothalamic opioid peptides.
Suppression of endogenous opioid activity may free noradrenergic
neurons from inhibition. The norepinephrine secretion would then
stimulate GnRH release. Further discussion of the role of endogenous
opioids in bulimia can be found in Chapters 6 and 7.

NOREPINEPHRINE

In addition to its possible role as a modulator of endogenous opioid
action, there is direct evidence that central nervous system norepinephrine metabolism is altered in bulimia (see Chapter 9). Of particular relevance to the regulation of menstruation amenorrheic bulimic patients had lower cerebrospinal fluid norepinephrine levels
than did bulimic patients with regular menses (Kaye et al. 1986b).
Increased hypothalamic norepinephrine turnover rate is closely correlated with LH surges in animal studies (Kalra 1981). The lower
cerebrospinal fluid norepinephrine levels in amenorrheic bulimic patients likely reflects decreased norepinephrine secretion, which in
turn would diminish LH secretion.

Several neuroendocrine mechanisms could cause diminished central nervous system norepinephrine secretion in bulimic patients. Food intake itself leads to decreased hypothalamic norepinephrine secretion. Feeding in rats has been shown to diminish neuronal release of previously stored radiolabeled norepinephrine from the ventromedial hypothalamus (McCaleb et al. 1979). Norepinephrine is a major regulator of appetite in rats. Instillation of physiologic concentrations of norepinephrine into the paraventricular nucleus of rats provokes feeding behavior (Leibowitz 1984). This action can be blocked by alpha-adrenergic antagonists. A diminution of ventromedial hypothalamic noradrenergic neuronal activity may accompany bingeing in bulimic patients. It is not clear if bingeing also affects those noradrenergic neurons that regulate GnRH release.

Platelet alpha$_2$-adrenoreceptors have been studied as a reflection of noradrenergic metabolism. The number of receptors for a neurotransmitter will decrease if the neurotransmitter concentration increases. Receptor number was found to be increased in patients with anorexia nervosa and bulimia (Heufelder et al 1985). It is likely that these increases represent a response to decreased peripheral norepinephrine concentrations. Decreased peripheral norepinephrine turnover occurs in starvation as well as in anorexic and bulimic patients. It is unlikely that these peripheral changes in norepinephrine turnover mirror central nervous system norepinephrine activity. Cerebrospinal fluid 3-methoxy-4-hydroxyphenyl-ethyleneglycol (MHPG) levels would serve as a more direct index of central nervous system norepinephrine activity. MHPG is a metabolite of norepinephrine. Cerebrospinal fluid MHPG levels are decreased in weight-recovered anorexic patients (WH Kaye, personal communication). This abnormality may reflect a pervasive "trait" marker of decreased central nervous system norepinephrine secretion in anorexia nervosa.

Measures of adrenoreceptors in the central nervous system also suggest diminished noradrenergic activity in anorexia nervosa and bulimia. Administration of clonidine, an alpha$_2$-adrenoreceptor agonist, elicits an increase in growth hormone mediated by post-synaptic alpha$_2$-adrenoreceptors. The response of growth hormone to clonidine was greater in low-weight than in weight-recovered anorexic patients (Kaye et al. submitted); however, the interpretation of this result is complicated by the known basal accentuation of growth hormone release in starvation. Growth hormone stimulates the production of somatomedin C in the liver and other tissues. Somatomedin C exerts feedback inhibition of growth hormone release both at the level of the hypothalamus and at the pituitary (Berelowitz et al. 1981; Tannenbaum et al. 1983). In starvation, the liver produces less somatomedin C in response to growth hormone (Clemmons et al. 1981; Hintz et al. 1976). The decreased somatomedin C levels yield reduced feedback inhibition and thus increased growth hormone levels (Brown et al. 1977). Therefore, elevated growth hormone release does not simply reflect increased alpha$_2$-adrenoreceptor activity in low weight individuals.

The MHPG response to clonidine is another measure of central alpha$_2$-adrenoreceptor activity. Clonidine acts presynaptically to decrease norepinephrine release and thereby reduce plasma levels of the metabolite MHPG. Underweight anorexic patients had greater percentage reductions in plasma MHPG than did normal weight controls (WH Kaye, personal communication). The interpretation of this result is difficult since baseline MHPG levels are lower in underweight anorexic patients (Halmi et al. 1978). Presynaptic alpha$_2$-adrenoreceptor sensitivity may be greater at low weights. Alternatively, a reduction in norepinephrine release quantitatively similar to controls may have resulted in a greater percentage reduction in plasma MHPG for underweight anorexic patients.

Although measures of central alpha$_2$-adrenoreceptor activity are fraught with confounding metabolic influences, the bulk of the evidence favors reduced central norepinephrine turnover in anorexia nervosa and bulimia (see also Chapter 9). Since GnRH secretion depends on stimulation by noradrenergic neurons, a decrease in norepinephrine release could disrupt GnRH secretion in eating disorder patients.

PROLACTIN AND SEROTONIN

Hyperprolactinemia causes amenorrhea due to diminished GnRH release. Opiate receptor blockade with naloxone has reestablished LH pulses in patients with hyperprolactinemia (Grossman et al. 1982).

Excess prolactin is secreted in pregnancy and in some patients with pituitary tumors, hypothalamic disturbances, hypothyroidism; by physical stimulation of the chest wall; or with drugs that release serotonin or block dopamine receptors. Prolactin is also physiologically increased following a meal (Ishizuka et al. 1983). The mechanism of this increase is not fully established, but it probably relates to the stimulatory role of serotonin in prolactin secretion. Direct ingestion of tryptophan, a precursor of serotonin, also elicits increased prolactin secretion (Ishizuka et al. 1983). In normal subjects, brain uptake of tryptophan is enhanced by carbohydrate ingestion (see also Chapter 14). Carbohydrate promotes the release of insulin, which leads to peripheral cellular uptake of most amino acids, but not of tryptophan. L-tryptophan enters the brain in competition with large neutral amino acids (tyrosine, phenylalanine, valine, leucine, isoleucine); as the blood concentration of large neutral amino acids falls, after insulin release, more l-tryptophan enters the brain (Fernstrom and Wurtman 1972). Tryptophan availability is a regulator of the synthesis of serotonin.

Kaye et al. (see Chapter 10) allowed bulimic patients to binge and vomit for up to five hours. Bulimic patients who voluntarily self-terminated bingeing showed an increase in their plasma ratio of l-tryptophan to large neutral amino acids with bingeing. Those bulimic patients who wished to continue the binge–purge episodes even after bingeing and vomiting up to four times over a span of up to five hours, did not have an increase in this ratio. The bulimic patients who self-terminated the bingeing and had an increased ratio of l-tryptophan to large neutral amino acids also had a greater peak increase in plasma prolactin than did the bulimics who had no increase in this ratio. The increase in brain tryptophan may be related to a satiety signal that terminates the desire to binge. Increases in brain serotonin are strongly implicated in regulation of satiety (Leibowitz and Shor-Posner, 1986). Some bulimic patients failed to show an increased ratio of l-tryptophan to large neutral amino acids with food ingestion despite raised insulin levels (see Chapter 10). This failure suggests an abnormality in the action of insulin or another regulator of amino acid metabolism.

Bulimia may be a behavioral attempt to compensate for a pathologic central nervous system serotonin deficiency (see also Chapter 10). A study of weight-recovered anorexic patients revealed a difference in serotonin metabolism between bulimic and nonbulimic patients (Kaye et al. 1984). Probenecid was administered to block the egress of 5-hydroxyindoleacetic acid (5-HIAA), a serotonin metabolite, from the cerebrospinal fluid. Cerebrospinal fluid levels of 5-HIAA were higher in bulimic than in nonbulimic weight-recovered anorexic patients. These patients were prevented from bingeing prior to the study. The lower 5-HIAA cerebrospinal fluid levels may reflect decreased serotonin turnover in the bulimic patients. Bingeing may serve to enhance serotonin synthesis by increasing brain tryptophan levels.

The postulated increase in brain serotonin synthesis after bingeing correlates with prolactin release. Serotonergic activity stimulates prolactin release. Prolactin is also released in stress. Food-induced prolactin release is distinguished from stress-induced release in that the former is enhanced by dexamethasone while the latter is diminished by dexamethasone (Copeland et al. 1985). Dexamethasone also enhances suckling-induced release of prolactin in mother rats (Riskind et al. 1984). Suckling-induced prolactin release is mediated by serotonin.

The postulated increase in brain serotonin synthesis with bingeing may also directly inhibit LH release (Moguilevsky et al. 1985). Stimulation of the midbrain dorsal raphe nucleus inhibited LH release in ovariectomized rats (Arendash and Gallo 1978). The dorsal raphe nucleus contains a large population of serotonergic neurons. Inhibition of serotonin synthesis with para-chlorphenylalanine blocked the effects of raphe nucleus stimulation (Arendash and Gallo 1978). Repletion of brain serotonin levels with 5-hydroxytryptophan restored the effect of raphe stimulation. Increased brain entry of tryptophan with bingeing in bulimics could, therefore, inhibit LH release without mediation by increased prolactin secretion.

CORTICOTROPIN-RELEASING HORMONE AND CORTISOL

The hypothalamic-pituitary-adrenal (HPA) axis is hyperfunctioning in many bulimics. This overactivity may be demonstrated by a failure of dexamethasone to normally suppress plasma cortisol levels with cortisol nonsuppression seen in 20 to 67 percent of bulimics (Gwirtsman et al. 1983; Hudson et al. 1983; Mitchell et al. 1984; Lindy et al. 1985; Musisi and Garfinkel 1985; see also Chapter 1). Overactivity of the HPA axis is also seen in virtually all low weight anorexic patients and in approximately half of patients with major depression (reviewed in Hudson and Hudson 1984). Studies have suggested that corticotropin-releasing hormone (CRH) hypersecretion causes the HPA axis overactivity in low-weight anorexic patients and depressed patients, since the ACTH response to a bolus of CRH is blunted (Gold et al. 1986a, 1986b). The blunting is ascribed to feedback inhibition from high circulating levels of cortisol. A postulated increase in endogenous CRH secretion or a non-ACTH-dependent increase in cortisol secretion could account for this finding (Copeland et al. 1986). Precedents for the latter mechanism have been described in animal studies and in normal human subjects. Morning cortisol pulses have been observed without antecedent ACTH pulses (Fehm et al. 1984).

Adrenocorticotropic hormone and cortisol responses to CRH have been reported in 10 patients with bulimia (Gold et al. 1986a). These patients all had normal responses to CRH. It should be noted, however, that urinary free cortisol levels were normal in all of these patients. It appears that the HPA axis was relatively quiescent in this group of bulimic patients. These patients had voluntarily abstained from bingeing and purging for at least 10 days before the study. It is possible that refraining from bulimic behavior restored more normal HPA axis dynamics.

Corticotropin-releasing hormone is found in the hypothalamus and in other brain regions (Kaye et al. 1987). It is secreted by the brain during stress and stimulates the release of ACTH from the pituitary. To accomplish this release, CRH is carried by the hypophyseal portal blood vessels from the hypothalamus to the pituitary. Corticotropin-releasing hormone is also released within the brain where it can affect other neuronal systems.

Corticotropin-releasing hormone acts centrally to inhibit GnRH release in rats. Administration of low doses of CRH into the lateral ventricle of the brains of ovariectomized rats inhibited LH secretion (Rivier and Vale 1984). Adrenalectomy did not prevent this effect, and therefore cortisol release does not seem to be the mechanism of the inhibition. Dexamethasone suppression of pituitary ACTH and beta-endorphin also did not reverse the CRH effect. Naltrexone, an opiate receptor blocker, did not alter the effect. Thus, CRH appears to exert a distinct inhibition of LH secretion.

Stress-induced inhibition of LH release is probably mediated by CRH. Luteinizing hormone release in castrated male rats is blunted following electric foot shocks. Administration of a CRH antagonist (alpha-helical ovine CRH residues 9 to 41) into the lateral ventricles of the brain reelicited LH pulsations (Rivier et al. 1986). Increased secretion of CRH may underlie the menstrual disturbances of patients with bulimia and other conditions of high psychological stress.

Elevated serum cortisol concentrations per se can inhibit GnRH secretion. When serum cortisol levels were raised to 75 to 100 μg/100 ml in Rhesus monkeys, LH release was inhibited (Dubey and Plant 1985). LH secretion could be restored by pulsatile administration of GnRH. The high cortisol levels appear to be acting directly or indirectly within the central nervous system to suppress GnRH release.

Direct measurements of cerebrospinal fluid CRH have shown elevated levels in patients with anorexia nervosa (Hotta et al. 1986; Kaye et al. 1987). In weight-recovered anorexic patients, cerebrospinal fluid CRH levels were positively correlated with scores on depression scales (Kaye et al. 1987). This association supports the concept that an HPA axis abnormally similar to that observed in depression is present in some eating disorder patients. Cerebrospinal fluid CRH levels have not been reported in normal weight bulimic patients.

EXERCISE

Excessive exercise itself can produce amenorrhea (Bullen et al. 1985). Women distance runners with amenorrhea have decreased LH pulse frequency with intact pituitary responsiveness to GnRH (Veldhuis et al. 1985). The mechanism for the apparent disruption in GnRH generation is not clear. Weight loss itself does not appear to be responsible, since temporary inactivity without increased body weight can reverse the amenorrhea (Warren 1980).

Increased activity may be additive to other factors in the amenorrhea of bulimia. Among anorexics, those who participated in vigorous athletics regained menses later after weight recovery and at a higher body weight (Litt and Glader 1986). No correlation was found between degree of exercise and amenorrhea among a population of bulimic patients (Copeland et al. 1984).

CONSEQUENCES OF MENSTRUAL DISTURBANCES

Osteopenia can be a long-term consequence of anorexia nervosa (Rigotti et al. 1984; Ayers et al. 1984). Vertebral compression fractures occur in some patients. It is not known if bulimic patients are similarly afflicted. Diminished estrogen may be only one factor in the osteoporosis of anorexia nervosa. The degree of osteopenia and the magnitude of the estrogen deficiency were not correlated. Most, but not all, of these patients were markedly estrogen deficient. In one study (Ayers et al. 1984), dehydroepiandrosterone sulfate (DHEA-S) levels were lower in those anorexics with the most severe osteopenia. DHEA-S is primarily secreted by the adrenal cortex and acts as an androgen, although it is far less potent than testosterone. The synthesis of DHEA-S falls in anorexia nervosa (Zumoff et al. 1983). The low DHEA-S levels may simply represent a marker of the severity of the anorexia nervosa. Alternatively, since androgens do help maintain bone mass, it is possible that low DHEA-S levels may predispose to osteoporosis. Elevated cortisol levels and poor nutrition with concomitant decreased somatomedin C levels may also contribute to bone loss. Bulimic patients who share these features of anorexia nervosa may be at risk for osteopenia. An assessment of bone density in bulimic patients is needed.

In patients with anorexia nervosa, normal fertility is usually achieved after weight restoration and recovery of menses. Some weight-recovered anorexic women who remain amenorrheic can regain menstruation and fertility with clomiphene therapy (Marshall and Fraser 1971). Clomiphene blocks estrogen receptors in the hypothalamus and thereby can produce a surge in gonadotropin secretion that leads to ovulation. Such treatment should be reserved for patients close to ideal body weight who have made a substantial psychiatric recovery.

CONCLUSION

Menstrual disturbances in bulimia include a range of defects from inadequate luteal phase, to oligomenorrhea, to amenorrhea. As in anorexia nervosa, the crucial disturbance appears to be decreased gonadotropin secretion. It is likely that disrupted GnRH secretion underlies the abnormality in gonadotropin secretion. GnRH in turn may be affected by a variety of factors stemming from binge-eating, episodic starvation, weight fluctuations, excessive exercise, stress, and depression. Possible neuroendocrine mediators of these phenomena include serotonin, norepinephrine, endogenous opioids, carotene, prolactin, CRH, cortisol, and diminished peripheral estrogen production. The actual roles of these and other factors in producing menstrual disturbances in bulimia remain to be determined.

REFERENCES

Abraham SF, Beumont PJV: How patients describe bulimia or binge eating. Psychological Med 12:625-635, 1982

Arendash GW, Gallo RV: Serotonin involvement in the inhibition of episodic luteinizing hormone release during electrical stimulation of the midbrain dorsal raphe nucleus in ovariectomized rats. Endocrinology 102:1199-1206, 1978

Ayers JWT, Gidwani GP, Schmidt IMV, et al: Osteopenia in hypoestrogenic young women with anorexia nervosa. Fertil Steril 41:224-228, 1984

Bachman GA, Kemmann E: Prevalence of oligomenorrhea and amenorrhea in a college population. Am J Obstet Gynecol 144:98-102, 1982

Baranowska B, Roxbicka G, Jeske W, et al: The role of endogenous opiates in the mechanism of inhibited luteinizing hormone (LH) secretion in women with anorexia nervosa: the effect of naloxone on LH, follicle-stimulating hormone, prolactin, and beta-endorphin secretion. J Clin Endocrinol Metab 59:412-416, 1984

Berelowitz M, Szabo M, Frohman LA, et al: Somatomedin-C mediated growth hormone negative feedback by effects on both the hypothalamus and the pituitary. Science 212:1279-1281, 1981

Boyar RM, Katz J, Binkelstein JW, et al: Anorexia nervosa: immaturity of the 24-hour luteinizing hormone secretory pattern. N Engl J Med 29:861-865, 1974

Brown GM, Garfinkel PE, Jeuniewic N, et al: Endocrine profiles in anorexia nervosa, in Anorexia Nervosa. Edited by Vigersky R. New York, Raven Press, 1977, pp 123-135

Bullen BA, Skrinar GS, Beitins I, et al: Induction of menstrual disorders by strenuous exercise in untrained women. N Engl J Med 312:1349-1353, 1985

Casper RC: Hypothalamic dysfunction and symptoms of anorexia nervosa. Psychiatr Clin North Am 7:201-213, 1984

Clemmons DR, Klibanski A, Underwood LE, et al: Reduction of plasma immunoreactive somatomedin-C during fasting in humans. J Clin Endocrinol Metab 53:1247-1250, 1981

Copeland PM, Ridgway E, Pepose M, et al: Amenorrhea in Bulimia. Presented at the First International Conference on Eating Disorders, New York, April 1984

Copeland PM, Herzog DB, Carr DB, et al: Effect of dexamethasone on cortisol and prolactin responses to meals in bulimic and normal women. Presented at the 8th International Congress for Psychosomatic Medicine, Chicago, September 1985

Copeland PM, Herzog DB, Carr DB, et al: Pulsatile ACTH and cortisol secretion after dexamethasone in bulimic and normal women. Presented at the 2nd International Conference on Eating Disorders, New York, April 1986

Curran-Celentano J, Erdman JW Jr, Nelson RA, et al: Alterations in vitamin A and thyroid hormone status in anorexia nervosa and associated disorders. Am J Clin Nutr 42:1183-1191, 1985

Dubey AK, Plant TM: A suppression of gonadotropin secretion by cortisol in castrated male Rhesus monkeys (*Macaca mulatta*) mediated by the interruption of hypothalamic gonadotropin-releasing hormone release. Biol Reprod 33:423-431, 1985

Fairburn CG, Cooper PJ: Self-induced vomiting and bulimia nervosa: an undetected problem. Br Med J 284:1153-1155, 1982

Fairburn CG, Cooper PJ: The clinical features of bulimia nervosa, Br J Psychiatry 144:238-246, 1984

Falk JR, Halmi KA: Amenorrhea in anorexia nervosa: examination of the critical body weight hypothesis. Biol Psychiatry 17:799-806, 1982

Fehm HL, Klein E, Hall R, et al: Evidence for extropituitary mechanisms mediating the morning peak of plasma cortisol in man. J Clin Endocrinol Metab 58:410-414, 1984

Feighner J, Robins S, Guze S, et al: Diagnostic criteria for use in psychiatric research. Arch Gen Psychiatry 26:57-63, 1972

Fernstrom JD, Wurtman RJ: Brain serotonin content: physiologic regulation by plasma neutral amino acids. Science 178:414-416, 1972

Fichter MM, Pirke KM: Hypothalamic pituitary function in starving healthy subjects, in The Psychobiology of Anorexia Nervosa. Edited by Pirke KM, Ploog D. New York, Springer-Verlag, 1984, pp 124-135

Fishman J, Boyar RM, Hellman L: Influence of body weight on estradiol metabolism in young women. J Clin Endocrinol Metab 41:989-991, 1975

Flint N, Stewart RB: Amenorrhea in psychiatric inpatients. Arch Gen Psychiatry 40:589, 1983

Frisch RE, McArthur JW: Menstrual cycles: fatness as a determinant of minimum weight for height necessary for their maintenance or onset. Science 185:949-951, 1974

Frumar AM, Meldrum DR, Judd HL: Hypercarotenemia in hypothalamic amenorrhea. Fertil Steril 32:261-264, 1979

Garner DM, Garfinkel PE, O'Shaugnessey M: The validity of the distinction between bulimia with and without anorexia nervosa. Am J Psychiatry 142:581-587, 1985

Gold PW, Gwirtsman HE, Averginos PC, et al.: Abnormal hypothalamic–pituitary–adrenal function in anorexia nervosa: pathophysiologic mechanisms in underweight and weight-corrected patients. N Engl J Med 314:1335-1342, 1986a

Gold PW, Loriaux DL, Roy A, et al: Responses to corticotropin-releasing hormone in the hypercortisolism of depression and Cushing's disease: pathophysiologic and diagnostic implications. N Engl J Med 314:1329-1335, 1986b

Grossman A, Moult PJA, McIntyre H, et al: Opiate mediation of amenorrhea in hyperprolactinemia and in weight-loss related amenorrhea. Clin Endocrinol 17:379-388, 1982

Gwirtsman HE, Roy-Byrne P, Yager J, et al: Neuroendocrine abnormalities in bulimia. Am J Psychiatry 140:559-563, 1983

Halmi K, Sherman BM: Gonadotropin response to LH-RH in anorexia nervosa. Arch Gen Psychiatry 32:875-878, 1975

Halmi KA, Dekirmenjian H, Davis JM, et al: Catecholamine metabolism in anorexia nervosa. Arch Gen Psychiatry 35:458-460, 1978

Heufelder A, Warnhoff M, Pirke KM: Platelet alpha$_2$-adrenoceptor and adenylate cyclase in patients with anorexia nervosa and bulimia. J Clin Endocrinol Metab 61:1053-1060, 1985

Hintz RL, Suskind R, Amatayakul K, et al: Plasma somatomedin and growth hormone values in children with protein-calorie malnutrition. J Pediatr 92:153-156, 1976

Hotta M, Shibasaki T, Masuda A, et al: The responses of plasma adreno-corticotropin and cortisol to corticotropin-releasing hormone (CRH) and cerebrospinal fluid immunoreactive CRH in anorexia nervosa. J Clin Endocrinol Metab 62:319-324, 1986

Hsu LKG: The aetiology of anorexia nervosa. Psychol Med 13:231-238, 1983

Hudson JI, Hudson MS: Endocrine dysfunction in anorexia nervosa and bulimia: comparison with abnormalities in other psychiatric disorders and disturbances due to metabolic factors. Psychiatr Devel 4:237-272, 1984

Hudson JI, Pope HJ Jr, Jonas JM, et al: Hypothalamic–pituitary–adrenal axis hyperactivity in bulimia. Psychiatry Res 8:111-118, 1983

Ishizuka B, Quigley ME, Yen SSC: Pituitary hormone release in response to food ingestion: evidence for neuroendocrine signals from gut to brain. J Clin Endocrinol Metab 57:1111-1118, 1983

Johnson CL, Stuckey MK, Lewis LD, et al: A survey of 509 cases of self-reported bulimia, in Anorexia Nervosa: Recent Developments in Research. Edited by Darby PL, Garfinkel PE, Garner DM, et al. New York, Alan R. Liss, 1983

Kalra SP: Neural loci involved in naloxone-induced luteinizing hormone release: effect of a norepinephrine synthesis inhibitor. Endocrinology 109:1805-1810, 1981

Kaplan SL, Grumbach MM: Physiology of puberty, in The Gonadotropins: Basic Science and Clinical Aspects in Females. Edited by Flamigini C, Givens JR. New York, Academic Press, 1982, pp 167-176

Katz JL, Boyar R, Roffwarg H, et al: Weight and circadian luteinizing hormone secretory pattern in anorexia nervosa. Psychosom Med 40:549-567, 1978

Kaye WH, Pickar D, Naber D, et al: Cerebrospinal fluid opioid activity in anorexia nervosa. Am J Psychiatry 139:643-645, 1982

Kaye WH, Ebert MH, Gwirtsman HE, et al: Differences in brain seroto-nergic metabolism between nonbulimic and bulimic patients with anorexia nervosa. Am J Psychiatry 141:1598-1601, 1984

Kaye WH, Jimerson DC, Lake CR, et al: Altered norepinephrine metabolism following long-term weight recovery in patients with anorexia nervosa. Psychiatry Res 14:333-342, 1985

Kaye WH, Berrettini WH, Gwirtsman HE, et al: Alterations of CSF CRH and POMC in anorexia nervosa [NR 26]. Presented at the 139th Annual Meeting of the American Psychiatric Association, Washington, DC, May 1986a

Kaye WH, Gwirtsman HE, Lake CR, et al: Noradrenergic disturbances in normal weight bulimia [NR 27]. Presented at the 139th Annual Meeting of the American Psychiatric Association, Washington, DC, May 1986b

Kaye WH, Gwirtsman HE, George DT, et al: Elevated cerebrospinal fluid levels of immunoreactive corticotropin-releasing hormone in anorexia nervosa: relation to state of nutrition, adrenal function and intensity of depression. J Clin Endocrinol Metab 64:203-208, 1987

Kemmann E, Pasquale SA, Skaf R: Amenorrhea associated with carotenemia. JAMA 249:926-929, 1983

Khuri R, Gehi M: Psychogenic amenorrhea: an integrative review. Psychosomatics 22:883-893, 1981

Kuderling I, Dorsch G, Warnhoff M, et al: The actions of prostaglandin E_2, naloxone and testosterone on starvation-induced suppression of luteinizing hormone-releasing hormone and luteinizing-hormone secretion. Neuroendocrinology 39:530-537, 1984

Lacey JH: The bulimic syndrome at normal body weight: reflections on pathogenesis and clinical features. International Journal of Eating Disorders 2:59-65, 1982

Leadem CA, Crowley WR, Simpkins JW, et al: Effects of naloxone on catecholamine and LHRH release from the perifused hypothalamus of the steroid-primed rat. Neuroendocrinology 40:497-500, 1985

Leibowitz SF: Noradrenergic function in the medial hypothalamus: potential relation to anorexia nervosa and bulimia, in The Psychobiology of Anorexia Nervosa. Edited by Pirke KM, Ploog D. New York, Springer-Verlag, 1984

Leibowitz SF, Shor-Posner G: Brain serotonin and feeding behavior. Appetite 7: suppl 1-14, 1986

Lindy DC, Walsh BT, Roose SP, et al: The dexamethasone suppression test in bulimia. Am J Psychiatry 142:1375-1376, 1985

Litt IF, Glader L: Anorexia nervosa, athletics, and amenorrhea. J Pediatr 109:150-153, 1986

Marshall JC, Fraser TR: Amenorrhea in anorexia nervosa: assessment and treatment with clomiphene citrate. Br Med J 4:590-592, 1971

Marshall JC, Kelch RP: Low dose pulsatile gonadotropin-releasing hormone in anorexia nervosa: a model of human pubertal development. J Clin Endocrinol Metab 49:712-718, 1979

McCaleb ML, Myers RD, Singer G, et al: Hypothalamic norepinephrine in the rat during feeding and push–pull perfusion with glucose, 2-DG, or insulin. Am J Physiol 236:R312-R321, 1979

Metropolitan Life Insurance Company: New weight standards for men and women. Statistical Bulletin 40:1, 1959

Mitchell JE, Pyle RL, Hatsukami D, et al: The dexamethasone suppression test in patients with bulimia. J Clin Psychiatry 45:508-511, 1984

Moguilevsky JA, Faigon MR, Scacchi P, et al: Effect of serotonergic system on luteinizing hormone secretion in prepubertal female rats. Neuroendocrinology 40:135-138, 1985

Moshang T, Parks JS, Baker L, et al: Low serum triidothyronine in patients with anorexia nervosa. J Clin Endocrinol Metab 40:470-473, 1975

Musisi S, Garfinkel P: Comparative dexamethasone suppression test measurements in bulimia, depression, and normal controls. Can J Psychiatry 30:190-194, 1985

Nakai Y, Plant TM, Hess DL, et al: On the sites of the negative and positive feedback action of estradiol in the control of gonadotropin secretion in the Rhesus monkey. Endocrinology 102:1008-1014, 1978

Piran N, Kennedy S, Garfinkel PE, et al: Affective disturbance in eating disorders. J Nerv Ment Dis 173:395-400, 1984

Pirke KM, Schweiger U: Disturbance of the hypothalamic–pituitary–gonadal axis in bulimia. Acta Endocrinologica, in press

Pirke KM, Fichter MM, Warnhoff M, et al: Hypothalamic regulation of gonadotropin secretion in anorexia nervosa and in starvation. International Journal of Eating Disorders 2:151-158, 1983

Pirke KM, Pahl J, Schweiger U, et al: Metabolic and endocrine indices of starvation in bulimia: a comparison with anorexia nervosa. Psychiatry Res 15:33-39, 1985a

Pirke KM, Schweiger U, Lemmel W, et al: The influence of dieting on the menstrual cycle of healthy young women. J Clin Endocrinol Metab 60:1174-1179, 1985b

Pops MA, Schwabe AD: Hypercarotenemia in anorexia nervosa. JAMA 205:533-534, 1968

Pyle RL, Mitchell JE, Eckert ED: Bulimia: a report of 34 cases. J Clin Psychiatry 42:60-64, 1981

Rigotti NA, Nussbaum SR, Herzog DB, et al: Osteoporosis in women with anorexia nervosa. N Engl J Med 311:1601-1606, 1984

Riskind PN, Millard WJ, Martin JB: Opiate modulation of the anterior pituitary hormone response during suckling in the rat. Endocrinology 114:1232-1237, 1984

Rivier C, Vale W: Influence of corticotropin-releasing factor on reproductive functions in the rat. Endocrinology 114:914-921, 1984

Rivier C, Rivier J, Vale W: Stress-induced inhibition of reproductive functions: role of endogenous corticotropin-releasing factor. Science 231:607-609, 1986

Russell GFM: Bulimia nervosa: an ominous variant of anorexia nervosa. Psychol Med 9:429-448, 1979

Silverman JA: Medical consequences of starvation, the malnutrition of anorexia nervosa: caveat medicus, in Anorexia Nervosa: Recent Developments in Research. Edited by Darby PL, Garfinkel PE, Garner DM, et al: New York, Alan R. Liss, 1983

Spaulding SW, Chopra IJ, Sherwin RS, et al: Effect of caloric restriction and dietary composition of serum T_3 and reverse T_3 in man. J Clin Endocrinol Metab 42:197-200, 1976

Tannenbaum GS, Guyda HJ, Posner PI: Insulin-like growth factors: a role in growth hormone negative feedback and body weight regulation via brain. Science 220:77-79, 1983

Veldhuis JD, Evans WS, Demers LM, et al: Altered neuroendocrine regulation of gonadotropin secretion in women distance runners. J Clin Endocrinol Metab 61:557-563, 1985

Wakeling, A, DeSouza VFA: Differential endocrine and menstrual response to weight change in anorexia nervosa, in Anorexia Nervosa: Recent Developments in Research. Edited by Darby PL, Garfinkel PE, Garner DM, et al: New York, Alan R. Liss, 1983

Wakeling A, DeSouza VA, Beardwood CJ: Assessment of the negative and positive feedback effects of administered oestrogen on gonadotropin release in patients with anorexia nervosa. Psychol Med 7:397-405, 1977

Warren MP: The effects of exercise on pubertal progression and reproductive function in girls. J Clin Endocrinol Metab 51:1150-1157, 1980

Warren MP, Vande Wiele RL: Clinical and metabolic features of anorexia nervosa. Am J Obstet Gynecol 117:435-449, 1973

Warren MP, Jewelewicz R, Dyrenfurth I, et al: The significance of weight loss in the evaluation of pituitary response to LH-RH in women with secondary amenorrhea. J Clin Endocrinol Metab 40:601-611, 1975

Weiss SR, Ebert MH: Psychological and behavioral characteristics of normal-weight bulimics and normal-weight controls. Psychosom Med 45:293-303, 1983

Yen SSC, Quigley ME, Reid RL, et al: Neuroendocrinology of opioid peptides and their role in the control of gonadotropin and prolactin secretion. Am J Obstet Gynecol 152:485-493, 1985

Zumoff B, Walsh BT, Katz JL, et al: Subnormal plasma dehydroisoandrosterone to cortisol ratio in anorexia nervosa: a second hormonal parameter of ontogenic regression. J Clin Endocrinol Metab 56:668-672, 1983

Chapter 4

Thyroid Function in Bulimia

Allan S. Kaplan, M.D., F.R.C.P. (C)

Chapter 4

Thyroid Function in Bulimia

Thyroid function has not been extensively or rigorously studied in patients with the syndrome of bulimia. Yet there is clinical and theoretical value in conducting such investigations. After first reviewing some basic thyroid physiology, I shall discuss the rationale for conducting studies of thyroid function in bulimic patients, then review such studies that have been done, and conclude with the therapeutic significance of these studies.

REVIEW OF THYROID PHYSIOLOGY AND FUNCTION

The thyroid gland normally produces L-tetraiodothyronine (T_4, or thyroxine) and L-triiodothyronine (T_3). The thyroid gland is the only source of endogenous T_4; however, thyroid secretion accounts for only 20 percent of T_3 produced, with the remaining 80 percent being generated in the peripheral tissues from T_4 through peripheral deiodination (Ingbar and Woeber 1979). Reverse T_3, an isomer of T_3, is also produced in periphery through peripheral deiodination. Whereas T_3 is about three times more potent than T_4, reverse T_3 is metabolically inert (Chopra et al. 1975). These hormones are synthesized and secreted by the thyroid gland upon stimulation by thyroid-stimulating hormones (TSH, or thyrotropin), glycopeptides secreted by the anterior pituitary gland. Thyrotropin secretion, in turn, is regulated by TRH (thyrotropin-releasing hormone), a tripeptide secreted by the ventral medial hypothalamus into the portal venous system. The effects of TRH are inhibited by the extent of thyroid hormone effect on the pituitary, and this is closely related to the concentration of free thyroid hormone in the blood.

The thyroid gland also provides some autoregulatory control that is dependent on a supply of iodine. When iodine is unavailable, the

This research was supported in part by the Medical Research Council of Canada. I would like to thank Dr. Paul Garfinkel for reviewing the manuscript and Mrs. Linda Westecott for help in preparation of the manuscript.

gland secretes more T_3 than T_4, utilizing fewer iodine atoms and producing a more potent isomer (Robbins et al. 1974). Peripheral tissues also play a role in this regulation through the conversion of T_4 to T_3, as described earlier. Basal levels of thyroid hormone in the blood reflect the dynamic state of the thyroid gland, which is under direct control of the pituitary and indirect control of the hypothalamus and brain.

The monoamine neurotransmitters norepinephrine, serotonin, and dopamine regulate various neuroendocrine axes, including the hypothalamic–pituitary–thyroid (HPT) axis. Specifically, norepinephrine and dopamine appear to stimulate, and serotonin to inhibit, TRH release (Martin et al. 1977). These same neurotransmitters are also thought to play a role in the pathophysiology of psychiatric illnesses such as affective and eating disorders. This interface justifies the use of tests of neuroendocrine function as windows into the brain which may further elucidate the neurobiology of psychiatric illness.

RATIONALE FOR STUDIES OF THYROID FUNCTION IN BULIMIA

There are many reasons to examine the relationship between thyroid function and psychiatric illness in general, and bulimia in particular. The thyroid gland has been known to play a role in mental illness for almost 200 years (Rush 1806). It has become increasingly evident that the thyroid gland and the brain have a mutual relationship, with disturbed function in one area affecting the other. Concomitant with this increased knowledge has been an emerging literature related to the neurobiology and neurochemistry of appetitive behaviors. The rationale for examining thyroid function in bulimia relates to the possibility that as part of this brain–thyroid relationship, 1) thyroid function may be disturbed in some way in bulimia and an understanding of the nature of this disturbance may lead to an understanding of pathophysiology and pathogenesis, and 2) thyroid hormone may have clinical utility as a therapeutic agent.

PATHOPHYSIOLOGIC SIGNIFICANCE

Thyroid hormone influences a variety of metabolic processes, including protein synthesis and oxygen consumption. Disturbance in these areas often leads to a wide range of symptoms, including changes in mood, weight, and cognition—symptoms that are common in bulimia. In addition, assessment of thyroid function, especially the HPT axis, can provide access to neurotransmitter systems (described earlier) that are involved in appetitive behaviors and that could be disturbed in bulimia. Abnormalities in both basal levels of thyroid hormone and functioning of the HPT axis have been described in two closely related conditions, depression and anorexia nervosa. A review of these findings may shed light on mechanisms related to pathophysiology and pathogenesis of these disorders and provide rationale for similar studies in bulimia.

Depression and Thyroid Function

There is much evidence linking bulimia and depression. They share a common phenomenology, with high rates of depression and dysphoria reported among bulimic patients (Russell 1979; Pyle et al. 1981; Hudson et al 1983b; Piran et al. 1985). They share a common family history, with higher than expected rates of affective illness in the family members of bulimic probands (Strober et al. 1982; Hudson et al. 1983a). They share responsiveness to treatment, with a percentage of bulimic patients responding to conventional antidepressant pharmacotherapy (Pope et al. 1983a, 1983b; Walsh et al. 1984; Kennedy et al. 1985; Hughes et al. 1986).

Another area of possible linkage is shared neuroendocrine disturbances, such as are found in thyroid function. Recent studies suggest that thyroid hormone plays a role in affective disorders, probably as a modulator of central nervous system neurotransmission, and thereby indirectly influences affective state (Whybrow et al. 1981). Thyroid dysfunction, either hypo- or hyperthyroidism, is associated with changes in mood (Whybrow et al. 1969), and affective illness in turn seems to be associated with changes in thyroid function (Whybrow et al. 1981). These include alterations in levels of T_3, T_4, and reverse T_3 and in HPT axis function.

Transiently elevated levels of thyroxine have been reported in acute psychiatric illness generally: Anywhere from 4 to 38 percent of acute psychiatric admissions present with euthyroid hyperthyroxinemia (Spratt et al. 1982). Most authors report thyroid indices to be either in the high normal or normal range in depressed patients (Prange et al. 1984). The consensus is that the thyroid axis is interacting with a host of other biologic factors responsible for mood alteration.

The euthyroid sick syndrome (Carter et al. 1974; Chopra 1983), which occurs in starvation and chronic medical illness, is characterized by low normal T_4, decreased T_3, increased reverse T_3, and normal TSH. One specific aspect of this syndrome, elevated reverse T_3 levels, has been found to be present in some depressed patients (Linnoila et al. 1982). Others report a state-dependent increase in reverse T_3 in depression (Kjellman et al. 1983). The mechanism for this is not understood but may relate to reduced food intake.

Approximately 25 percent of patients with affective illness demonstrate blunting of the peak TSH response to TRH, despite the fact that such patients are clinically and metabolically euthyroid (Loosen and Prange 1982). Blunting, as defined by these authors, is a maximal change from baseline to peak TSH following TRH of less than 5 μU/ml (Δ max < 5μU/ml) in response to 500 μg intravenous TRH. Loosen and Prange (1982) hypothesized that hypersecretion of TRH, secondary to central neurotransmitter disturbance, leads to down-regulation of pituitary receptors and hyporesponsiveness to TRH. This finding is not specific to depression, however; it has been reported to occur in associated conditions such as alcoholism (Loosen and Prange 1979), mania (Kirkegaard et al. 1978), and borderline personality disorder (Garbutt et al. 1983).

Anorexia Nervosa and Thyroid Function

The relationship between anorexia nervosa and bulimia remains somewhat obscure. Bulimia has been characterized as a subtype of anorexia nervosa (Russell 1979; Garfinkel et al. 1980; Casper et al. 1980). More recently, bulimia has been identified as a separate syndrome (American Psychiatric Association 1980).

Thyroid function has been studied extensively in patients with anorexia nervosa; however, such studies have not distinguished between restricting and bulimic patterns of intake, and have generally been conducted on patients in an underweight state.

The pattern of thyroid hormone seen in underweight anorexics includes

1. T_4 levels usually within the normal range (Brown et al. 1977; Moshang et al. 1975; Miyai et al. 1975), although lower than those found in matched controls (Miyai et al. 1975), with an apparent correlation between resting T_4 levels and levels of cortisol (Brown et al. 1977);
2. normal T_3 resin uptake, suggesting normal T_4-binding globulin (Brown et al. 1977);
3. abnormally low levels of serum T_3 (Moshang et al. 1977);
4. increased levels of inactive reverse T_3 (Leslie et al. 1978);
5. normal levels of TSH in most studies, with very few studies finding decreased TSH levels (Hurd et al. 1977); and
6. usually normal (Brown et al. 1977), but in some studies delayed (Vigersky and Loriaux 1977; Wakeling et al. 1979) or blunted (Travaglini et al. 1976), TSH responses to TRH. Delayed and blunted responses also occur in conditions of simple weight loss (Vigersky et al. 1977) and these responses, for the most part, return to normal after weight gain (Leslie et al. 1978).

This pattern of thyroid indices occurs in other states of malnutrition and low carbohydrate intake or chronic illness, and is a physiologic adaptation to starvation. The pattern of low normal T_4, decreased T_3, increased reverse T_3, and normal TSH has been found in individuals who lose weight rapidly. It is often called a "low T_3" syndrome or, as mentioned earlier "euthyroid sick" syndrome (Carter et al. 1974; Chopra 1983).

Teleologically, there appears to be an explanation for these findings. On the basis of metabolic needs, thyroid hormones regulate metabolism, and in conditions of low metabolic need, such as starvation, there is an alteration of cellular mechanisms involved in the control of deiodination of T_4. This would reduce the production of T_3 and increase the production of reverse T_3, a much less calorigenic hormone. The pituitary thyrotrophs would not interpret low levels of T_3 as being insufficient for metabolic needs, as this alteration would occur in the pituitary as well. Therefore TSH levels would remain normal and not increase (Moshang and Utiger 1977).

In summary, the pattern of thyroid indices seen in anorexia nervosa is a physiologic adaptation to starvation. A recent study of healthy control subjects starved over a three-week period demonstrated that basal TSH levels were lowered and the TSH response to TRH was blunted compared with prefasting levels (Fichter et al. 1986). These abnormalities normalized during the period of weight gain. This study supports previous findings (Vinik et al. 1975) in five of nine normal males, who initially had a normal TSH response to TRH, of displayed blunted responses following a 36-hour fast. In both the Fichter et al. study and the Vinik et al. study, the definition of blunted response was not clearly stated. In addition, both studies utilized 200 μg of TRH, a submaximal stimulation dose (Anderson et al. 1971). Nevertheless, these studies illustrate the importance of assessing caloric intake at the time of testing.

It has been suggested that studying similar indices in patients with bulimia at a normal weight will reveal abnormalities that are not explained by weight loss or other metabolic factors, and that these abnormalities, if present, could possibly be indicative of a primary neuroendocrine defect. However, although most bulimic patients are at a normal weight (as defined by average body weight for age and height), many, if not all, such patients have lost weight from a premorbidly heavier state (Garfinkel et al. 1980). Biologically, they may be in a starvation state similar to underweight anorexic patients. This hypothesis is supported by a recent study (Pirke et al. 1985; see Chapter 8) that demonstrates that a majority of patients with bulimia show evidence of elevated plasma beta-hydroxybutyric acid and free fatty acids, both of which are indices of starvation, similar to emaciated anorexic patients and unlike controls at a similar weight. Alternatively, chaotic eating associated with abnormal patterns of nutrient intake could indirectly alter central nervous system neurotransmission and manifest by a disturbance in the HPT axis.

Despite these considerations, assessment of thyroid function, both absolute hormone levels and responsiveness of the HPT axis, could help to more accurately determine whether any disturbance does exist and, if so, whether such a disturbance is secondary to the metabolic effects of disordered eating or represents a primary disturbance with pathophysiologic or pathogenetic significance.

STUDIES OF THYROID FUNCTION IN BULIMIA

Studies of thyroid function in bulimia can be divided into a) those that focus on basal levels of thyroid hormones T_4, T_3, and reverse T_3, and b) those that focus on the TSH response to TRH.

T_3, T_4, and Reverse T_3 Studies

A small number of studies have been focused on the basal levels of thyroid hormones in bulimia. Mitchell and Bantle (1983) examined thyroid function in six bulimic subjects. Five had normal T_4 and T_3 concentrations and normal T_3 resin uptake; one had mildly depressed T_4 and T_3 levels. The authors comment on the normal T_3 levels found in the five patients as reflecting the improved nutritional status of bulimic patients compared with patients with anorexia nervosa, for whom lower T_3 is believed to be a result of decreased peripheral conversion of T_4 to T_3 as an adaptation to starvation.

In contrast, Pirke et al. (1985) assessed endocrine and metabolic indices of starvation in bulimic patients compared with anorexic patients and control subjects and found levels of T_3 in bulimic patients that were significantly lower compared with both control and anorexic subjects. The authors interpret this finding, in combination with their findings of decreased levels of glucose, decreased elevation of noradrenalin in response to an orthostatic challenge, and significantly increased levels of free fatty acids and beta-hydroxybutyric acid, as indicative of starvation and evidence of intermittent inadequate energy supply in bulimic patients (see also Chapter 8).

In another study (Mitchell et al. 1983), 16 of 168 patients with normal weight bulimia were found to have abnormal thyroid function upon screening, usually a decreased thyroxine index (the product of the resin T_3 uptake and serum T_4). Two of the 16 patients had documented preexisting thyroid disease. Only one of the remaining 14 patients had, on physical examination and further laboratory testing, evidence of thyroid dysfunction; in this case, a diagnosis of hypothyroidism was made, and thyroid supplementation was provided. The authors do not comment on the 16 percent rate of low thyroxine index in these patients. A possible explanation is that 18 (11 percent) of the 168 patients were under 90 percent of ideal body weight. It would be important to assess whether the thyroid abnormalities occurred with greater frequency in this underweight group of patients.

In my own series of bulimic patients at normal weight seen in consultation, 40 had T_3 resin uptake and serum T_4 values taken as part of the screening process prior to entering a research protocol (1983-1986). All patients were within 90 to 110 percent of ideal body weight for height. All were moderately to severely ill, with 70 percent of the patients engaging in daily binge eating and purging. One patient had a low T_3 resin uptake with a normal T_4; all other patients had values in the normal range.

In summary, the small amount of available literature supports the notion that bulimic patients are clinically and by laboratory standards euthyroid. A decrease in T_3 reported by one group of investigators in normal weight bulimic patients is an important finding and requires replication. It is important because it supports the concept that bulimic patients, although over 90 percent of ideal body weight, are biologically in a starved state. This could have implications for interpretation of other parameters in the study of normal weight bulimia.

Studies of Thyroid-Stimulating Hormone Response to Thyroid-Releasing Hormone

There are four published and several unpublished studies on the TSH response to TRH in bulimia. They report on small numbers of patients and offer somewhat conflicting results. Gwirtsman et al. (1983) studied 10 normal weight bulimic patients who were between 83 and 110 percent of ideal body weight. They were part of a larger group of 18 bulimics, 15 of whom were closely monitored as inpatients for one week prior to any investigations. The remaining three were outpatients with no monitoring of their eating prior to testing. The authors do not state how many of the 10 patients tested with TRH were unmonitored outpatients. They found that 8 of the 10 demonstrated a blunted TSH response to TRH as defined by previously established criteria (Loosen and Prange 1982). No control group was used. Blunting was not related to other variables, such as a history of anorexia nervosa, positive result on the dexamethasone suppression test, weight below or above 95 percent of ideal body weight, menstrual status, or positive family history. The authors do not state whether the outpatients were more likely to show a blunted response. They also do not specify the dose of intravenous TRH used. This is important, because it is known that for maximum stimulation, at least 400 μg of TRH are required (Anderson et al. 1971).

In another study, the same group of investigators (Gwirtsman et al. 1984) described three cases of bulimia in men. All patients were at least 85 percent of ideal body weight at time of testing. All three had normal basal levels of TSH; one of the three showed a blunted response on the basis of the previously described criteria. Interestingly, at the time of testing, all three patients were considerably below their premorbid maximum weight. The patient with the blunted response was 13 kg thinner than his premorbidly heaviest weight, while the two normal responders were 10 to 9 kg thinner, respectively. The dose of TRH used was not stated.

Mitchell and Bantle (1983) conducted the TRH stimulation test on six normal weight bulimic patients, all within 10 percent of their ideal body weight. The six patients were hospitalized for an undefined period of time prior to testing but were allowed to eat as they wished and were actively binge-eating during the testing. Five of the six subjects who had normal basal TSH levels showed normal responses to TRH. One subject, who demonstrated elevated basal concentrations of TSH, had no response to TRH. The authors do not comment on the possible reasons for the elevated baseline TSH, although this particular subject had normal serum T_4 and T_3 and normal T_3 resin uptake. The absence of a response to TRH seems explainable by the elevated baseline TSH.

Finally, Norris et al. (1985) performed the TRH stimulation test in 10 outpatients with bulimia, 9 inpatients with anorexia nervosa, and a group of healthy subjects. The bulimic patients' eating pattern was not regulated in any matter. Although their weight varied from 95 to 119 percent of ideal body weight, there was no mention of percent of present weight compared with premorbid weight. There were no significant group differences between the bulimic subjects and healthy controls with regard to various aspects of the TRH test, including the degree and timing of the peak response. However, 3 out of the 10 bulimic patients produced a blunted response, as defined by Δ max TSH $< 5 \mu U/ml$. Interestingly, 2 of the 10 healthy control subjects produced responses that were close to blunted, with a peak rise in TSH from baseline of exactly 5 μU/ml. There were no significant correlations with weight for basal TSH level, peak TSH level, peak incremental TSH response and area under the response curve, as well as peak-to-basal ratio. The anorexic group demonstrated a significantly later peak TSH level compared with either controls or themselves after weight restoration. Only one of the anorexic patients showed a blunted response.

Some unpublished studies report TSH responses to TRH in bulimia. Levy et al. (1986) found one of seven inpatients with bulimia to demonstrate a blunted response, as defined by Δ max TSH < $5\mu U/ml$. However, four of the seven demonstrated a delayed peak TSH response. The authors found no significant association between percentage of ideal body weight and peak response.

Finally, our group (Kaplan et al. 1986) examined the TSH response to TRH in 19 normal weight bulimic patients compared to 12 age- and sex-matched controls. The bulimic patients were moderately to severely ill, with 70 percent binge-eating and purging at least daily. All were within 90 to 110 percent of ideal body weight. A standard dose of 500 μg intravenous TRH was given and samples were drawn every 15 minutes for 60 minutes. The bulimic patients and controls did not differ in their TSH response to TRH. Moreover, no bulimic or control subject produced a blunted response. Hormonal responses in the bulimic group did not correlate with various indices of depression (Beck Depression Inventory scores, past personal or family history of depression, or Diagnostic Interview Schedule diagnosis of major depression) or weight (current weight, percent average body weight, percent premorbid weight, or percent maximum weight).

To summarize, in six studies examining TSH response to TRH 55 subjects have been tested. Of these 14 (25 percent) have demonstrated a blunted response. Approximately 4 percent (Anderson et al. 1971) of the normal population as compared with 25 percent (Loosen and Prange 1982) of depressed patients produce a blunted response. Five of the six studies report a range of blunting from 0 to 33 percent, quite dissimilar to the 80 percent blunted rate found by one group of investigators (Gwirtsman et al. 1983). If this study is excluded, the rate of blunted responses falls to 13 percent, or six blunted responses out of 45 subjects tested. It would seem then that normal weight bulimic patients demonstrate a blunted response at a rate similar to, or slightly below, that seen in a depressed population, but above the rate seen in normal individuals.

There are methodologic difficulties with these studies that limit conclusions at this time. Not all researchers used the recommended maximally stimulating dose of TRH. Few studies controlled for the immediate and recent nutritional status of the patient. As referred to earlier, brief periods of caloric restriction can alter the TSH response to TRH (Vinik et al. 1975). Bulimic patients commonly go through cycles of binge-eating and fasting; even though their weight remains stable, their caloric intake does not. The criteria for blunted response in four of the six studies were those established by other investigators, possibly under different experimental conditions. As shown in the study by Norris et al. (1985), inclusion of a control group is important, as it allows for comparison under similar conditions.

Despite these limitations, the data from these studies do provide valuable information. It does appear as if bulimic patients respond differently than do patients with anorexia nervosa to this neuroendocrine challenge test. It remains unclear from these studies whether the response in bulimia is similar to that found in depression, and further comparisons of bulimic, depressed, and normal populations under controlled conditions are required to more accurately assess this.

THERAPEUTIC SIGNIFICANCE

The status of the thyroid gland and the hypothalamic–pituitary–thyroid axis in bulimia may have implications for its treatment. Identifying a subpopulation of bulimic patients with thyroid abnormalities may identify a subgroup of biologically homogeneous patients more likely to respond to antidepressant therapy. There is some support for this hypothesis with respect to depression. Langer et al. (1983, 1986) reported that blunted TSH response to TRH predicted response to antidepressant medication, and Kirkegaard et al. (1975) found that patients who reverted from a blunted to a responsive state tended to be those who had the greatest antidepressant response to tricyclic antidepressants. No such studies have been reported in bulimic patients.

Theoretically, thyroid hormone could play a therapeutic role in bulimia, as it has in affective disorders. Studies have suggested that T_3 accelerates tricyclic antidepressant response (Coppen et al. 1972; Wheatley 1972) and that it can convert tricyclic antidepressant nonresponders to responders (Goodwin et al. 1981). On the other hand, others (Joffe et al. 1984) suggest that the antidepressant effect of drugs such as lithium and carbamazepine is due to their antithyroid effect. There have been case reports of the effectiveness of carbamazepine (Kaplan et al. 1983) and lithium (Hsu 1984) in bulimia. There have also been anecdotal reports of the use of T_3 as an adjunct to other antidepressant drugs in bulimic patients (Pope et al. 1983b). However, when thyroid hormone is taken by a bulimic patient, it is often being self-administered to increase metabolism and lower weight, as was described in "the Case of Ellen West" (Binswanger 1944) and as has been described in a recent report (Ferner et al. 1986) of T_3 abuse in a female body-builder.

Until the efficacy of antidepressant pharmacotherapy is more clearly established for bulimia, novel and unproved treatments such as adjunct thyroid supplementation should be used with caution in a clinical setting. However, on the basis of the experience with depressed patients, there may be merit in assessing the thyroid state of antidepressant unresponsive bulimic patients, and in considering the addition of thyroid hormone in such patients.

CONCLUSION

No consistent abnormalities have been found in thyroid function in bulimia. The studies in which various aspects of thyroid function have been examined have been methodologically inconsistent, few in number, and performed on small samples of patients. The abnormalities that have been reported could reflect altered pathophysiology that may elucidate underlying pathogenic mechanisms. Alternatively, such abnormalities could represent epiphenomena, that is, physiologic alterations due to factors nonspecific for bulimia. Future studies examining thyroid indices should help identify a more biologically homogeneous group of patients with bulimia. Intensive study of such a group will ideally lead to greater understanding of the biology of bulimia and to more efficacious treatment.

REFERENCES

American Psychiatric Association: Diagnostic and Statistical Manual of Mental Disorders (Third Edition). Washington, DC, American Psychiatric Association, 1980

Andersen MS, Bowers CJ, Kastin AJ, et al: Synthetic TRH, a potent stimulator of thyrotropin secretion in man. N Engl J Med 285:1279-1283, 1971

Binswanger L: Der Fall Ellen West [The case of Ellen West]. Schweiz Arch Neurol Psychiat 54:69-117, 1944

Brown GM, Garfinkel PE, Jeunlewic N, et al: Endocrine profiles in anorexia nervosa, in Anorexia Nervosa. Edited by Vigersky R. New York, Raven Press, 1977

Carter JN, Corcoran JM, Eastman CJ, et al: Effect of severe, chronic illness on thyroid function. Lancet 2:971-974, 1974

Casper RC, Eckert ED, Halmi KA: Bulimia: its incidence and clinical importance in patients with anorexia nervosa. Arch Gen Psychiatry 37:1030-1035, 1980

Chopra IJ: Thyroid function in nonthyroidal illnesses. Ann Intern Med 98:946-957, 1983

Chopra IJ, Smith SR: Circulating thyroid hormones and thyrotropin in adult patients with protein-calorie malnutrition. J Clin Endocrinol Metab 40:221-227, 1975

Chopra IJ, Sack J, Fisher DA: Reverse T_3 in the fetus and newborn, in Perinatal Thyroid Physiology and Disease. Edited by Fisher PA, Burrow GN. New York, Raven Press, pp. 33-48 1975

Coppen A, Whybrow PC, Noguera R, et al: The comparative antidepressant value of L-tryptophan with and without attempted potentiation by liothyromine. Arch Gen Psychiatry 26:239-241, 1972

Ferner RE, Burnett A, Rawlins MD: Triiodothyroacetic acid abuse in a female body builder. Lancet 1:383, 1986

Fichter MM, Pirke KM, Holsboer F: Weight loss causes neuroendocrine disturbances: experimental study in healthy starving subjects. Psychiatry Res 17:61-72, 1986

Garbutt JC, Loosen PT, Tipermas A, et al: The TRH test in patients with borderline personality. Psychiatry Res 9:107-113, 1983

Garfinkel PE, Moldofsky H, Garner DM: The heterogeneity of anorexia nervosa: bulimia as a distinct subgroup. Arch Gen Psychiatry 37:1036-1040, 1980

Goodwin FK, Prange AJ, Post RM, et al: L-triiodothyromine converts tricyclic antidepressant non-responders to responders. Am J Psychiatry 139:337-338, 1981

Gwirtsman HE, Roy-Byrne P, Yager J, et al: Neuroendocrine abnormalities in bulimia. Am J Psychiatry 140:559-563, 1983

Gwirtsman HE, Roy-Byrne P, Lerner L, et al: Bulimia in men: report of three cases with neuroendocrine findings. J Clin Psychiatry 45:78-81, 1984

Hsu LKG: Treatment of bulimia with lithium. Am J Psychiatry 191:1260-1262 1984

Hudson JI, Pope HG Jr, Jonas JM, et al: Family history study of anorexia nervosa and bulimia. Br J Psychiatry 142:133-138, 1983a

Hudson JI, Pope HG Jr, Jonas JM, et al: Phenomenologic relationship of eating disorders to major affective disorder. Psychiatry Res 9:345-354, 1983b

Hughes PL, Wells LA, Cunningham CJ, et al: Treating bulimia with desipramine. Arch Gen Psychiatry 43:182-186, 1986

Hurd HP, Palumbo PJ, Gharib H: Hypothalamic–endocrine dysfunction in anorexia nervosa. Mayo Clin Proc 52:711-716, 1977

Ingbar SH, Woeber KA: The thyroid gland, in Textbook of Endocrinology. Edited by Williams RH. Philadelphia, WB Saunders, 1974

Joffe RT, Roy-Byrne PP, Uhde T, et al: Thyroid function and affective illness: a reappraisal. Biol Psychiatry 19:1685-1691, 1984

Kaplan AS, Garfinkel PE, Darby PL, et al: Carbamazepine in the treatment of bulimia. Am J Psychiatry 140:1225-1226, 1983

Kaplan AS, Garfinkel PE, Warsh JJ, et al: The DST and TRH Stimulation Test in Normal Weight Bulimia. Presented at the 2nd International Conference on Eating Disorders, New York, April 1986

Kennedy S, Piran N, Garfinkel PE: Monoamine oxidase inhibitor therapy for anorexia nervosa and bulimia—a preliminary trial of isocarboxazid. J Clin Psychopharmacol 5:279-285, 1985

Kirkegaard C, Norlem N, Lauridson VB, et al: Protirelin stimulation test and thyroid function during treatment of depression. Arch Gen Psychiatry 32:1115-1118, 1975

Kirkegaard C, Bjorum N, Cohn D, et al: TRH stimulation test in manic depressive disease. Arch Gen Psychiatry 35:1017-1023, 1978

Kjellman BF, Ljunggren JG, Beck Friis J, et al: Reverse T_3 levels in affective disorders. Psychiatry Res 10:1-9, 1983

Langer G, Aschaver H, Koinig G, et al: The TSH response to TRH: a possible predictor of outcome to antidepressant and neuroleptic treatment. Prog Neuropsychopharmacol Biol Psychiatry 7:335-342, 1983

Langer G, Koinig G, Hatzinger R, et al: Response of thyrotropin to TSH as a predictor of treatment outcome. Arch Gen Psychiatry 43:861-868, 1986

Leslie RD, Isaacs AJ, Gomer J, et al: Hypothalamic–pituitary–thyroid function in anorexia nervosa: influence of weight gain. Br Med J 2:526-528, 1978

Levy A, Dixon K, Malarkey WB: Pathological GH and PRL responses to TRH in bulimia. Presented at the 139th Annual Meeting of the American Psychiatric Association, Washington, DC, May 1986

Linnoila M, Lamberg BA, Potter WZ, et al: High reverse T_3 levels in mania and unipolar depressed women. Psychiatry Res 6:271-276, 1982

Loosen PT, Prange AJ: TRH in alcoholic men: endocrine responses. Psychosom Med 41:584-585, 1979

Loosen PT, Prange AJ: Serum thyrotropin response to thyrotropin-releasing hormone in psychiatric patients: a review. Am J Psychiatry 139:405-416, 1982

Martin JB, Reichlin S, Brown GM: Clinical Neuroendocrinology. Philadelphia, F. A. Davis, 1977

Mitchell JE, Bantle JP: Metabolic and endocrine investigations in women of normal weight with bulimia syndrome. Biol Psychiatry 18:355-365, 1983

Mitchell JE, Pyle RL, Eckert ED, et al: Electrolyte and other physiologic abnormalities in patients with bulimia. Psychol Med 13:273-278, 1983

Miyai K, Yamamoto T, Azukizawa M, et al: Serum thyroid hormones and thyrotropin in anorexia nervosa. J Clin Endocrinol Metab 40:334-338, 1975

Moshang T, Utiger RD: Low T_3 euthyroidism in anorexia nervosa, in Anorexia Nervosa. Edited by Vigersky R. New York, Raven Press, 1977

Moshang T, Parks JS, Baker L: Low serum T_3 in patients with anorexia nervosa. J Clin Endocrinol Metab 40:470-473, 1975

Norris PD, O'Malley BP, Palmer RL: The TRH test in bulimia and anorexia nervosa: a controlled study. J Psychiatr Res 19:215-219, 1985

Piran N, Kennedy S, Garfinkel PE, et al: Affective disturbance in eating disorders. J Nerv Ment Dis 173:395-400, 1985

Pirke KM, Pahl J, Schweiger U, et al: Metabolic and endocrine indices of starvation in bulimia: a comparison with anorexia nervosa. Psychiatry Res 15:33-39, 1985

Pope HG Jr, Hudson JI, Jonas JM, et al: Bulimia treated with imipramine: a placebo-controlled double-blind study. Am J Psychiatry 140:554-558, 1983a

Pope HG Jr, Hudson JI, Jonas JM: Antidepressant treatment of bulimia: preliminary experience and practical recommendations. J Clin Psychopharmacol 3:274-281, 1983b

Prange AJ, Loosen PT, Wilson IC, et al: Therapeutic use of hormones of the thyroid axis in depression, in Neurobiology of Mood Disorders. Edited by Post RM, Ballenger JC. Baltimore, Williams and Wilkins, 1984

Pyle RL, Mitchell JE, Eckert ED: Bulimia: a report of 34 cases. J Clin Psychiatry 42:60-64, 1981

Robbins J, Rall JE, Groden P: The thyroid and iodine metabolism, in Duncan's Disease of Metabolism: III. Endocrinology. Edited by Bondy PK, Rosenberg LE. Philadelphia, WB Saunders, 1974

Rush B: An inquiry into the functions of the spleen, liver, pancreas and thyroid gland. Med Physic J London 16:193-208, 1806

Russell G: Bulimia nervosa: an ominous variant of anorexia nervosa. Psychol Med 9:429-448, 1979

Spratt D, Pont A, Miller M, et al: Hyperthyroxinemia in patients with acute psychiatric disorders. Am J Med 73:41-47, 1982

Strober M, Salkin B, Burroughs J, et al: Validity of the bulimia-restricter distinction in anorexia nervosa: parental personality characteristics and family psychiatric morbidity. J Nerv Ment Dis 170:345-351, 1982

Travaglini P, Beck-Peccoz P, Ferrari C, et al: Some aspects of hypothalamic-pituitary function in patients with anorexia nervosa. Acta Endocrinol 81:252-262, 1976

Vigersky RA, Loriaux DL: Anorexia nervosa as a model of hypothalamic dysfunction, in Anorexia Nervosa. Edited by Vigersky R. New York, Raven Press, 1977, pp 109-122

Vigersky RA, Andersen AE, Thompson RH, et al: Hypothalamic dysfunction in secondary amenorrhea associated with simple weight loss. N Engl J Med 297:1141-1145, 1977

Vinik AF, Kalk WJ, McLaren H, et al: Fasting blunts the TSH response to synthetic TRH. J Clin Endocrinol Metab 40:509-511, 1975

Wakeling A, De Souza VA, Gore MB, et al: Amenorrhea, body weight and serum hormone concentrations, with particular reference to prolactin and thyroid hormones in anorexia nervosa. Psychol Med 9:265-272, 1979

Walsh BT, Stewart JW, Roose SP, et al: Treatment of bulimia with phenelzine. Arch Gen Psych 41:1105-1109, 1984

Wheatley D: Potentiation of amitryptiline by thyroid hormone. Arch Gen Psychiatry 26:229-233, 1972

Whybrow PC, Prange AJ: A hypothesis of thyroid-catecholamine receptor interaction. Arch Gen Psychiatry 38:106-113, 1981

Whybrow PC, Prange AJ, Treadway CR: Mental changes accompanying thyroid gland dysfunction: a reappraisal using objective psychological measurements. Arch Gen Psychiatry 20:48-63, 1969

Chapter 5

Melatonin Regulation in Bulimia

Sidney Kennedy, M.B., F.R.C.P.(C)
Daniel Costa, M.D.
Victor Parienti, M.D.
Gregory M. Brown, M.D., Ph.D., F.R.C.P.(C)

Chapter 5

Melatonin Regulation in Bulimia

I n this chapter, historical developments in understanding the role of the pineal gland, regulation of its hormone melatonin, and the application of this knowledge to the study of psychiatric populations are considered. Three distinct ways in which measurement of melatonin may provide new information about bulimia involve its role as a marker for a) the circadian system, b) the noradrenergic system, and c) light sensitivity.

THE PINEAL GLAND AND MELATONIN

Historical Perspective

The pineal gland occupies a prominent place in the history of psychiatry. Its median position in the brain has always fascinated neuroscientists and psychiatrists. Descartes described the pineal as the seat of rational thought (Descartes 1953), and Thomas Arnold (1786) concluded that calcification of the pineal represented one cause of insanity. The discovery that people free of mental disorders also invariably had pineal calcification (Crowther 1811) introduced a prolonged period when the pineal was thought to be a vestigial organ (Mullen and Silman 1977).

Modern interest in this endocrine gland began when Aaron Lerner and his colleagues discovered the pineal hormone melatonin (Lerner et al. 1958, 1959), at that time characterized by its ability to lighten the color of amphibian melanocytes. This extract was shown to inhibit

We wish to thank Drs. Paul Garfinkel and Niva Piran for their helpful comments and the staff of the Clinical Investigation Unit at Toronto General Hospital for their excellent nursing care. We also thank Erika Johansson for laboratory assistance and Brenda Lediett and Carrol Whynot for their help in the preparation of the manuscript. Physicians' Services Incorporated provided grant support.

gonadal maturation in animals (Wurtman et al. 1963a). Previous experiments with pineal extract (Wurtman et al. 1961) suggested that the production of pineal hormone was inhibited by continuous exposure to light. In the late 1960s, the mammalian pineal was already known to function as a neuroendocrine transducer, producing melatonin in response to the release of the neurotransmitter norepinephrine from its sympathetic nerve supply. Equally exciting was the discovery of the pineal's unique role in transducing the succession of light and dark into typical patterns of melatonin plasma levels secreted almost exclusively during darkness (Wurtman 1985).

Pineal Anatomy and Melatonin Biosynthesis

In primitive animals, the pineal is nicknamed "the third eye" because it is situated on the dorsal face of the skull and its neurons are directly stimulated by light (Kappers 1979). In man it is a component of the diencephalic roof located between the habenular and posterior commissures (Kappers et al. 1979). Although it is connected to the brain and is derived from neural tissue, the pineal lies outside the blood–brain barrier. The melatonin-secreting pinealocytes are thought to be innervated mainly by the sympathetic fibers of nervi conarii. These adrenergic fibers originate from the superior cervical ganglia (Kappers 1965).

Melatonin is synthesized from serotonin, in two stages involving N-acetylation and 5-0-methylation (Axelrod and Weisbach 1960). The concentration of serotonin in the pineal is approximately 50 times greater than in the rest of the brain (Quay 1974). N-acetylation is thought to be the rate-limiting step in this process (Klein and Weller 1970), and the maintenance of its activity requires continued beta-adrenergic stimulation (Deguchi and Axelrod 1972). Thus melatonin production may serve as a marker for noradrenergic activity.

In early attempts to measure melatonin, researchers used bioassay techniques that were quite insensitive (Pelham et al. 1973; Pang et al. 1977). Subsequently, radioimmunoassay (Arendt et al. 1975, 1977; Wetterberg et al. 1976) and negative chemical ionization mass spectrometry–gas chromatography (Lewy and Markey 1978) techniques have been developed and are available in a limited number of research laboratories.

Regulation and Circadian Rhythm of Melatonin

The pineal is the only major source of circulating melatonin in humans (Lewy and Newsome 1983; Chik et al. 1985; Neuwelt et al. 1985). Sympathetic inflow is regulated by the suprachiasmatic nucleus of the hypothalamus, which in turn receives impulses of retinal origin via the retino–hypothalamic tract (Hendrickson et al. 1972). The retino–hypothalamic tract is the neural substrate of the light/dark cycle's influence on melatonin secretion. Situated at the beginning of this multisynaptic adrenergic pathway, the suprachiasmatic nucleus is capable of endogenous, self-sustained oscillation (Stephen and Zucker 1972; Moore and Eichler 1972) that is light sensitive.

The suprachiasmatic–pineal pathway is multisynaptic and as yet incompletely mapped. It includes the lateral and tuberal hypothalamus, the medial forebrain bundle, and the oral part of the mesencephalic tegmentum. This long pathway terminates in the thoracic intermediolateral nuclei of the spinal cord grey matter (Kappers 1979). These nuclei harbor the pineal's preganglionic sympathetic neurons, which terminate in the superior cervical ganglia. In addition, animal experiments suggest that circulating melatonin may exert a negative feedback on the pineal (Brown et al. 1983).

It is now established that in normal human subjects melatonin secretion is low during the day (<10 pg/ml), increasing to a peak between 30 and 100 pg/ml by 2:00 to 3:00 A.M. before falling again to daytime levels. This rhythm is an endogenous one that persists in the absence of any light cues. Melatonin is now considered to be one of several markers of the human circadian system (Anders 1982; Lewy 1984; Hallonquist et al. 1986).

The human circadian system is a central integrative mechanism by which specialized physiological and behavioral states prepare an individual for and are timed to recurring environmental changes (Hallonquist et al. 1986).

The rhythms controlled by the human circadian system are believed to be generated by "oscillators" or "internal clocks" that can measure time when no external cues are present (Moore-Ede et al. 1983). In addition to melatonin, other endogenous rhythms, that is rhythms that persist in the absence of external cues, include sleep/wakefulness, rapid eye movement sleep, body temperatures, cortisol, renal function, perceptual–motor performance, and menstruation (Anders 1982; Hallonquist et al. 1986).

Pineal rhythm is regulated by the interaction between an endogenous pacemaker, likely in the suprachiasmatic nucleus (Lewy 1984) and environmental light/dark changes. Thus melatonin secretion demonstrates alterations both on a circadian and seasonal basis as the ratio of light to darkness alters (Lewy 1984). The light-induced changes of the melatonin circadian rhythm are probably comparable to the effects induced by light on other circadian rhythms, but only melatonin secretion is acutely suppressed by light (Wurtman et al. 1963b).

Although circadian rhythm disturbances are generally not associated with pineal tumors (Moore-Ede et al. 1983), there are individual case reports of a syndrome resembling jet lag in the presence of pineoblastoma, with symptom improvement after pinealectomy (Neuwelt et al. 1985). In addition, administration of exogenous melatonin to normal subjects can induce sleep (Lieberman et al. 1984; Vollrath et al. 1975), and melatonin has been used as a treatment for jet lag (Arendt et al. 1986). For these reasons, plasma melatonin levels serve as a marker for both circadian rhythm and light sensitivity.

Knowledge of melatonin's effects on other endocrine glands (for example, gonads, thyroid) is increasing (Wurtman 1985; Nir 1985; Vriend 1983). Melatonin has been shown to regulate the timing of the annual reproductive cycle in animals with seasonal breeding patterns, such as sheep and hamsters (Bittman et al. 1983; Carter and Goldman 1983). In humans it may have a role in timing the onset of puberty, although this is not clearly established (Waldhauser et al. 1984).

STUDIES OF MELATONIN IN AFFECTIVE DISORDER

Melatonin as a Marker for Rhythm Disturbance

Affectively ill patients have abnormalities of several biological rhythms, including diurnal mood variations, alterations in the sleep–wake cycle, as well as altered secretion of pituitary hormones (Papousek 1975; Hawkins and Mendels 1966; Lohrenz et al. 1969; Sachar 1975). These findings suggest an underlying disturbance in circadian rhythm, which may be studied using the timing and duration of melatonin production as a marker for circadian rhythm.

Two types of circadian rhythm disturbances might be present in patients with major affective disorder. The first type, described as complete or partial internal desynchronization, has been reported in bipolar depression (Kripke et al. 1978; Pflug et al. 1976; Beersma et al. 1983). The second type, described as phase advancement of circadian rhythms, has been observed in both unipolar and bipolar affective disorders (Papousek 1975; Wehr and Goodwin 1983). In several instances, the peak level of plasma melatonin occurred earlier during the night in subjects with major depression (Wetterberg et al. 1981; Branchey et al. 1982; Nair et al. 1985). These findings support the phase-advance hypothesis, although others (Claustrat et al. 1984; Beck-Friis et al. 1985) have reported no difference between patients and controls.

Melatonin as an Adrenergic Marker

There is also extensive evidence to suggest abnormalities in the noradrenergic neurotransmitter system in patients with affective disorder (Schildkraut 1965; Maas 1975). Thus, by measuring melatonin as an index of noradrenergic activation of the pineal, this system can also be studied. The amplitude peak of plasma melatonin in depressive patients has been found to be lower than that of control subjects in a number of studies (Beck-Friis et al. 1984; Claustrat et al. 1984; Steiner and Brown 1985), particularly in those with melancholia (American Psychiatric Association 1980; Frazer et al. 1985).

The adrenoreceptors in the proximity of the pinealocytes are of the alpha-2 presynaptic type and the beta-1 postsynaptic type. A norepinephrine uptake mechanism is also present (Lewy 1983). In humans, neuropharmacological research data suggest that both alpha-2 and beta-1 adrenoreceptors participate in the regulation of melatonin production (Hanssen et al. 1977; Cowen et al. 1983; Lewy 1983, 1984). Hence, melatonin levels were considered suitable to provide an accurate "window" to assess adrenergic function (Lewy 1984; Thompson et al. 1985). Although controversial, there is evidence to suggest that an acute, but not necessarily chronic, increase in nocturnal melatonin levels occurs in control subjects following treatment with desipramine (Cowen et al. 1985). Desipramine also produced a significant increase of plasma melatonin after three weeks of treatment in depressed patients (Thompson et al. 1985). In depressed patients who are responsive to desipramine, there is also a significant inverse correlation between the plasma levels of desipramine and melatonin-like immunoreactivity (Halbreich et al. 1981). This finding is consistent with the hypothesis of down-regulation of beta-adrenergic receptors in man by chronic high plasma levels of desipramine. Similarly, beta blockers (Hanssen et al. 1977; Cowen et al. 1983) decrease plasma melatonin concentration in humans, as does clonidine, an alpha-adrenergic agonist (Lewy 1983).

A relationship has also been proposed between melatonin and cortisol abnormalities in depression. A "low melatonin syndrome" in depression proposed by Beck-Friis et al. (1985) included low melatonin levels together with a lower plasma melatonin/cortisol ratio in depressed patients who had a positive dexamethasone suppression test (DST) compared with depressed patients who had a normal DST. However, others have reported that melatonin profiles remain abnormal after clinical recovery while cortisol patterns normalize (Branchey et al. 1982; Steiner and Brown 1985).

Melatonin and Light Sensitivity

There is preliminary evidence to suggest that manic depressive patients may show a supersensitivity to light. Lewy et al. (1981) initially reported that nighttime melatonin levels fell twice as much in acutely ill manic patients compared with normal subjects following exposure to bright light. Similar results were reported with euthymic bipolar patients (Lewy et al. 1985a), suggesting that supersensitivity to light may be a trait marker for bipolar affective disorder.

Seasonal Affective Disorder

Before considering bulimia, it is worth reviewing recent descriptions of the seasonal affective disorder (SAD) syndrome, since both of these disorders share affective and eating disturbances. (See Chapter 13 for a comprehensive discussion of this disorder.) Seasonal affective disorder has been described both in adults, predominantly women (Rosenthal et al. 1984), and children and adolescents (Rosenthal et al. 1986). During the winter, an individual characteristically experiences recurrent episodes of feeling moderately depressed, oversleeping, and overeating, which is associated with carbohydrate craving. This may alternate with mild elation and overactivity during spring and summer months. However, these subjects appear to differ from bulimic patients in their lack of a pathological preoccupation about body weight and body image.

Controlled studies comparing the effects of bright light versus dim light on such patients during their "winter depression" have shown significant improvement in mood and level of psychosocial functioning only during bright light exposure (Rosenthal et al. 1985; also see Chapter 13). Since bright light, but not dim light, suppresses melatonin (Lewy et al. 1980), it has been proposed that the melatonin system and its response to light may play some role in this syndrome (Lewy et al. 1985b), although there may not be a direct relationship (Wehr et al. 1986).

STUDIES OF MELATONIN IN STARVATION AND ANOREXIA NERVOSA

Both underfed rats (Blask et al. 1981) and pinealectomized rats (Sorrentino et al. 1971) experience a delay in puberty related to inhibition of gonadal maturity; this is partly reversed by the administration of melatonin (Blask et al. 1980; Lang et al. 1983). During such underfeeding, rats typically show an increase in amplitude and duration of nocturnal circulatory melatonin (Chik and Brown 1983).

Other investigators have looked at the influence of weight loss on biological measures. The DST has been found to be altered by weight loss (Berger et al. 1983; Edelstein et al. 1983). There are contradictory reports on the relationship between weight and melatonin among depressed subjects. In two studies (Ferrier et al. 1982; Arendt et al. 1982), a significant positive correlation was found between melatonin and body weight, while in a third (Beck-Friis et al. 1984) a negative correlation was found between serum melatonin and both body weight and height.

There is also evidence in underweight patients with anorexia nervosa that peripheral noradrenergic activity is reduced. These studies measured norepinephrine and its major metabolite 3-methoxy-4-hydroxyphenylglycol in urine and plasma (Gerner and Gwirtsman 1981; Biederman et al. 1984; Darby et al. 1979). If there is a similar reduction in noradrenergic activity on the pineal, then low levels of melatonin would be predicted in anorexia nervosa. However, results of melatonin studies in anorexia nervosa are also conflicting. In emaciated patients, low nocturnal melatonin levels were reported by Birau et al. (1984), normal levels were reported by Dalery et al. (1985), and elevated levels were reported by Brown et al. (1979). Ferrari et al. (1985) also reported the absence of a significant circadian rhythm of melatonin in all but 27 percent of the anorexic patients studied.

OTHER FACTORS INFLUENCING MELATONIN PRODUCTION

Other factors can influence pineal and plasma melatonin levels (Pang 1985). Melatonin levels decrease with age (Iguchi et al. 1982; Pang 1985). Physical and biochemical stress induces an increase in the synthesis and secretion of melatonin in birds and mammals (Pang 1985). Melatonin has generally been reported as being insensitive to psychological stress in humans (Vaughan et al. 1975, 1978). The influence of the menstrual cycle on melatonin remains controversial (Vaughan 1984; Arendt 1985). In a recent study of young women with normal menstrual function, melatonin levels were lowest at ovulation (Hariharasubramanian et al. 1985).

Finally, there is a great interindividual variation of melatonin levels, in spite of their substantial intraindividual stability (Arato et al. 1985).

BULIMIA—ITS RELATIONSHIP TO ANOREXIA NERVOSA AND AFFECTIVE DISORDER

Although bulimia has been recognized in association with anorexia nervosa for many years (Casper 1983), the case for a distinct syndrome to be called "bulimia nervosa" was first made in 1979 (Russell 1979). It was modified in 1980 to become the syndrome of bulimia (American Psychiatric Association 1980) and again in 1987 to become "bulimia nervosa" (American Psychiatric Association 1987). There is considerable overlap between anorexia nervosa and bulimia. About 50 percent of patients meeting criteria for anorexia nervosa currently report frequent binge eating and purging behavior (Garfinkel et al. 1980); in addition, significant numbers of normal weight bulimic patients have a past history of anorexia nervosa (Pyle et al. 1981; Cooper and Fairburn 1983). There is, therefore, agreement that the two syndromes are closely related. Nevertheless, biological studies suggest that the two groups may show different neurochemical disturbances (Kaye et al. 1984).

A second area of overlap involves the relationship between bulimia and depression. This has been extensively reviewed elsewhere (Kennedy and Walsh 1987). In summary, similarities between the two groups of disorders have been reported involving a) clinical phenomenology (Hudson et al. 1983c; Cooper and Fairburn 1986; Piran et al. 1985); b) shared family history of affective disorder (Hudson et al. 1983b; Pyle et al. 1981; Fairburn and Cooper 1984); c) biological abnormalities, including abnormal DSTs (Gwirtsman et al. 1983; Hudson et al. 1983a; Kennedy et al. 1984; Lindy et al. 1985; also see Chapter 1) and shared neurotransmitter abnormalities (Kaye et al. 1984); and d) shared response to antidepressant medications (Pope et al. 1983; Walsh et al. 1984; Kennedy et al. 1986; Hughes et al. 1986).

Melatonin Disturbances in Bulimia

Rationale for Study.   If bulimia as a syndrome is related to affective disorder, then similar disturbances of melatonin production would be expected to occur in the two disorders. Also, since bulimia has close clinical, and perhaps endocrine, links to anorexia nervosa, melatonin may also serve as a marker for comparisons between these two syndromes, particularly regarding the influence of weight on findings.

So far, it is not known whether rhythmic patterns of bingeing behavior occur on a circadian or annual basis. However, we have observed clinically that many of our patients binge mainly in the evening, often following periods of restriction. Sequential measurement of melatonin would provide information on a possible disturbance in circadian rhythm in bulimic patients. We proposed that bulimic patients would show lower melatonin levels and an earlier peak compatible with phase advance compared with control subjects.

Method of Study.   To test our hypothesis, we studied three groups of young women ages 18 to 35 who had been admitted to the Clinical

Investigation Unit at Toronto General Hospital: those with bulimia in the presence of anorexia nervosa (AB) ($n = 6$), those with bulimia at normal weight (NWB) ($n = 6$), and normal control subjects (NC) ($n = 6$).

During the study, hourly sampling from 6:00 P.M. to 6:00 A.M. of melatonin and cortisol (to enable comparison of the melatonin/cortisol ratio) was carried out using an in-dwelling angiocatheter. All subjects wore an "overnight flight" eye mask from 10:00 P.M. to 6:00 A.M. to ensure standardized darkness. Serum was separated by centrifugation, and the samples were frozen for analysis within three months. Serum melatonin and cortisol assays were carried out using radioimmunoassay techniques described elsewhere (Brown et al. 1983; Wong et al. 1977). All samples were obtained between April and September 1986.

Statistical analysis involved two-way analysis of variance on three groups looking at two dimensions (group × time). Where significant differences were found, one-way analysis of variance was used together with the Duncan multiple range test.

Results. Only weight measures distinguished the anorexic bulimic from the normal weight bulimic groups (see Table 4).

Mean hourly serum melatonin levels (in pg/ml) were plotted for each of the three groups from 6:00 P.M. to 6:00 A.M. (see Figure 9). Although both bulimic groups compared with controls showed a trend toward lower nighttime levels (between 12:00 midnight and 4:00 A.M.), there were no significant differences between the groups at any time point.

As shown in Figure 10, hourly values of serum cortisol for the three groups showed similar, but inverted, patterns (compared with melatonin profiles), with significant group differences at 12:00 midnight between NWB and NC ($F = 3.97$; $df = 2, 17$; $p < .05$) and at 4:00 P.M. between AB and NC ($F = 4.15$; $df = 2, 17$; $p < .05$).

Repeated-measure analysis of variance for the ratio of melatonin to cortisol showed significant differences between the AB and NC groups at two time points: 9:00 P.M. ($F = 4.32$; $df = 2, 17$; $p < .05$) and 5:00 A.M. ($F = 5.66$; $df = 2, 17$; $p < .05$) (see Figure 11).

Peak melatonin levels and the hour of occurrence were noted. Although there was a wider time distribution for peak melatonin levels in bulimic subjects, there was no trend toward an earlier or later peak. Similarly, the lowest cortisol values were noted, and the ratio of peak melatonin levels to lowest cortisol values calculated (see Table 5).

Table 4. Descriptive Characteristics of Subjects

Characteristics	Normal Weight Bulimia (n = 6) Mean ± SD	Anorexia Nervosa, Bulimic Subtype (n = 6) Mean ± SD	Normal Control (n = 6) Mean ± SD
Age (years)	26.7 ± 5.9	26.3 ± 6.1	24.3 ± 3.1
Duration of eating disorder (years)	10.5 ± 6.8	7.5 ± 4.2ᵃ	0.0 ± 0.0 ᵃ
Height (cm)	163.5 ± 8.1	163.0 ± 2.8	161.8 ± 3.1
Weight (kg)	56.1 ± 8.1ᵃ	43.5 ± 3.0ᵃ	64.1 ± 8.2
Weight as percent of ideal body weight	95.2 ± 9.7ᵃ	73.9 ± 3.8ᵃ	111.8 ± 13.8 ᵃ
No. of binges per week	7.2 ± 4.9	4.7 ± 8.0	0.0 ± 0.0

ᵃSignificant ($p < .05$) difference from the group to the immediate right.

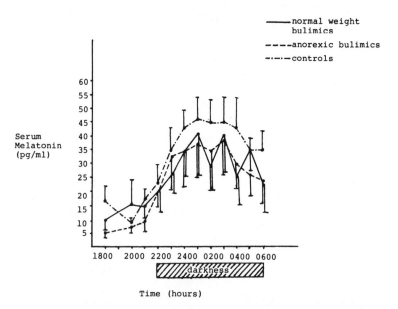

Figure 9. Mean (± SEM) serum melatonin levels in normal weight bulimic subjects ($n = 6$), anorexic bulimic subjects ($n = 6$), and normal controls ($n = 6$).

Absolute weight and percent of ideal body weight did not correlate with the total melatonin levels for subjects in any of the three groups. We also compared the 2:00 A.M. melatonin level with total 12-hour melatonin and found a significant correlation in each of the three groups. (For NWB, $r = .98, p < .001$; for AB, $r = .97, p < .001$; for NC, $r = .95, p < .002$.)

Conclusion. In our study of 12 bulimic subjects (six with an additional diagnosis of anorexia nervosa) and six female control subjects, levels of melatonin were not significantly reduced in either bulimic group, suggesting two preliminary conclusions. First, normal me-

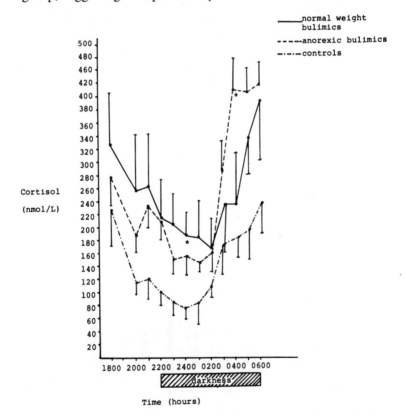

Figure 10. Mean (± SEM) serum cortisol levels in normal weight bulimic subjects ($n = 6$), anorexic bulimic subjects ($n = 6$), and normal controls ($n = 6$). *Significant difference ($p < .05$) from controls.

latonin levels imply normal functioning of pineal beta-adrenergic receptors in bulimia. Second, low weight did not appear to alter melatonin levels. Dalery et al. (1985) also found normal melatonin levels in nondepressed emaciated anorexic women. These women were on average 30 percent below ideal body weight, compared with the 27 percent below in our anorexic bulimic group and the 20 to 56 percent below in the study by Birau et al. (1984). In all cases, the percentage weight loss was considerably less than in animal starvation studies. Where significant differences occurred in melatonin/cortisol ratios, the differences were due to cortisol values; hence, we found no evidence that measuring the ratio provided any additional information.

Our findings of elevated nocturnal cortisol in both low weight and normal weight bulimic subjects are in agreement with other reports on hypothalamic–pituitary–adrenal axis dysfunction in bu-

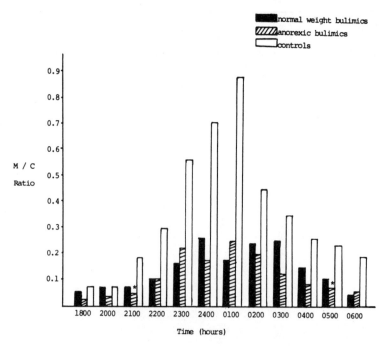

Figure 11. Mean (± SEM) serum melatonin/cortisol ratios in normal weight bulimic subjects (*n* = 6), anorexic bulimic subjects (*n* = 6), and normal controls (*n* = 6). *Significant difference (*p* < .05) from controls.

limia (Gwirtsman et al. 1983; Hudson et al. 1983a; also see Chapter 1). These findings have been used to support the hypothesis that affective disorder and bulimia are etiologically linked. In contrast, we did not find abnormal melatonin levels in bulimia, as have been reported in depressed patients (Claustrat et al. 1984). However, the recent study by Brown et al. (1985) found significantly reduced

Table 5. Value and Time of Maximum Serum Melatonin (MT max) and Minimum Cortisol (C min) Levels, and MT max/C min Ratio for Subject Groups

ID	MT max (pg/ml)		C min(ηmol/L)		MT max/C min
	Value	Time	Value	Time	
Normal Weight Bulimia ($n = 6$)					
03	11.9	0500	117.0	0400	0.10
06	30.9	2300	69.0	0300	0.45
09	33.9	0500	94.0	2300	0.36
11	65.2	0100	267.0	0200	0.24
12	84.6	0300	91.0	0200	0.93
13	93.3	0100	50.1	0100	1.86
Mean	53.3	0200	114.7	0200	0.66
Anorexia Nervosa, Bulimic Subtype ($n = 6$)					
01	17.6	0500	93.0	0200	0.19
02	40.4	0300	42.0	2400	0.96
05	68.2	0300	151.0	0200	0.45
10	30.2	0100	120.0	2400	0.25
16	107.2	0200	154.0	2300	0.70
17	32.6	0400	94.0	0200	0.35
Mean	49.4	0300	109.0	0100	0.48
Normal Control ($n = 6$)					
18	25.8	2400	53.0	0100	0.49
19	55.9	0400	87.0	0100	0.64
20	74.9	0100	42.8	0100	1.75
21	37.2	0100	108.0	2200	0.34
22	60.9	2400	47.0	0100	1.30
24	69.6	0400	37.0	0100	1.88
Mean	54.1	0200	62.5	0100	1.07

melatonin levels only in the subgroup with melancholia. In our study, diagnostic and rating scale data on depression have been collected, but small numbers prevent comparisons between depressed and non-depressed bulimics, although this will be of particular interest at a later stage.

Since melatonin levels show both a good intraindividual consistency and a wide interindividual variation (Grof et al. 1985), the relatively small sample size limits between-group comparisons. However, in a second phase of the study we will retest the same anorexic bulimic subjects when they are weight restored.

Because all groups showed a suppression of melatonin after the lights were on, it is not possible to assess whether any of the bulimic (or control) subjects would have continued to produce melatonin. However, we found no differences between the three groups with respect to the time at which nocturnal melatonin reached its peak value. This is potentially a second way in which bulimic subjects may differ from those with major depression (where phase advance or phase delay of circadian rhythms has been proposed to occur). However, it will be necessary to include a group of subjects with major depression and to separate bulimic subjects with and without depression before this issue can be further explored.

In conclusion, we found normal regulation of melatonin in small samples of normal weight and anorexic patients with bulimia. Further studies involving larger samples and repeat measures within groups are necessary to confirm these findings.

REFERENCES

American Psychiatric Association: Diagnostic and Statistical Manual of Mental Disorders (Third Edition). Washington, DC, American Psychiatric Association, 1980

American Psychiatric Association: Diagnostic and Statistical Manual of Mental Disorders (Third Edition–Revised). Washington, DC, American Psychiatric Association, 1987

Anders TF: Biological rhythms in development. Psychosom Med 44:61-72, 1982

Arato M, Grof E, Lalso I, et al.: Reproducibility of the overnight melatonin secretion pattern in healthy men, in The Pineal Gland: Endocrine Aspects. Edited by Brown GM, Wainwright S. Oxford, England, Pergamon, 1985

Arendt J: Mammalian pineal rhythms. Pineal Res Rev 3:161-213, 1985

Arendt J, Paunier L, Sizonenko PC: Melatonin radioimmunoassay. J Clin Endocrinol Metab 40:347-350, 1975

Arendt J, Wetterberg L, Heyden T, et al: Radioimmunoassay of melatonin: human serum and cerebrospinal fluid. Horm Res 8:65-75, 1977

Arendt J, Hampton S, English J, et al: 24-hour profiles of melatonin, cortisol, insulin, C-peptide and GIP following a meal and subsequent fasting. Clin Endocrinol 16:89-95, 1982

Arendt J, Aldhous M, Marks V: Alleviation of jet lag by melatonin: preliminary results of a controlled double blind trial. Br Med J 292:1170, 1986

Arnold T: Observation on the Nature, Kinds, Causes and Prevention of Insanity, Lunacy or Madness [Volume 2]. Leicester, 1786

Axelrod J, Weisbach W: Enzymatic O-methylation of N-acetylserotonin to melatonin. Science 131:1312, 1960

Beck-Friis J, von Rosen D, Kjellman BF, et al: Melatonin in relation to body measures, sex, age, season and the use of drugs in patients with major affective disorders and healthy subjects. Psychoneuroendocrinology 9:261-277, 1984

Beck-Friis J, Kjellman BF, Aperia B, et al: Serum melatonin in relation to clinical variables in patients with major depressive disorder and a hypothesis of a low-melatonin syndrome. Acta Psychiatr Scand 71:319-330, 1985

Beersma DGM, van den Hoofdakker RH, van Berkesteijn WBM: Circadian rhythms in affective disorders: body temperature and sleep physiology in endogenous depressives, in Biological Rhythms and Behaviour [Volume 2 in the Advances in Biological Psychiatry Series]. Edited by Mendelwicz J, van Praag HM. Basel, Switzerland, S. Karger, 1983

Berger M, Pirke KM, Doerr P, et al: Influence of weight loss on the dexamethasone suppression test. Arch Gen Psychiatry 40:585-586, 1983

Biederman J, Herzog DB, Rivinus TM, et al: Urinary MHPG in anorexia nervosa patients with and without a concomitant major depressive disorder. J Psychiatr Res 18:149-160, 1984

Birau N, Alexander D, Bertholdt S, et al: Low nocturnal melatonin serum concentration in anorexia nervosa—further evidence for body weight influence. IRCS Med Sci 12:477, 1984

Bittman EL, Dempsey RJ, Karsch RJ: Pineal melatonin secretion drives the reproductive response to daylength in ewes. Endocrinology 113:2276-2283, 1983

Blask DE, Nodelman JL, Leadem C, et al: Influence of exogenously administered melatonin on the reproductive system and prolactin levels in underfed male rats. Biol Reprod 22:507-512, 1980

Blask DE, Leadem C, Richardson BA: Nutritional status, time of day and pinealectomy: factors influencing the sensitivity of the neuroendrocrine reproductive axis of the rat to melatonin. Horm Res 14:104-113, 1981

Branchey L, Weinberg U, Branchey M, et al: Simultaneous study of 24-hour patterns of melatonin and cortisol secretion in depressed patients. Neuropsychobiology 8:225-232, 1982

Brown GM, Kirwan P, Garfinkel PE, et al: Overnight patterning of prolactin and melatonin in anorexia nervosa [Abstract]. Presented at the 2nd International Symposium on Clinical Psychoneuroendocrinology in Reproduction, Venice, 1979

Brown GM, Grota LJ, Pulido O, et al: Application of immunologic techniques to the study of pineal indolealkylamines, in Pineal Research Reviews. Edited by Reiter RJ. New York, Alan Liss, 1983

Brown R, Kocsis JH, Caroff S, et al: Differences in nocturnal melatonin secretion between melancholic depressed patients and control subjects. Am J Psychiatry 142:811-816, 1985

Carter DS, Goldman BD: Antigonadal effects of timed melatonin infusion in pinealectomized male djungarian hamsters (Phodopus sungarus sungarus): duration is the critical parameter. Endocrinology 113:1261-1267, 1983

Casper R: On the emergence of bulimia nervosa as a syndrome. International Journal of Eating Disorders 2:3-16, 1983

Chik CL, Brown GM: Pineal–gonadal interaction in underfeeding. Clin Invest Med 6:40, 1983

Chik CL, Talalla A, Brown GM: Effect of pinealectomy on serum melatonin, lutenizing hormone and prolactin: a case report. Clin Endocrinol 23:367-372, 1985

Claustrat B, Chazot G, Brun J, et al: A chronobiological study of melatonin and cortisol secretion in depressed subjects: plasma melatonin, a biochemical marker in major depression. Biol Psychiatry 19:1216-1228, 1984

Cooper PJ, Fairburn CG: Binge-eating and self-induced vomiting in the community: a preliminary report. Br J Psychiatry 142:139-144, 1983

Cooper PJ, Fairburn CG: The depressive symptoms of bulimia nervosa. Br J Psychiatry 148:268-274, 1986

Cowen PJ, Fraser S, Sammons R, et al: Atenolol reduces plasma melatonin concentration in man. Br J Clin Psychiatry 15:579-581, 1983

Cowen PJ, Green AR, Grahame-Smith DG, et al: Plasma melatonin during desmethylimipramine treatment: evidence for changes in noradrenergic transmission. Br J Clin Pharmacol 19:799-805, 1985

Crowther B: Practical remarks on insanity. London, Thomas Underwood, 1811

Dalery J, Claustrat B, Brun J, et al: Plasma melatonin and cortisol levels in 8 patients with anorexia nervosa [letter]. Neuroendocrinology 7:159-164, 1985.

Darby PL, Van Loon G, Garfinkel PE, et al: LH, growth hormone, prolactin and catecholamine responses to LHRF and bromocriptine in anorexia nervosa. Psychosom Med 41:585, 1979

Deguchi T, Axelrod J: Induction and superinduction of serotonin N-acetyltransferase by adrenergic drugs and denervation in rat pineal organ. Proc Nat Acad Sci USA 69:2208-2211, 1972

Descartes R: Oeuvres et lettres. Biblioteque de la Pleiade. Paris, Gallimard, 1953, pp 710-712

Edelstein CK, Roy-Byrne P, Fawzy FI, et al: Effects of weight loss on the dexamethasone suppression test. Am J Psychiatry 140:338-341, 1983

Fairburn CG, Cooper PJ: The clinical features of bulimia nervosa. Br J Psychiatry 144:238-246, 1984

Ferrari E, Bossolo PA, Marelli G, et al: Chronobiological aspects of anorexia nervosa [Abstract]. Presented at the International Symposium on Disorders of Eating Behaviour, Pavio, Italy, September 1985

Ferrier IN, Arendt J, Johnstone EC, et al: Reduced nocturnal melatonin secretion in chronic schizophrenia: relation to body weight. Clin Endocrinol 17:181-187, 1982

Frazer A, Brown R, Kocsis J, et al: Patterns of melatonin rhythms in depression, in Melatonin in Humans. Edited by Wurtman RJ, Waldhauser F. Cambridge, MA, Centre for Brain Sciences and Metabolism Charitable Trust, 1985

Garfinkel PE, Moldofsky H, Garner DM: The heterogeneity of anorexia nervosa: bulimia as a distinctive subgroup. Arch Gen Psychiatry 37:1036-1040, 1980

Gerner RH, Gwirtsman HE: Abnormalities of dexamethasone suppression test and urinary MHPG in anorexia nervosa. Am J Psychiatry 138:650-653, 1981

Grof E, Grof P, Brown GM, et al: Investigations of melatonin secretion in man. Prog Neuropsychopharmacol Biol Psychiatry 9:602-612, 1985

Gwirtsman HE, Roy-Byrne P, Yager J, et al: Neuroendocrine abnormalities in bulimia. Am J Psychiatry 140:559-563, 1983

Halbreich U, Weinberg U, Stewart J, et al: An inverse correlation between like immunoreactivity in DMI-responsive depressives. Psychiatry Res 4:109-113, 1981

Hallonquist JD, Goldberg MA, Brandes JS: Affective disorders and circadian rhythms. Can J Psychiatry 31:259-272, 1986

Hanssen T, Heyden T, Sundberg IL, et al: Effect of propanolol on serum melatonin. Lancet 2:309-310, 1977

Hariharasubramanian N, Nair NPV, Pilapil C: Circadian rhythm of plasma melatonin and cortisol during the menstrual cycle, in The Pineal Gland: Endocrine Aspects. Edited by Brown GM, Wainwright S. Oxford, England, Pergamon, 1985

Hawkins D, Mendels J: Sleep disturbance in depressive syndromes. Am J Psychiatry 123:682-690, 1966

Hendrickson AE, Wagoner N, Cowan WM: Autoradiographic and electron microscopic study of retino–hypothalamic connections. Z Zellerforsch, Mikrosk Auat 135:1-26, 1972

Hudson JI, Pope HG Jr, Jonas JM, et al: Hypothalamic–pituitary–adrenal axis hyperactivity in bulimia. Psychiatry Res 8:111-117, 1983a

Hudson JI, Pope HG Jr, Jonas JM, et al: Family history study of anorexia nervosa and bulimia. Br J Psychiatry 142:133-138, 1983b

Hudson JI, Pope HG Jr, Jonas JM, et al: Phenomenologic relationship of eating disorders to major affective disorder. Psychiatry Res 9:345-354, 1983c

Hughes PL, Wells LA, Cunningham CJ, et al: Treating bulimia with desipramine. Arch Gen Psychiatry 43:182-186, 1986

Iguchi H, Kato KI, Ibayashi H: Age-dependent reduction in serum melatonin concentrations in healthy human subjects. J Clin Endocrinol Metab 55:27-29, 1982

Kappers JA: The Structure and Function of the Epiphysis Cerebri. Amsterdam, Elsevier, 1965

Kappers JA: Short history of pineal discovery and research, in The Pineal Gland of Vertebrates Including Man—Progress in Brain Research. Edited by Kappers JA, Pevet P. Amsterdam, Elsevier/North Holland Biomedical Press, 1979

Kappers JA, Smith AR, De Vries RAC: The mammalian pineal gland and its control of hypothalamic activity, in The Pineal Gland of Vertebrates Including Man—Progress in Brain Research. Edited by Kappers JA, Pevet P. Amsterdam, Elsevier/North Holland Biomedical Press, 1979

Kaye WH, Ebert MH, Gwirtsman HE, et al: Differences in brain serotonergic metabolism between nonbulimic and bulimic patients with anorexia nervosa. Am J Psychiatry 141:1598-1601, 1984

Kaye WH, Ebert MH, Raleigh M, et al: Abnormalities in CNS monoamine metabolism in anorexia nervosa. Arch Gen Psychiatry 41:350-355, 1984

Kennedy SH, Stokl S, Garfinkel PE, et al: Effects of Weight Change on the Dexamethasone Suppression Test. Presented at the 34th Annual Meeting of the Canadian Psychiatric Association, Banff, 1984

Kennedy SH, Piran N, Garfinkel PE: Isocarboxazid in the treatment of bulimia. Am J Psychiatry 143:1495-1496, 1986

Kennedy SH, Walsh BT: Monoamine oxidase inhibitors, in The Role of Drug Treatment for Eating Disorders. Edited by Garfinkel PE, Garner DM. New York, Bruner/Mazel, 1987

Klein DC, Weller J: Indole metabolism in the pineal gland: a circadian rhythm in N-acetyltransferase. Science 169:1093-1095, 1970

Kripke DF, Mullaney DJ, Atkinson M, et al: Circadian rhythm disorders in manic-depressives. Biol Psychiatry 13:335-351, 1978

Lang U, Aubert ML, Conne BS, et al: Influence of exogenous melatonin on melatonin secretion and the neuroendocrine reproductive axis of intact male rats during sexual maturation. Endocrinology 112:1578-1584, 1983

Lerner AB, Case JD, Takashashi Y, et al: Isolation of melatonin, the pineal gland factor that lightens melanocytes. J Am Chem Soc 80:2587, 1958

Lerner AB, Case JD, Heinzelman RV: Structure of melatonin. J Am Chem Soc 81:6084-6085, 1959

Lewy AJ: Mammalian melatonin production, in The Pineal Gland. Edited by Relkin R. Amsterdam, Elsevier, 1983

Lewy AJ: Human melatonin secretion: a marker for the circadian system and the effects of light, in Neurobiology of Mood Disorders. Edited by Post RM, Ballenger JC. Baltimore, Williams and Wilkins, 1984

Lewy AJ, Markey SP: Analysis of melatonin in human plasma by gas chromatography negative chemical ionization mass spectrometry. Science 201:741-743, 1978

Lewy AJ, Newsome DA: Different types of melatonin circadia secretory rhythms in some blind subjects. J Clin Endocrinol Metab 56:1103-1107, 1983

Lewy AJ, Wehr TA, Goodwin FK, et al: Light suppresses melatonin secretion in humans. Science 210:1267-1269, 1980

Lewy AJ, Wehr TA, Goodwin FK, et al: Manic-depressive patients may be supersensitive to light. Lancet 1:383-384, 1981

Lewy AJ, Nurnberger JI, Wehr TA, et al: Supersensitivity to light: possible trait marker for manic-depressive. Am J Psychiatry 142:725-727, 1985a

Lewy AJ, Sack RL, Miller LS, et al: The use of plasma melatonin levels and light in the assessment and treatment of chronobiologic sleep and mood disorders, in Melatonin in Humans. Edited by Wurtman RJ, Waldhauser F. Cambridge, MA, Centre for Brain Sciences and Metabolism and Charitable Trust, 1985b

Lieberman MR, Waldhauser F, Garfield G, et al: Effects of melatonin on human mood and performance. Brain Res 323:201-207, 1984

Lindy C, Walsh BT, Roose SP, et al: The dexamethasone suppression test in bulimia. Am J Psychiatry 142:1375-1376, 1986

Lohrenz RN, Fullerton DT, Wenzel FJ, et al: Circadian rhythm of adrenal cortical activity in depression. Behavioral Neuropsychiatry 1:10-13, 1969

Maas JW: Biogenic amines and depression: biochemical and pharmacological separation of two types of depression. Arch Gen Psychiatry 32:1357-1361, 1975

Moore RY, Eichler VB: Loss of circadian adrenal corticosterone rhythm following suprachiasmatic lesions in the rat. Brain Res 42:201-206, 1972

Moore-Ede MC, Czeisler CA, Richardson GS: Circadian timekeeping in health and disease: Part I. Basic properties of circadian pacemakers. N Engl J Med 309:469-476, 1983

Mullen PE, Silman RE: The pineal and psychiatry: a review. Psychol Med 7:407-417, 1977

Nair NPV, Hariharasubramanian N, Pilapil C: Circadian rhythm of plasma melatonin and cortisol in endogenous depression, in The Pineal Gland: Endocrine Aspects. Edited by Brown GM, Wainwright S. Oxford, England, Pergamon Press, 1985

Neuwelt EA, Mickey B, Lewy AJ: The importance of melatonin and tumor markers in pineal tumors, in Melatonin in Humans. Edited by Wurtman RJ, Waldhauser F. Cambridge, MA, Centre for Brain Sciences and Metabolism Charitable Trust, 1985

Nir I: The central nervous system, peripheral glands and the pineal, in The Pineal Gland: Endocrine Aspects. Edited by Brown GM, Wainwright S. Oxford, England, Pergamon Press, 1985

Pang SF: Melatonin concentrations in blood and pineal gland. Pineal Res Rev 3:115-159, 1985

Pang SF, Brown GM, Grota LJ, et al: Determination of N-acetylserotonin and melatonin activities in the pineal gland, retina, harderian gland, brain and serum of rats and chickens. Neuroendocrinology 23:1-13, 1977

Papousek M: Chronobiologische Aspekte der Zyklothymie [Chronobiologic aspects of cyclothymia]. Forschr Neurol Psychiat 53:381-440, 1975

Pelham RW, Vaughan GM, Sandock KL, et al: Twenty-four hour cycle of a melatonin-like substance in the plasma of human males. J Clin Endocrinol Metab 37:341-344, 1973

Pflug B, Erikson R, Johnson A: Depression and daily temperature: a long-term study. Acta Psychiatr Scand 54:254-266, 1976

Piran N, Kennedy SH, Garfinkel PE, et al: Affective disturbance in eating disorders. J Nerv Ment Dis 173:395-400, 1985

Pope HG Jr, Hudson JI, Jonas JM, et al: Bulimia treated with imipramine: a placebo-controlled double-blind study. Am J Psychiatry 140:554-558, 1983

Pyle RL, Mitchell JE, Eckert ED: Bulimia: a report of 34 cases. J Clin Psychiatry 42:60-64, 1981

Quay WB: Pineal Chemistry. Springfield, MA, Thomas, 1974

Rosenthal NE, Sack DA, Gillin JC, et al: Seasonal affective disorder. Arch Gen Psychiatry 41:72-80, 1984

Rosenthal NE, Sack DA, Carpenter CJ, et al: Antidepressant effect of light in seasonal affective disorder. Am J Psychiatry 142:163-170, 1985

Rosenthal NE, Carpenter CJ, James SP, et al: Seasonal affective disorder in children and adolescents. Am J Psychiatry 143:356-358, 1986

Russell GFM: Bulimia nervosa: an ominous variant of anorexia nervosa. Psychol Med 9:429-448, 1979

Sachar EJ: Twenty-four hour cortisol secretory patterns in depressed and manic patients. Prog Brain Res 42:81-91, 1975

Schildkraut JJ: The catecholamine hypothesis of affective disorders: a review of supporting evidence. Am J Psychiatry 122:509-522, 1965

Sorrentino S, Reiter RJ, Schalch DS: Interaction of the pineal gland, blinding and underfeeding on reproductive organ size and radioimmunoassayable growth hormone. Neuroendocrinology 7:105-115, 1971

Steiner M, Brown GM: Melatonin/cortisol ratio and the dexamethasone suppression test in newly admitted psychiatric inpatients, in The Pineal Gland: Endocrine Aspects. Edited by Brown GM, Wainwright S. Oxford, England, Pergamon, 1985

Stephan FK, Zucker I: Circadian rhythms in drinking behavior and locomotor activity of rats are eliminated by hypothalamic lesions. Proc Nat Acad Sci USA 69:1583-1586, 1972

Thompson C, Mezey G, Corn T, et al: The effect of desipramine upon melatonin and cortisol secretion in depressed and normal subjects. Br J Psychiatry 147:389-393, 1985

Vaughan G: Melatonin in humans. Pineal Res Rev 2:141-201, 1984

Vaughan GM, McDonald SD, Jordan RM, et al: Melatonin concentration in human blood and cerebrospinal fluid: relationship to stress. J Clin Endocrinol Metab 47:220-224, 1978

Vaughan GM, Taylor T, Lasko J, et al: The human melatonin rhythm and lack of influence by sympathetic activation, in The Pineal Gland: Endocrine Aspects. Edited by Brown GM, Wainwright S. Oxford, England, Pergamon, 1985

Vollrath L, Semm P, Gammel G: Sleep induction by intranasal application of melatonin, in Melatonin: Current Studies and Perspective. Edited by Birau N, Schloot W. Oxford, England, Pergamon Press, 1975

Vriend J: Evidence for pineal gland modulation of the neuroendocrine thyroid axis. Neuroendocrinology 36:68-78, 1983

Waldhauser F, Wieszenbacher G, Zeithuber U, et al: Fall in nocturnal serum melatonin levels during pre-puberty and pubescence. Lancet 1:362-365, 1984

Walsh BT, Stewart JW, Roose SP, et al: Treatment of bulimia with phenelzine: a double-blind placebo-controlled study. Arch Gen Psychiatry 41:1105-1109, 1984

Wehr TA, Goodwin FK: Biological rhythms in manic-depressive illness, in Circadian Rhythms in Psychiatry. Edited by Wehr TA, Goodwin FK. Pacific Grove, CA, Boxwood, 1983

Wehr TA, Jacobsen FM, Sack DA, et al: Phototherapy for seasonal affective disorder: time of day and suppression on melatonin are not critical for antidepressant effects. Arch Gen Psychiatry 43:870-875, 1986

Wetterberg L: Clinical importance of melatonin. Prog Brain Res 52:539-57, 1979

Wetterberg L, Arendt J, Paunier L, et al: Human serum melatonin changes during the menstrual cycle. J Clin Endocrinol Metab 42:185-188, 1976

Wetterberg L, Aperia B, Beck-Friis J, et al: Pineal-hypothalamic pituitary function in patients with depressive illness, in Steroid Hormone Regulation of the Brain. Edited by Fuxe K, Gustafsson VA, Wetterberg L. Oxford, England, Pergamon Press, 1981

Wong PY, Mee AV, Ho FFK: A direct radioimmunoassay of serum cortisol with in-house 125I-tracer and pre-conjugated double antibody. Clin Chem 25:914-917, 1979

Wurtman RJ: Melatonin as a hormone in humans: a history. Yale J Biol Med 58:547-552, 1985

Wurtman RJ, Roth W, Altschule MD, et al: Interaction of the pineal and exposure to continuous light on organ weights of female rats. Acta Endocrinol 36:617-624, 1961

Wurtman RJ, Axelrod J, Chu EW: Melatonin, a pineal substance: effect on the rat ovary. Science 141:277-278, 1963a

Wurtman RJ, Axelrod J, Philips LS: Melatonin synthesis in the pineal gland: control by light. Science 142:1071-1073, 1963b

Chapter 6

Endogenous Opioid Peptides and Feeding

James E. Mitchell, M.D.
John E. Morley, M.B., B.Ch.

Chapter 6

Endogenous Opioid Peptides and Feeding

Over the last few decades there has been an increasing interest in studying the basic biological mechanisms that regulate feeding behavior in both the human and infrahuman species. In this time it has become clear that peptides play an important modulating role in feeding behavior. In particular, two peptide systems have been linked to feeding control. One is a peripheral satiety system that is best illustrated by the gastrointestinal hormone cholecystokinin. The other is a central system, which is illustrated by two families of peptides known to increase feeding behavior after central administration: the opioid peptides and neuropeptide Y (Morley et al. 1985b). A large literature has accumulated implicating these various substances in the control of feeding behavior (Morley et al. 1985a; Morley et al. 1985b), and although the data in humans to date are limited, researchers are now attempting to translate the findings from basic animal models into pharmacological approaches with patients who have eating problems. In this chapter we shall explore the relationship between the opioid system and feeding, reviewing the main findings from the animal literature and discussing in more detail the human studies that have been completed to date. As will be seen, the practical clinical application of the findings in animals is of yet limited, but some interesting findings have emerged from these studies that suggest that this line of research should be pursued further.

STUDIES IN ANIMALS

In the early 1970s it was demonstrated that the analgesic effects of administered opiates resulted from specific interactions between opiates and identifiable receptors in the central nervous system (Pert and Snyder 1973; Terenius 1973). Subsequently, endogenous opiatelike substances were isolated and identified, and eventually a large family of opioid peptides was described that included beta-lipotropin, beta-endorphin, met-enkephalin and leu-enkephalin.

Martin et al. (1963) first reported that opiate agonists could stimulate feeding, noting that morphine-dependent rats consumed large quantities of food following daily morphine injections. This hyperphagia was reversible using the short-acting narcotic antagonist naloxone, suggesting that the effect was mediated through a direct interaction with opiate receptors (Lowy et al. 1981).

The first study that clearly documented that opiate antagonists possessed anorexic properties and could suppress feeding behavior in the absence of exogenously administered opiates was reported by Holtzman (1974), who demonstrated that naloxone would decrease feeding in rats following food deprivation. This observation was confirmed in subsequent reports (Brands et al. 1979; Brown and Holtzman 1979; Frenk and Rogers 1979) and was found to be dose-related and stereospecific, again suggesting direct interaction with opiate receptors (Lowy et al. 1981; Sanger et al. 1981). In addition, it was shown that opiate antagonists would attenuate other types of hyperphagia, including diazepam-induced eating (Stapleton et al. 1979), tail-pinch induced eating (Lowy et al. 1980; Morley and Levine 1980), and feeding induced by the administration of glucose antimetabolite 2-deoxy-D-glucose (Lowy et al. 1980; Levine and Morley 1981). It was also shown that the anorexic effect was not secondary to a suppression of water intake (Lowy and Yim 1981) or suppression of activity (Carey et al. 1981) and was not mediated primarily by conditioned taste aversion (Ostrowski et al. 1980; Wu et al. 1979).

Of particular interest in considering the relevance of these studies for clinical purposes is the tail-pinch model of stress-induced eating. In 1975 Antelman et al. developed a model whereby mild, sustained tail pinch in the rat would induce a variety of oral behaviors including eating, licking, and gnawing (Antelman and Szechtman 1975; Antelman et al. 1975). Levine and Morley (1982) subsequently showed this model to be effective in mice. Studies using this model have suggested that activation of the endogenous opioid system is involved in tail-pinch induced feeding. It has been demonstrated that naloxone will suppress tail-pinch induced feeding in untrained rats and mice, although there is also evidence that other systems, including the dopamine system, are involved in these behavioral changes (Lowy et al. 1980; Morley and Levine 1980). The tail-pinch model has been suggested as a possible model of stress-induced overeating in humans, suggesting that opioid suppression might suppress overeating in response to stress.

Also of relevance to the present discussion are studies in which certain genetically obese strains of mice and rats have been identified that have enhanced sensitivity to the appetite suppressant effects of naloxone and to have elevated levels of opioid peptides in their pituitaries (Coleman and Hummel 1973; Zucker and Zucker 1961; Margules et al. 1978). These studies suggest that abnormally elevated levels of endogenous opioids, perhaps genetically determined, may be responsible for some types of obesity and overeating in humans.

Much of the literature on opiates and feeding has concerned rats and mice. However, opiate antagonists have been shown to suppress food intake in many other animal species, ranging from certain invertebrates such as the giant garden slug *(Limax maximus)* (Kavaliers et al. 1985) to various vertebrates including cats (Foster et al. 1981), guinea pigs (Schulz et al. 1980), sheep (Baile et al. 1981), wolves (Morley et al. 1983a); and monkeys (Herling 1981). However, the ingestive behaviors of hamsters appear to be relatively resistant to suppression by opiate antagonists (Lowy and Yim 1982, 1983).

OPIATE ANTAGONISTS AND FEEDING IN HUMANS

Pharmacological studies using predominantly opiates have suggested that the kappa opiate receptor plays a primary role in feeding initiation (Morley et al. 1982). Other studies have identified the endogenous kappa agonists dynorphin (Morley and Levine. 1981) and alpha-neo-endorphin (Schulz et al. 1984) as the primary opioids involved in the activation of feeding. These findings are particularly pertinent to the chronic studies in humans, because naloxone and naltrexone are relatively poor kappa opioid antagonists.

Dunger et al. (1980) and Fraioli et al. (1981) reported cases of individuals found to have elevated endogenous opioid activity who were also obese. Krotkiewski et al. (1983) found an increase in opioid fraction 2 of the cerebrospinal fluid in Prader-Willi syndrome patients compared with lean controls. In two subjects a decrease in food intake and body weight occurred when they were given 0.4 mg naloxone daily. Kyriakides et al. (1980) reported that two of three subjects with Prader-Willi syndrome who were profoundly hyerphagic had a reduction of food intake following naloxone infusion, and Morley and Levine (1982) reported a patient who developed obesity following traumatic damage to the hypothalamus and who demonstrated a significant decrease in food intake following naloxone infusion. Schwartz (1981) reported a trial, using himself as subject, using oral naloxone, whereby he experienced significant weight loss over a period of 48 days.

Anecdotal reports concerning use of the long-acting narcotic antagonist naltrexone and weight change are also of relevance. Hollister et al. in 1981 reported that naltrexone therapy reduced food intake in 6 of 10 nonaddict normal subjects, and Sternbach et al. in 1982 reported anorectic effects with naltrexone in a series of four detoxified patients with opiate addiction.

Let us now turn to the controlled trials in humans. Trials involving administration of naloxone on a short-term basis have also indicated a significant suppressant effect on eating. Thompson et al. (1982) demonstrated that naloxone infusion decreased 2-deoxyglucose-stimulated liquid food intake by 26 percent in normal volunteers. Atkinson (1982) reported that seven out of seven obese subjects who received a 5 mg bolus of naloxone followed by a 5 mg per hour infusion for a total of two hours demonstrated a 27 percent decrease in caloric intake compared with placebo infusion. However, this reduction was not demonstrated in five normal weight subjects. Trenchard and Silverstone (1983) studied food intake in a series of 12 normal weight subjects and found that a 0.8 mg naloxone infusion resulted in a nonsignificant reduction in food intake, while a 1.6 mg infusion resulted in a significant reduction in food intake. Cohen et al. (1985) demonstrated that an infusion of 2 mg per kg of naloxone significantly reduced total food intake in seven normal volunteers. Wolkowitz et al. (1985) also demonstrated suppression of food intake in obese subjects following naloxone administration. Billington et al. (1985), using the long-acting opiate antagonist nalmifene, found that food intake could be reduced for up to 26 hours after drug administration, with a preferential reduction in fat intake.

Of particular interest is the observation that naloxone reduces food intake without altering the perception of satiety or fullness (Thompson et al. 1982). O'Brien et al. (1982) found no effect on subjective perception of hunger when naloxone was infused in dosages of 10 mg/70 kg and 30 mg/70 kg in seven massively obese subjects. Another study in which enhanced feeding was demonstrated in normal subjects using the opiate agonist butorphanol tartrate again showed no effect on hunger (Morley et al. 1985c). These studies suggest that opioid modulation of feeding does not directly involve perception of hunger and satiety.

Taken together the reports of short-term reductions in feeding suggested that long-acting narcotic antagonists should be evaluated in longer term clinical trials in patients who overeat, in particular in patients with obesity and patients with bulimia. Naltrexone, the long-acting orally active antagonist, became a logical choice for investigation. The studies on obesity will be reviewed first.

OPIATE ANTAGONISTS IN HUMAN OBESITY

Five studies have systematically examined the use of chronic narcotic antagonists in individuals with obesity. Atkinson et al. (1985) reported their results on naltrexone therapy for weight loss. These investigators studied 60 obese subjects who were a minimum of 30 percent over ideal body weight. Subjects received placebo, 50 mg of naltrexone, or 100 mg of naltrexone for a total of eight weeks. Fifty-four of the 60 subjects completed the protocol, and compliance with the medication regimen was thought to be excellent. Comparisons of the weight changes for the combined populations of men and women revealed no significant weight loss during the eight weeks of medication therapy, weight change being -0.02, -1.65, and -0.5 kg for the placebo, 50 mg naltrexone, and 100 mg naltrexone groups, respectively. However, an analysis of the data by sex indicated that women taking the active drug lost a mean of 1.7 kg, compared with a mean gain of 0.1 kg in the placebo group, a significant difference. There did not appear to be a dose–response relationship, however.

We subsequently reported a placebo-controlled, double-blind high dose trial of naltrexone in males (Mitchell et al. 1987). The original design called for 40 obese males to finish the entire protocol; however, the study was terminated prematurely because of the development of liver toxicity in several subjects. High-dose therapy of 300 mg/day had been chosen in an attempt to maximize the likelihood of effective opioid blockade. The first two weeks of medication therapy consisted of single-blind placebo. At the end of this period subjects were stratified according to the amount of weight loss to that point and then randomized to either active drug or placebo condition; the remainder of the protocol (eight weeks) was double blind. Of the 56 subjects who were initiated into the study, 33 finished the entire protocol. Eight were terminated for medical reasons, and four were terminated prematurely when the study was discontinued. The mean ± SD weight loss for the active drug group in the double-blind phase was 5.03 ± 4.01 kg and for the placebo group was 4.73 ± 3.60 kg, indicating no significant difference in the amount of weight loss between the two groups. Six patients developed elevations on liver function tests that were presumed to be related to the drug. The results indicated that naltrexone was not superior to placebo in producing weight loss in overweight males who were also undergoing dietary counseling for weight reduction.

The hepatic toxicity that developed in a subgroup of patients indicated that the dosage used in this study and higher dosages of the drug could not be used safely in this population.

The third report, by Maggio et al. (1985), detailed a dose-ranging inpatient trial of naltrexone in moderately obese men. Eight subjects were studied over the course of a 28-day protocol that began with a 7-day habituation period, during which placebo was administered. Subsequently, using a Latin square design, subjects were randomly assigned to three-day periods when they received placebo, 100 mg, 200 mg, or 300 mg dosages of naltrexone. Administration of each dosage of naltrexone resulted in some decreased daily caloric intake compared with that in the placebo condition, but the intake reductions were neither statistically significant nor dose related. In fact, the 100 mg dose resulted in the largest reduction, and virtually the same pattern of meal and snack intake was observed during placebo and naltrexone administration. All subjects showed a tendency toward weight loss during at least one of the three-day naltrexone administration periods, but analysis of variance indicated that these differences were not significantly different from that seen during placebo. The authors concluded that the naltrexone administration was relatively ineffective in inducing weight loss in obese males.

Malcolm et al. (1985) found no effect on weight loss using 200 mg/day of naltrexone or placebo in an eight-week trial involving 27 females and 14 males. Billington and Morley (unpublished data) found that 200 mg of naltrexone administered daily for two weeks failed to alter weight or glucose tolerance in a double-blind, placebo-controlled trial in patients with type II diabetes mellitus.

Taken together, these reports indicate that naltrexone does not appear to be a particularly effective agent in inducing weight loss in overweight individuals, with the possible exception of the overweight women studied in the Atkinson et al. study (1985). These results suggest that chronic antagonism of endogenous opioid receptors may not be useful as a weight control technique. However, it should be remembered that animal studies have shown that the kappa opioid receptor plays a particularly important role in the stimulation of appetite, although other opioid receptors are apparently involved (Morley et al. 1985b; Morley et al. 1982). Kappa receptors have been shown to be present in highest densities at brain sites known to be involved in gustatary and feeding control (Lynch et al. 1985). However, naltrexone and naloxone poorly antagonize the kappa receptor. It is certainly possible that more specific kappa antagonists may be more useful as appetite suppressants in overweight patients. Also, opiate antagonists appear to be particularly effective in reducing certain types of hyperphagia, such as that associated with stress (Terenius 1973; Lowy et al. 1980). Therefore, opiate antagonists might be found to be particularly beneficial for a subpopulation of obese individuals.

Unfortunately, in humans the picture becomes ever more complex when we consider other observations concerning opioids and eating. For example, a recent study showed a marked decrease in weight in subjects given the mixed agonist/antagonist nalorphine (Bulkanyi et al. 1985). This is not surprising when it is remembered that in rats opiate agonist can cause weight loss (Morley et al. 1983b) and subjects on methadone maintenance are generally below ideal body weight while demonstrating hyperphagia (Tallman et al. 1984). The mechanism by which chronic administration of opiate agonists induces weight loss is unclear but may involve alterations in activity and thermogenesis as well as inhibition of lipogenic enzymes and activation of lipolytic processes. Therefore, in certain situations, opiates and opiate antagonists may cause the same result, albeit by different mechanisms.

OPIATE ANTAGONISTS IN BULIMIA

The effects of opiate antagonists in bulimia have been studied in two investigations. We evaluated the effects of naloxone on binge-eating behavior in patients of normal weight with bulimia (Mitchell et al. 1986). Subjects were five female volunteers who were actively binge-eating and self-inducing vomiting at a minimum frequency of once a day for several months prior to admission. Each subject was hospitalized in the Clinical Research Center at the University of Minnesota in a private room. Subjects were instructed prior to admission that they would be allowed one binge-eating episode each day, and each selected a predetermined time when she would initiate each binge-eating episode.

Four of the hospital days were designated as experimental medication days. Subjects received all drugs intravenously and double-blind in a randomly determined sequence. On two days, subjects received placebo; on one day, the octapeptide of cholecystokinin; and on one day, naloxone. In addition to naloxone, cholecystokinin was studied because of its possible role as a satiety factor and the previous demonstration that this drug decreases food intake in a variety of animal species including the rat, the dog, the Rhesus monkey, and, in certain circumstances, humans (Gibbs et al. 1973, 1976; Goetz and Sturdevant 1975; Kissileff et al. 1981; Pi-Sunyer et al. 1982). Naloxone was administered as a 6 mg bolus over two minutes followed by .1 mg per minute intravenously to a maximum of 120 minutes. Cholecystokinin was administered as a 20 ng/kg bolus over 2 minutes followed by an infusion of 1 ng/kg per minute to a maximum of 120 minutes.

There was considerable variability in the number of kilocalories consumed during the binge-eating episodes across subjects. However, the naloxone drug administration episode was the episode of lowest food intake for four of the five subjects, and for the fifth subject the naloxone administration episode was the second lowest. Expressed as a percent of the mean ± SD value of the placebo days, intake on naloxone was 77.1 ± 13.5, a significant reduction ($p = .02$, paired t-test, two-tailed). There was no apparent effect for cholecystokinin. There were no significant side-effects associated with the administration of the experimental medications. Although the effects were not dramatic, they were statistically significant, and it was our assumption that the structure of the protocol implicitly encouraged patients to attempt to replicate the same eating pattern day after day. Therefore, the protocol was biased against showing any drug effect, and the effect that was shown, although modest, may be important.

In another study, Jonas and Gold (1986) conducted an open-label trial of naltrexone in five bulimic women treated for six weeks. The subjects demonstrated significant reductions in the frequency of binges, frequency of purging, and duration of binges, with evidence of improvement in binge-eating frequency by the second week and continued improvement during the remainder of the study. Although these authors reported that liver function tests remained stable during the trial, the mean dosage administered was 200 mg/day. In view of other reports of dose-related hepatotoxicity when using this drug in amounts above a mean daily dose of 50 mg/day, which is the dose approved by the U.S. Food and Drug Administration for maintenance opioid blockade in opiate addiction (Atkinson et al. 1985; Mitchell et al. 1984; Maggio et al. 1985), considerable caution should be exercised at this time in using this drug in high dosages in this population, until controlled trials involving careful monitoring of liver functions have been completed.

CONCLUSIONS

The involvement of the opioid peptide in the control of feeding is now well established in several animal species. To this point, attempts to find practical clinical applications of the knowledge gleaned from basic research have yielded mixed results. Particularly disappointing have been trials in obese humans, which have shown minimal or no effect. In part this may reflect the lack of specificity of the available narcotic antagonists; in part it may reflect the complexity of factors that influence eating behavior in humans. Another possibility would be that humans rapidly habituate to the effects of opioid blockade. This would explain why the results in short-term studies often have suggested a significant effect, while results of longer term studies generally have been negative. The results to date, however, have been encouraging enough to suggest possible directions for future research. The effects of alternative narcotic antagonists that are more specific for the kappa receptor should be studied when they are available, and consideration should be given to studying patients who binge-eat in response to stress, whether overweight or of normal weight, with narcotic antagonists. The two investigations involving bulimic patients are particularly interesting and raise the hope that opiate antagonists may help this condition. However, controlled trials using naltrexone are yet to be reported, and investigators working in the area must take careful note of the potential hepatotoxicity of this drug.

REFERENCES

Antelman SM, Szechtman H: Tail-pinch induces eating in sated rats which appears to depend on nigrostriatal dopamine system. Science 189:731-733, 1975

Antelman SM, Szechtman H, Chin P, et al: Tail-pinch induced eating, gnawing and licking behavior in rats: dependence on the nigrostriatal dopamine system. Brain Res 99:319-337, 1975

Atkinson RL: Naloxone decreases food intake in obese humans. J Clin Endocrinol Metab 55:196-198, 1982

Atkinson RL, Berke LK, Drake CR, et al: Effects of long-term therapy with naltrexone on body weight in obesity. Clin Pharmacol Ther 38:419-422, 1985

Baile CA, Keim DA, Della-Fera MA, et al: Opiate antagonists and agonists and feeding in sheep. Physiol Behav 26:1019-1023, 1981

Billington CJ, Shafer RB, Morley JE: Effects of opioid blockade with nalmefene on older impotent men. Endocrinology 116:946A, 1985

Brands B, Thornhill JA, Hirst M, et al: Suppression of food intake and body weight gain by naloxone in rats. Life Sci 24:1773-1778, 1979

Brown DR, Holtzman SG: Suppression of deprivation-induced food and water intake in rats and mice by naloxone. Pharmacol Biochem Behav 11:567-573, 1979

Bulkanyi I, Mohai L, Ralkanyi L: A New Approach to Diminish the Hunger of Hyperphagic Obese Patients. Abstracts of 4th Congress of the Hungarian Pharmacological Society, Budapest, Hungary, 1985

Carey MP, Ross JA, Enns MP: Naloxone suppresses feeding and drinking but not wheel running in rats. Pharmacol Biochem Behav 14:569-571, 1981

Cohen MR, Cohen RM, Pickar D: Naloxone reduces food intake in humans. Psychosom Med 47:132-138, 1985

Coleman DL, Hummel KP: The influence of background on the expression of the obese (ob/ob) mouse. Diabetologia 9:287-293, 1973

Dunger DG, Leonard JV, Wolff OH, et al: Effect of naloxone in a previously undescribed hypothalamic syndrome. Lancet 1:1277-1281, 1980

Foster JA, Morrison M, Dean SJ, et al: Naloxone suppresses food/water consumption in the deprived cat. Pharmacol Biochem Behav 14:419-421, 1981

Fraioli F, Fabbri A, Moretti C, et al: Endogenous opioid peptides and neuroendocrine correlations in a case of congenital indifference to pain. Endocrinology 108:238A, 1981

Frenk H, Rogers GH: The suppressant effect of naloxone on food and water intake in the rat. Behav Neural Biol 25:23-40, 1979

Gibbs J, Young RC, Smitch GP: Cholecystokinin decreases in food intake in rats. J Comp Psychol 84:488-495, 1973

Gibbs J, Falasco JD, McHugh PR: Cholecystokinin-decreased food intake in rhesus monkeys. Am J Physiol 230:15-18, 1976

Goetz H, Sturdevant R: Effect of cholecystokinin on food intake in man. Clin Research 23:98A, 1975

Herling S: Effects of naltrexone dose and history of naltrexone exposure on food-and codeine-maintained responding in rhesus monkeys. J Pharm Exp Ther 217:105-113, 1981

Hollister LE, Johnson K, Bookhabza D, et al: Adverse effects of naltrexone in subjects not dependent on opiates. Drug Alcohol Depend 8:37-41, 1981

Holtzman SG: Behavioral effects of separate and combined administration of naloxone and d-amphetamine. J Pharm Exp Ther 189:51-60, 1974

Jonas JM, Gold MS: Naltrexone reverses bulimic symptoms. Lancet 1:807, 1986

Kavaliers M, Hirst M, Teskey GC: Opioid systems and feeding in the slug, Limax maximus: similarities to and implications for mammalian feeding. Brain Res Bull 14:681-685, 1985

Kissileff HR, Pi-Sunyer FX, Thornton J, et al: C-Terminal octapeptide of cholecystokinin decreases food intake in man. Am J Clin Nutr 34:154-160, 1981

Krotkiewski M, Fagerberg B, Bjomtorp P, et al: Endorphins in genetic human obesity. Int J Obesity 7:597-598, 1983

Kyriakides M, Silverstone T, Jeffcoate W, et al: Effect of naloxone on hyperphagia in the Prader-Willi syndrome. Lancet 1:876-877, 1980

Levine AS, Morley JE: Peptidergic control of insulin-induced feeding. Peptides 2:261-264, 1981

Levine AS, Morley JE: Tail-pinch induced eating: is it the tail or the pinch? Physiol Behav 28:565-567, 1982

Lowy MT, Starkey C, Yim GKW: Stereoselective effects of opiate agonists and antagonists on ingestive behavior in rats. Pharmacol Biochem Behav 14:591-596, 1981

Lowy MT, Yim GKW: The anorexic effect of naltrexone is independent of its suppressant effect on water intake. Neuropharmacology 20:883-886, 1981

Lowy MT, Yim GKW: Drinking, but not feeding is opiate sensitive in hamsters. Life Sci 30:1639-1644, 1982

Lowy MT, Yim GKW: Stimulation of food intake following opiate agonists in rats but not hamsters. Psychopharmacology 81:28-32, 1983

Lowy MT, Maickel RP, Yim GKW: Naloxone reduction of stress-related feeding. Life Sci 26:2113-2118, 1980

Lynch WC, Watt J, Krall S, et al: Autoradiographic localization of kappa opiate receptors in CNS taste and feeding areas. Pharmacol Biochem Behav 22:699-705, 1985

Maggio CA, Presta E, Bracco EF, et al: Naltrexone and human eating behavior: a dose-ranging inpatient trial in moderately obese men. Brain Res Bull 14:657-664, 1985

Malcom R, O'Neil PM, Sexaues JD, et al: A controlled trial of naltrexone in obese humans. Int J Obesity 9:347-353, 1985

Margules DL, Moisset B, Lewis MJ, et al: B-endorphin is associated with overeating in genetically obese mice (ob/ob) and rats (fa/fa). Science 202:988-991, 1978

Martin WR, Wikler A, Eades CG, et al: Tolerance to and physical dependence on morphine in rats. Psychopharmacology 4:247-260, 1963

Mitchell JE, Laine DE, Morley JE, et al: Naloxone but not CCK-8 may attenuate binge-eating behavior in patients with the bulimia syndrome. Biol Psychiatry 21:1399-1406, 1986

Mitchell JE, Morley JE, Levine AS, et al: High-dose naltrexone therapy and dietary counseling for obesity. Biol Psychiatry 22:35-42, 1987

Morley JE, Levine AS: Stress-induced eating is mediated through endogenous opiates. Science 209:1259-1261, 1980

Morley JE, Levine AS: Dynorphin (1-13) induces spontaneous feeding in rats. Life LSci 29:1901-1903, 1981

Morley JE, Levine AS: The role of the endogenous opiates as regulators of appetite. Am J Clin Nutr 35:757-761, 1982

Morley JE, Levine AS, Grace M, et al: An investigation of the role of kappa opiate receptor agonists in the initiation of feeding. Life Sci 31:2617-2626, 1982

Morley JE, Levine AS, Plotka ED, et al: The effect of naloxone on feeding and spontaneous locomotion in the wolf. Physiol Behav 30:331-334, 1983a

Morley JE, Levine AS, Yum GKW, et al: Opioid modulation of appetite. Neurosci Biobehav Rev 7:281-305, 1983b.

Morley JE, Bartness TJ, Gosnell BA, et al: Peptidergic regulation of feeding. Int Rev Neurobiol 27:207-298, 1985a

Morley JE, Levine AS, Gosnell BA, et al: Peptides and feeding. Peptides 6:181-192, 1985b

Morley JE, Parker S. Levine AS: Effect of butorphanol tartrate on food and water consumption in humans. Am J Clin Nutr 42:1175-1178, 1985c

O'Brien CP, Stunkard AJ, Ternes JW: Absence of naloxone sensitivity in obese humans. Psychosom Med 44:215-218, 1982

Ostrowski NL, Foley TL, Lind MD, et al: Naloxone reduces fluid intake: effects of water and food deprivation. Pharmacol Biochem Behav 12:431-435, 1980

Pert CB, Snyder SH: Opiate receptor: demonstration in nervous tissue. Science 179:1011-1014, 1973

Pi-LSunyer X, Kissileff HR, Thornton J, et al: C-terminal octapeptide of cholecystokinin decreases food intake in obese men. Physiol Behav 29:627-630, 1982

Sanger DJ, McCarthy PS, Metcalf G: The effects of opiate antagonists on food intake are stereospecific. Neuropharmacology 20:45-47, 1981

Schulz R, Wuster M, Herz A: Interaction of amphetamine and naloxone in feeding behavior in guinea pigs. Eur J Pharmacol 63:313-319, 1980

Schulz R, Wilhelm A, Dirlich G: Intracerebral injection of different antibodies against endogenous opioids suggests alpha-neoendorphin participation in control of feeding behavior. Naunyn Schmiedebergs Arch Pharmacol 326:222-226, 1984

Schwartz, TB: Naloxone and weight reduction: an exercise in introspection. Trans Am Clinic Climatol Assoc 92:103-110, 1981

Stapleton JM, Lind MD, Merriman VJ, et al: Naloxone inhibits diazepam-induced feeding in rats. Life Sci 24:2421-2426, 1979

Sternbach HA, Annitto W, Pottash ALC, et al: Anorexic effects of naltrexone in man. Lancet 1:388-389, 1982

Tallman JR, Willenburg MR, Carlson G, et al: Effect of chronic methadone use in humans on taste and dietary preference. Fed Proc 43:1058A, 1984

Terenius L: Stereospecific interaction between narcotic analgesics and a synaptic plasma membrane fraction of rat cerebral cortex. Acta Pharmacol Toxicol 32:317-320, 1973

Thompson DA, Welle SL, Lilavivat U, et al: Opiate receptor blockade in man reduces 2-deoxy-D-glucose induced food intake but not hunger, thirst and hypothermia. Life Sci 31:847-852, 1982

Trenchard E, Silverstone T: Naloxone reduces the food intake of normal human volunteers. Appetite: Journal of Intake Research 4:43-50, 1983

Wolkowitz O, Doran AR, Cohen MR: Effect of naloxone on food consumption in obesity. N Engl J Med 313:327, 1985

Wu MF, Cruz-Morales SE, Quinan JR, et al: Naloxone reduces fluid consumption: relationship of this effect to conditioned taste aversion and morphine dependence. Bulletin of the Psychonomic Society 14:323-325, 1979

Zucker LM, Zucker TF: Fatty—a new mutation in the rat. J Hered 52:275-278, 1961

Chapter 7

Opiate Antagonists as Clinical Probes in Bulimia

Jeffrey M. Jonas, M.D.
Mark S. Gold, M.D.

Chapter 7

Opiate Antagonists as Clinical Probes in Bulimia

The rationale for using the long-acting opiate antagonist naltrexone to treat individuals with bulimia comes largely from evidence implicating endogenous opioid peptides in the regulation of feeding behavior, as is summarized by Drs. James Mitchell and John Morley in Chapter 6.

The review by Drs. Mitchell and Morley makes clear that the precise role of opioid peptides in the regulation of human feeding behavior is unknown. However, from the studies in this area, three points concerning the effects of opiate blockade on ingestive behavior may be made. First, much of the animal literature suggests that administration of opiate antagonists diminishes food intake in situations of free feeding and stress-induced feeding. Second, in humans, short-term controlled trials of the antagonist naloxone have demonstrated suppression of food intake. And third, in contrast, longer term studies of naltrexone in obese humans have failed to show the weight loss that might be expected if naltrexone is an effective appetite suppressant.

The failure of naltrexone to cause weight loss in obese subjects does not exclude a role for opioid peptides in the pathogenesis of obesity and other eating disorders. Endogenous opioids may be involved in initiation of feeding or in dietary preference, for example, rather than in control of set point, satiety, or hunger. If this were so, administration of naltrexone might not affect weight so much as other aspects of feeding behavior. Preliminary data from our center and others tentatively support these conjectures.

A role of endogenous opioids in obesity is supported by demonstration of enhanced beta-endorphin response to glucose ingestion in obese subjects (Getto et al. 1984), as well as by certain clinical findings, such as differences in pain sensitivity seen in obese subjects (McKendall and Haier 1983) and in the reversal of sleep apnea in obese subjects treated with naloxone (Atkinson et al. 1985). In bulimia, sustained elevation of beta-endorphins unrelated to glucose ingestion has been observed (Fullerton et al. 1986), and naltrexone has been reported to ameliorate symptoms of bingeing and purging without significant weight loss in a small, open-label study (Jonas and Gold 1986a). Naltrexone has also been reported to reduce dietary preference for carbohydrates in normal and obese subjects (Fantino et al. 1986).

These reports and those reviewed by Drs. Mitchell and Morley in Chapter 6 support a role for endogenous opioids in the etiology of obesity and bulimia, but it appears that this role is not simply one of increased opioid peptides' causing increased appetite. We shall now summarize data from our center of open trials of naltrexone (Jonas and Gold 1986a, 1986b, 1986c, 1986d) that tentatively suggest that opiate blockade may alleviate bulimic symptoms, often without associated weight loss.

METHODS

Twenty-five consecutive normal weight individuals (80 to 120 percent of ideal body weight) diagnosed as having bulimia by criteria from the *Diagnostic and Statistical Manual of Mental Disorders (Third Edition)* (American Psychiatric Association 1980), who had failed at least one trial of an antidepressant medication, were entered into an open six-week trial of naltrexone, in which dosages of up to 300 mg/day were used. A trial of antidepressant was deemed adequate using the following criteria: 1) Dosages of heterocyclics were deemed adequate if they produced serum levels in the therapeutic range (Pope et al. 1983); an adequate dose of nomifensine was defined as 300 mg/day; and an adequate dose of monoamine oxidase inhibitors was that which yielded a minimum 80 percent suppression of platelet monoamine oxidase (with a minimal accepted dosage of 60 mg of tranylcypromine). 2) A minimum of four weeks' treatment on adequate dosages, as defined above, on any antidepressant was required. We studied antidepressant nonresponders, hypothesizing that if bulimia were a heterogeneous entity, selecting a population of thymoleptic nonresponders could enhance the chance of finding individuals for whom opiate systems, rather than monoamine systems, played a role in the disorder.

Patients were included in the study if they were between the ages of 15 and 40, if they were bingeing a minimum of five days each week, and if they had been ill a minimum of two years. Of the 25 subjects, 18 had no response whatsoever to antidepressants and were treated with naltrexone alone. Seven individuals had major depression that responded to antidepressants with no change in their eating patterns. In this group we added naltrexone to the subject's medication regimen. Data from the two groups were analyzed separately. All patients had initial physical exams that were normal, and all had normal initial blood work, including liver function tests. Liver functions were monitored weekly during the first six weeks of naltrexone, and biweekly thereafter.

Patients were administered naltrexone, beginning with an initial dose of 50 mg for two days and then increasing as tolerated to 150 mg for the first two weeks. If no response was noted at that time, the dose was increased to a maximum of 300 mg each day. Naltrexone was taken at night with a snack to lessen the nausea that may accompany its use.

Patients were rated weekly by one of the authors (JMJ) for the number of days each week when bingeing and purging occurred, along with the duration of bingeing and purging each day. This information was obtained during a clinical interview and on the basis of a daily log kept by each subject. Patients were also administered the Hamilton Rating Scale for Depression (HRSD) each week. Weights were obtained weekly. Follow-up interviews were obtained on each subject every two to four weeks, with follow-up obtained for 1 to 11 months.

RESULTS

Five patients (all in the group treated with naltrexone alone) could not complete the study due to nausea attributable to the naltrexone. Otherwise, adverse effects from the medication were relatively few. During the initial trial and on follow-up, only one subject displayed any liver function abnormalities, and this was a rise in LDH to 337 units and an elevation of SGPT to 64 units when the patient had been taking 300 mg of naltrexone for two months. Lowering the dose of naltrexone to 200 mg led to normalization of liver functions without alteration in response.

Results are summarized in Tables 6 and 7 for 13 subjects treated with naltrexone alone and in Tables 8 and 9 for 7 subjects treated with naltrexone and antidepressant. Tests of significance are by paired t test, two-tailed, unless otherwise noted.

The 13 subjects treated with naltrexone alone showed significant reductions in bingeing, purging, and duration of binge episodes by week 2, with continued reductions through the course of the six-week trial. There were also significant reductions in scores on the HRSD by week 4, but the presence or absence of major depression at the start of the study did not appear to have any effect on the response to naltrexone.

We found that improvement in symptoms did not occur after the sixth week. However, we could not determine the time course and dose range needed for response because of the study design, whereby the dosage of naltrexone was raised fairly quickly to 300 mg over a three-week period. It is possible that in some cases lower dosages than those used here would be sufficient, but in our experience, we have seen no cases in which response occurred at a dose of less than 150 mg.

We also rated the percent reduction of bingeing and purging seen in each subject at the end of the trial and on follow-up. Six subjects

Table 6. Response to Naltrexone in 13 Bulimic Subjects Treated With Naltrexone Alone

Week	No. of Days Bingeing per Week		No. of Days Purging per Week		Duration of Binge Episodes (Min.)		HRSD Scores	
	Mean	SD	Mean	SD	Mean	SD	Mean	SD
0	6.8	0.5	4.8	2.0	120	99	18.6	5.1
2	4.6***	1.3	3.2**	2.0	75*	67	15.8	4.7
4	3.0***	2.1	2.2***	2.5	48**	78	12.9**	5.9
6	1.8***	2.4	1.7***	2.4	33**	67	12.3**	5.2

Note: Test of significance, pretreatment versus posttreatment, by two-tailed, paired t-test. HRSD = Hamilton Rating Scale for Depresison.
* $p < .05$ ** $p < .01$ *** $p < .001$

Table 7. Number of Patients in Each Response Category at Six Weeks and After 2 to 11 Months Follow-Up on Naltrexone Alone

	Response Category			
	Complete (100%)	Marked (75%)	Moderate (50%)	None (<50%)
Week 6	6	4	1	2
Follow-up	5	3	2	3
Breakdown of length of follow-up in months	One each at 2, 4, 8, 10, 11 months	One each at 3, 7, 8 months	One each at 2, 5 months	—

Note: Global response given as percent reduction in days bingeing and purging.

had a 100 percent (complete) resolution of their bingeing and purging, and four experienced a 75 percent reduction ("marked") of their symptoms at the end of the trial, with three subjects displaying little or no response. On follow-up, five of six subjects maintained a complete response, and three of four maintained a marked response after 2 to 11 months.

There were no significant changes in weight noted among the group treated with naltrexone alone. After six weeks, the 13 subjects lost a mean 1.8 pounds. If we look only at those subjects with at

Table 8. Response to Naltrexone in Seven Bulimic Subjects Treated With Naltrexone in Combination With Thymoleptics

Week	No. of Days Bingeing per Week		No. of Days Purging per Week		Duration of Binge Episodes (Min.)		HRSD Scores	
	Mean	*SD*	*Mean*	*SD*	*Mean*	*SD*	*Mean*	*SD*
0	6.4	1.4	5.6	2.3	76	34	15.3	1.8
2	3.1**	2.4	3.0*	2.3	62	40	11.7	3.6
4	1.8**	2.4	2.0**	2.2	33**	33	10.8**	2.7
6	1.6**	2.4	1.6**	2.4	20**	26	9.4**	2.2

Note: Test of significance, pretreatment versus posttreatment, by two-tailed, paired t-test. HRSD = Hamilton Rating Scale for Depression.
* $p < .05$ ** $p < .01$ *** $p < .001$

Table 9. Number of Patients in Each Response Category at Six Weeks and After One to Three Months Follow-Up— Treatment With Naltrexone and Thymoleptic

	Response Category			
	Complete (100%)	Marked (75%)	Moderate (50%)	None (<50%)
Week 6	4	2	0	1
Follow-up	3	3	0	1
Breakdown of length of follow-up in months	One each at 1, 2, 3 months	Three at 2 months	0	—

Note: Global response given as percent reduction in days bingeing and purging.

least a 75 percent reduction of bingeing and purging (10 of the 13), no significant weight loss effect from naltrexone can be observed. In this group there was a mean weight loss of 2.3 pounds over six weeks. There was also no difference in weight loss in comparing subjects who experienced at least a 75 percent reduction in binge-eating and those who experienced no change in their bingeing patterns. Finally, we compared subjects who had greater than 75 percent reduction of bingeing with those whose bingeing did not stop to see whether individuals simply lost weight, gained weight, or remained the same. Subjects were no more likely to gain weight with a reduction in bingeing and purging of 75 percent or more than they were to lose or maintain their weight ($\chi^2 = .88$; n.s.).

The results for the seven subjects treated with naltrexone plus antidepressant were similar to those seen in the group treated with naltrexone alone, with significant reductions in bingeing, purging, and duration of bingeing. Even though none of these subjects met criteria for major depression, there nevertheless was a significant reduction in HRSD scores by week 6. This we shall discuss below. On follow-up of one to three months, most of the subjects had maintained their improvement.

The pattern of weight change in the naltrexone-plus-antidepressant group resembled that seen in the group treated with naltrexone alone. Overall, there was no significant change—a mean weight gain of .29 pounds over six weeks. For the six individuals who experienced at least a 75 percent reduction in bingeing and purging, there was an average weight gain of 2.33 pounds during the trial. As in the group treated with naltrexone alone, there was no demonstrable effect on weight from the naltrexone, and subjects were just as likely to gain weight as to lose weight, whether or not their bingeing was reduced ($\chi^2 = .001$; n.s.).

DISCUSSION

The data presented here must be interpreted with caution, since this was an open study. A double-blind, placebo-controlled study is required to confirm our early findings. Nevertheless, these preliminary data are encouraging and provide clinical evidence that endogenous opioids may be involved in the pathogenesis of bulimia.

The response of our subjects to treatment with naltrexone suggests that opiate blockage may be a useful clinical tool in treating bulimia by attenuating bulimic symptoms. In subjects with marked or complete responses, we observed decreased bingeing and purging, along with decreased preoccupation with food and resumption of normal eating patterns. These improvements appeared stable, and some of our patients have remained symptom free while being treated with naltrexone for nearly one year.

ROLE OF OPIOID PEPTIDES IN BULIMIA

How and why opiate blockade should be effective in treating bulimia is likely to remain a matter of conjecture until the role of endogenous opioids in regulating human feeding is better understood. However, because naltrexone is a nearly pure opiate antagonist (Gold et al. 1982), it is tempting to speculate that its efficacy supports the role of endogenous opioids in the pathogenesis of eating disorders. While this may be the case, we cannot exclude interactions between monoamine and opioid systems in humans. The efficacy of naltrexone may be due to its ability to alter the level of other neurotransmitters via its blockade of opiate peptides. From a clinical standpoint, there is little to distinguish a complete response to naltrexone from a complete response to antidepressants in bulimic individuals. In both instances there are global improvements in mood and eating symptoms. At this juncture, it is as hazardous to say that naltrexone treatment supports an isolated opiate defect in bulimia as it is to say that neuroleptic efficacy in schizophrenia supports excess dopamine activity as the primary cause of that disorder.

An interaction between dysregulation of monoaminergic and opioid systems in bulimia is suggested by a number of lines of evidence. In animals, there is a known interplay of these systems in the regulation of feeding (Morley et al. 1985; Liebowitz and Hor 1982). In bulimia, as already noted, response of eating symptoms to opiate blockade resembles response to antidepressant medications. Perhaps most interesting, our data suggest that naltrexone may have an effect on mood. In our sample, individuals with major depression experienced reduction of their HRSD scores along with improvement in their bulimic symptoms. While naltrexone has not been reported to have thymoleptic properties (Gold et al. 1982), dysregulation of endogenous opiates has been reported in major depression (Matthews et al. 1986). It may be that the extent of opioid dysregulation varies in different types of affective disorders and in cases in which dysfunction is most pronounced, eating symptoms become prominent (for example, loss of appetite in major depression) or actually predominate, as in bulimia.

If depression and bulimia do arise from dysfunction of monoamine and opioid systems, then naltrexone might be expected to be of use in augmenting antidepressant response in resistant cases of both bulimia and depression. While the use of naltrexone to augment antidepressant response in depression has yet to be reported, our data support this possibility in bulimic individuals who respond incompletely to antidepressants. In our small group of seven subjects, we added naltrexone to thymoleptics, believing that the patient's mood response was complete in the face of ongoing bulimic symptoms. We were therefore surprised to note further and significant reductions of HRSD scores along with reduction of bulimic symptomatology. This suggested that continued bulimic and undiagnosed depressive symptoms due to an incomplete response of a single (affective) disorder to antidepressants, both of which improved with addition of naltrexone. This interpretation is consistent with studies showing a relationship between bulimia and major affective disorder (Hudson et al. 1983; Pope and Hudson 1984). However, it is also possible that naltrexone was treating a second disorder distinct from affective disorder. Further studies of naltrexone in treating bulimia and affective disorders will be required to clarify these points.

On a phenomenologic level, involvement of opiate systems in the pathogenesis of bulimia might explain the compulsive and irresistible nature of bingeing and purging. If endogenous opioid systems were involved in generating bulimic symptoms, this could account for the observation that attitudes toward food among bulimic patients resembles the attitudes toward drugs seen in substance-abusing individuals. In both bulimia and substance abuse there is loss of control over a substance, adverse social and medical consequences from abuse of a substance, and preoccupation with obtaining the substance (Hatsukami et al. 1982).

If there were a biological link between substance abuse and eating disorders, we would expect these two types of disorders to frequently coexist. This has been shown to be the case in studies of individuals with eating disorders. In such studies, between 25 and 50 percent of individuals with either bulimia or anorexia nervosa have been shown to suffer from some form of substance abuse (Pyle et al. 1981; Hudson et al. 1983; Hatsukami et al. 1984; Mitchell et al. 1985; Jones et al. 1985). Fewer such studies have been performed on populations of drug abusers. Survey data obtained from cocaine abusers suggest a high incidence of eating disorders (Jonas et al. 1987), and children of alcoholics may also have an elevated incidence of eating disorders (Jonas and Gold in press). In all, there is an ample amount of empirical data linking substance abuse and eating disorders—but whether this linkage is on the basis of a common opioid mechanism remains to be seen.

OPIATE ANTAGONISTS AND REGULATION OF BODY WEIGHT

Another area of interest involves the effect of opiate antagonists on body weight. If opioid peptides are responsible for sustaining feeding behaviors in humans, then opiate blockade should result in weight loss. As Drs. Mitchell and Morley noted in Chapter 6, however, naltrexone has not proved effective in treating simple obesity. One possible explanation for this finding is that opiate dysfunction in simple obesity differs from the hypothetical dysfunction that causes eating disorders. However, in our sample of bulimic individuals, cessation of bingeing also did not regularly result in weight loss. These observations suggest that naltrexone is generally not useful as an appetite suppressant and that in the case of bulimia, the efficacy of naltrexone is not due to attenuation of appetite or food intake.

Because binge-eating may cease without attendant weight loss, factors other than total caloric intake, such as set point, metabolic rate, composition of diet, activity level, and efficacy of purging, must be influencing body weight. In these individuals, it may be that endogenous opioids are involved in the process of binge-eating, but not in other areas that have impact on weight regulation in humans. We have been studying the effect of naltrexone on obese, binge-eating individuals with and without bulimia, and our early data (Jonas and Gold 1986c) are similar to that described here. Naltrexone may be effective in decreasing binge-eating in obese subjects, but this occurs without weight loss. A detailed dietary analysis of bulimic individuals treated with naltrexone might provide answers to some of these questions.

SAFETY OF NALTREXONE

Finally, there is the question of the safety of high doses of naltrexone. Drs. Mitchell and Morley note in Chapter 6 that there may be a risk of developing liver function abnormalities after taking naltrexone for extended periods. We have not had similar experiences in our bulimic population. In only one instance has there been evidence of elevated liver enzymes. It may be that obese individuals and patients with opiate addiction, populations in whom naltrexone has been studied most, are at special risk for this adverse effect. Nevertheless, we believe that investigators should monitor liver function tests weekly during the first four to eight weeks of treatment with naltrexone, and biweekly thereafter, until the risks of hepatotoxicity are better defined.

As we noted at the start of this chapter, our data, although suggestive, are preliminary; they require confirmation in double-blind, placebo-controlled studies. However, the efficacy of naltrexone in treating bulimia, if confirmed, will provide the first convincing clinical evidence that endogenous opioids may be involved in the etiology of this disorder, and may provide new avenues for the treatment of all eating disorders.

REFERENCES

Atkinson RL, Suratt PM, Wilhoit SC, et al: Naloxone improves sleep apnea in obese humans. Int J Obes 9:233-239, 1985

Fantino M, Hosotte J, Apfelbaum M: An opioid antagonist, naltrexone, reduces preference for sucrose in humans. Am J Physiol 251(1):R91-R95, 1986

Fullerton DT, Swift WJ, Getto CJ, et al: Plasma immunoreactive beta-endorphin in bulimics. Psychol Med 16:59-63, 1986

Getto CJ, Fullerton DT, Carlson IH: Plasma immunoreactive beta-endorphin response to glucose ingestion. Appetite: Journal of Intake Research 5:329-335, 1984

Gold MS, Dackis CA, Pottash ALC, et al: Naltrexone, opiate addiction, and endorphins. Medical Res Rev 2:211-246, 1982

Hatsukami DK, Owen P, Pyle R, et al: Similarities and differences on the MMPI between women with bulimia and women with alcohol or drug abuse problems. Addict Behav 7:435-439, 1982

Hatsukami DK, Eckert ED, Mitchell JE, et al: Affective disorder and substance abuse in women with bulimia. Psychol Med 14:701-704, 1984

Hudson JI, Pope HG Jr, Jonas JM, et al: Phenomenologic relationship of eating disorders to major affective disorder. Psychiatry Res 9:345-354, 1983

Jonas JM, Gold MS: Naltrexone reverses bulimic symptoms. Lancet 1:807, 1986a

Jonas JM, Gold MS: Naltrexone in the treatment of bulimia. Presented at the 139th Annual Meeting of the American Psychiatric Association, Washington, DC, May 1986b

Jonas JM, Gold MS: Treatment of binge-eating: an open study of naltrexone. Society of Neuroscience Abstracts 12:595, 1986c

Jonas JM, Gold MS: Treatment of antidepressant-resistant bulimia with naltrexone. Int J Psychiatry Med 16:305-309, 1986d

Jonas JM, Gold MS: Naltrexone treatment of bulimia: clinical and theoretical findings linking eating disorders and substance abuse. Adv Alcohol Subst Abuse, in press

Jonas JM, Gold MS, Sweeney DR, et al: Eating disorders and cocaine abuse: a survey of 259 cocaine abusers. J Clin Psychiatry 48:47-50, 1987

Jones DA, Cheshire N, Moorhouse H: Anorexia nervosa, bulimia, and alcoholism—association of eating disorder and alcohol. J Psychiatry Res 19:377-380, 1985

Liebowitz SF, Hor L: Endorphinergic and alpha-noradrenergic systems in the paraventricular nucleus: effects on eating behavior. Peptides 3:421-428, 1982

Matthews J, Akil H, Greden J, et al: Beta-endorphin/beta-lipotropin immunoreactivity in endogenous depression: effect of dexamethasone. Arch Gen Psychiatry 43:374-381, 1986

McKendall MJ, Haier RJ: Pain sensitivity and obesity. Psychiatry Res 8:119-125, 1983

Mitchell JE, Hatsukami DK, Eckert ED, et al: Characteristics of 275 patients with bulimia. Am J Psychiatry 142:482-485, 1985

Morley JE, Gosnell BA, Krahn DD, et al: Neuropeptidergic regulation of feeding. Psychopharmacol Bull 21:400-405, 1985

Pope HG Jr, Hudson JI: New Hope for Binge Eaters: Advances in the Understanding and Treatment of Bulimia. New York, Harper and Row, 1984

Pope HG Jr, Hudson JI, Jonas JM: Antidepressant treatment of bulimia: preliminary experience and practical recommendations. J Clin Psychopharmacol 3:274-281, 1983

Pyle RL, Mitchell JE, Eckert ED: Bulimia: a report of 34 cases. J Clin Psychiatry 42:60-64, 1981

Chapter 8

Metabolic and Endocrine Consequences of Eating Behavior and Food Composition in Bulimia

Karl-M. Pirke, M.D.
Ulrich Schweiger, M.D.
Reinhold Laessle, Ph.D
Manfred M. Fichter, M.D.
Guenther Wolfram, M.D.

Chapter 8

Metabolic and Endocrine Consequences of Eating Behavior and Food Composition in Bulimia

Recurrent episodes of binge-eating characterize the syndrome of bulimia as defined by the *Diagnostic and Statistical Manual of Mental Disorders (Third Edition)* (*DSM-III*; American Psychiatric Association 1980). Since most bulimic patients are extremely concerned with their body weight and figure, they attempt to lose weight by vomiting and/or laxative abuse and by intermittently dieting, with or without the accompanying use of appetite-suppressing drugs. This disturbed eating behavior results in certain metabolic and endocrine consequences.

We studied 24 patients diagnosed as having bulimia by *DSM-III* criteria. The patients were between 20 to 35 years of age (mean = 25.6 years). Their body weight ranged from 85 to 120 percent of ideal body weight (IBW) (mean = 98.3 percent), calculated according to the Metropolitan Life Insurance tables (1959). Three patients were excluded from the study because of severe alcohol abuse (consumption of more than 40 ml of alcohol per day).

Patients completed nutritional diaries over a three-week period prior to hospital admission. Food diaries were evaluated using German food tables (Souci et al. 1981). Table 10 summarizes the average calorie consumption per day, the number of binge-eating episodes and the number of calories consumed during such an episode. The patients had an average of 16.8 binge-eating episodes per three weeks. During the observation period their food intake was lower than 1,500 kcal on an average of 6.0 days (SD-4.2), indicating that they were dieting. Since by vomiting patients lose a large amount of the calories

Table 10. Analysis of Eating Behavior in 24 Patients With Bulimia

	Average caloric intake/day (kcal)	No. of binge-eating episodes per 3 weeks	Average energy consumed per binge-eating episode (kcal)	No. of days with caloric intake < 1500 kcal per 3 weeks
Mean	3,091	16.8	1,947	6.0
SD	1,888	15.6	908	4.2
Range	1,718–7,959	3–54	1,106–4,330	1–14

consumed, the actual number of days with an insufficient supply of energy is certainly much greater.

Figure 12 shows the food composition in bulimic patients. Data from a healthy, age-matched control group ($n = 18$) who later participated in a study on dieting and menstrual cycle disturbances are also presented. The average carbohydrate, protein, and fat intake in the bulimic patients did not differ from that in the normal controls. When the food consumption during binge-eating episodes was compared with total food consumption, significant changes were observed. The fat content increased significantly ($p < .01$; Wilcoxon test for paired data), while the protein content decreased significantly ($p < .05$). The carbohydrate content remained constant. These changes are most likely the consequence of a loss of control during the binge-eating episode. Young women in general, and bulimic patients in particular, often try to avoid high-fat nutrients. This control probably erodes during binge-eating episodes.

THE CONSEQUENCES OF RESTRICTED FOOD INTAKE

The metabolic adaptation to starvation can be described in three phases: an overnight fast (12 to 14 hours), a short-term fast (three days), and a prolonged fast (three weeks and longer). During the first phase, glycogen reserves are utilized, and glucose and free fatty acids (FFA) from lypolysis contribute equal parts to the body's energy needs. Only 10 to 20 percent is provided by amino acid oxidation (Owen et al. 1978).

In the second phase, when glycogen stores have been depleted (Nilsson and Hultman 1974), 85 to 90 percent of the fuel requirement is met by substrates provided by lipids: FFA and their metabolites, as well as the ketone bodies beta-hydroxybutyric acid (BHBA) and acetoacetate. The remaining caloric requirement is met by amino acids, which are either directly oxidized or used in gluconeogenesis.

In the third phase, adaptation processes occur that reduce the basal energy consumption of the body: Body temperature is lowered, and blood pressure and heart rate are reduced. These changes are brought about by a decrease in triiodothyronine (T_3) levels and by a reduction of catecholamine production (Vagenakis et al. 1975; Young and Landsberg 1977). Blood glucose levels are reduced in starvation but do not reach hypoglycemic values. Only rarely does severe hypoglycemia develop in a state of extreme malnutrition, which may then be refractory to therapy (Elias and Gwinup 1982).

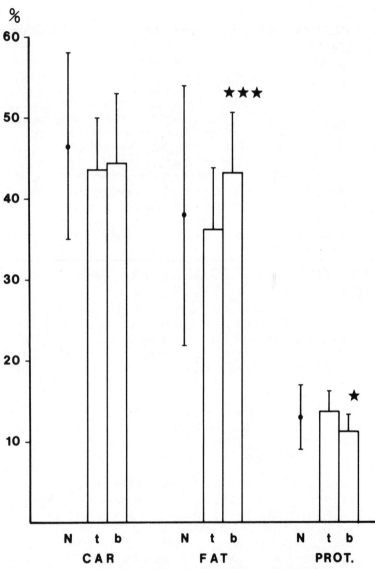

Figure 12. Composition of food (Mean ± SD) eaten by bulimic patients and controls. CAR = carbohydrates, PROT. = protein, N = control subjects, t = total food intake, b = food consumed during episodes of binge-eating. During bingeing, the fat content is significantly (***p < .01) increased while protein content is significantly decreased (*p < .05).

METABOLIC AND ENDOCRINE OBSERVATIONS IN BULIMIA

Figure 13 shows glucose, BHBA, and FFA levels in 15 bulimic patients and in 25 healthy age-matched young women studied earlier by our group (Pirke et al. 1985). Glucose levels were significantly decreased, while both BHBA and FFA levels were significantly increased, in patients with bulimia ($p < .01$). The endocrine adaptation to starvation was studied by our group in 20 patients with bulimia

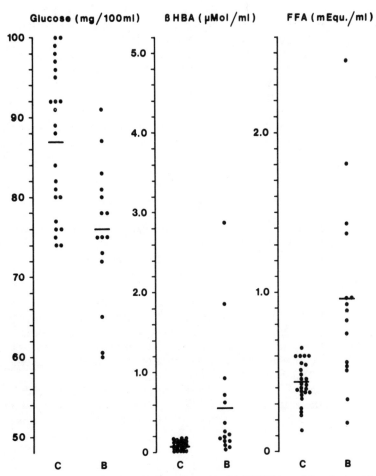

Figure 13. Glucose, beta-hydroxybutyric acid (BHBA), and free fatty acids (FFA) in patients with bulimia (B) and in controls (C).

and in 24 age- and sex-matched controls (Heufelder et al. 1985). Table 11 gives the results.

Triiodothyronine levels were significantly decreased in bulimia. Supine norepinephrine (NE) values in plasma were no different between patients and controls. The orthostatic response of NE, which represents the difference in values before and after standing up for 10 minutes, was significantly reduced in bulimia. Orthostatic response is considered a good indicator of the peripheral NE turnover (Kopin et al. 1978). Suppression of the NE turnover in bulimia is accompanied by a number of changes at the level of the adrenoreceptor and the postreceptor mechanisms, which have been discussed elsewhere in detail (Heufelder et al. 1985).

None of the metabolic and endocrine parameters reported here are specific for the state of starvation. Low glucose values also occur in states of hyperinsulinism; FFA increase in response to stress and high BHBA values are seen in diabetes mellitus that has been treated inadequately; low T_3 levels occur in various states of severe illness; and a decreased elevation of NE in response to standing is also observed in some forms of hypotonia. The simultaneous occurrence of all five symptoms, however, is specific to starvation. Since we observed significantly decreased levels of glucose, T_3 and NE and significantly increased values of FFA and BHBA in patients with bulimia, this finding is interpreted as evidence of an inadequate energy supply in these patients.

Despite the significant group differences between controls and bulimic patients, it is apparent (see Figure 13) that not all patients show all metabolic signs of starvation at all times. Earlier studies of patients with anorexia nervosa revealed that the metabolic and endocrine signs of starvation disappear with varying rapidity when starvation ceases and refeeding begins (Pahl et al. 1985). Elevated FFA and BHBA levels sink rapidly, while decreased T_3 values are normalized only slowly over a several-week period. Normalization of NE turnover is slower still. These differences in time schedule explain why not all patients demonstrate all metabolic and endocrine signs at a given point in time.

The low T_3 and NE values indicate that the basal metabolic rate in these patients is reduced. This fact probably presents an additional difficulty for bulimic patients who try to resume normal eating habits. The caloric intake calculated for a patient according to weight and age may lead to weight gain during the first one or two months of treatment.

Patients with bulimia appear to have normal body weight. It cannot be excluded that despite this, their weight may be below their in-

Table 11. Triiodothyronine and Norepinephrine Levels in Bulimic and Normal Women

	Bulimic women (n = 20) Mean ± SD	Normal women (n = 24) Mean ± SD	p
Triiodothyronine (ng/ml)	0.09 ± 0.10	1.52 ± 0.09	<.01
Norepinephrine supine (pmol/ml)	1.33 ± 0.26	1.42 ± 0.10	n.s.
Orthostatic norepinephrine response[a]	0.60 ± 0.14	1.11 ± 0.12	<.01

[a]Difference in norepinephrine levels before and after standing up for 10 minutes.

dividual set point. This assumption is, however, highly speculative, since it is unclear whether the set point hypothesis is applicable to human beings (for a review see Robbins 1986).

How can the metabolic and endocrine signs of starvation in patients without an obvious weight deficit be explained? In view of the clinical observations and the evaluation of the nutritional diaries (Table 10), the most plausible explanation is intermittent dieting.

We followed six bulimic patients over a four- to six-week period. Blood was drawn each Monday, Wednesday, and Friday after an overnight fast. The ketone body BHBA was measured and body weight recorded three times weekly. One example is given in Figure 14. Fluctuations in body weight are accompanied by changes in BHBA. These observations suggest that intermittent dieting leads to a metabolic and endocrine adaptation consistent with starvation in bulimia.

An example of how intermittent restriction of food intake and the composition of the food chosen influence metabolic and endocrine regulation is given in the final section of this chapter.

IMPAIRED GLUCOSE TOLERANCE IN BULIMIA

Impaired glucose tolerance with overshooting insulin secretion has been observed in starvation (Unger et al. 1963) and in low carbohydrate diets (Hales and Randle 1963). We therefore hypothesized that the glucose tolerance of bulimic patients is also impaired. The extent of this disturbance should be greater the more pronounced the metabolic and endocrine signs of starvation are and the lower the carbohydrate content of the food chosen is.

The same 24 bulimic patients whose nutritional diaries we evaluated participated in this study. Twelve healthy, age-matched women served as controls. After an overnight fast, a cannula was inserted into a forearm vein and kept open with a slow saline drip. After baseline sampling the test meal was consumed between 8:00 A.M. and 8:15 A.M. The test meal, a pudding, contained 500 kcal and consisted of 63.6 g carbohydrates (mainly oligosaccharides), 16.8 g protein, and 22.8 g fat. Further blood samples were drawn 30, 60, 90, and 120 min after termination of the meal.

Serum glucose was measured by the hexokinase method (Boehringer). Insulin and T_3 were measured by radioimmunoassay (Serono). All samples were run in the same assay. The coefficient of variation of determination of a quality control sample was 10.8 percent at an average concentration of 22.8 mIU/l insulin and 3.0 percent at an average concentration of 1.07 ng/ml T_3. Betahydroxybutyric acid was measured according to the method of Williamson and Mellonby (1974).

The test meal resulted in a significant rise in insulin levels (see Table 12) in both groups ($p < .01$). Yet in the patient group, insulin levels were significantly higher than those in the control group 30, 60, and 90 min after the end of the test meal ($p < .025$).

Glucose levels were significantly increased by the test meal only in the patient group ($p < .025$), and were significantly higher 90 min after the end of the test meal than those of the control group ($p < .025$). Within the patient group there was a significant correlation between the postprandial glucose increase and BHBA ($r_s = 0.41$; $p < .05$, Spearman rank correlation). The postprandial insulin increase correlated negatively with T_3 ($r = -0.38$; $p < .058$). Carbohydrate intake correlated negatively with the level of the glucose maximum ($r_s = -0.42$; $p < .05$).

These results support the hypothesis outlined above:

1. Bulimic patients have an impaired glucose tolerance as a consequence of intermittent dieting.
2. Food choice (low carbohydrate content) contributes to the development of impaired glucose tolerance.

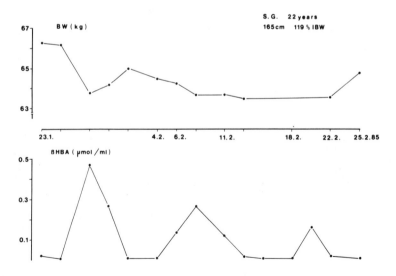

Figure 14. Body weight (BW) and beta-hydroxybutyric acid (BHBA) in a patient with bulimia followed over a five-week period.

Table 12. Glucose and Insulin Levels After a Standardized Test Meal in Patients With Bulimia and in Normal Controls

	Before Test (Mean ± SD)	At Test (Mean ± SD)	Minutes After Test (Mean ± SD)			
			30 (Mean ± SD)	60 (Mean ± SD)	90 (Mean ± SD)	120 (Mean ± SD)
Bulimic patients, n = 24						
Insulin (mIU/ml)	12.6 ± 2.8	13.2 ± 3.8	33.7 ± 17.4[a]	34.5 ± 19.9[a]	32.4 ± 21.7[a]	22.8 ± 9.2
Glucose (mg/100ml)	66.7 ± 11.7	74.8 ± 11.8	94.1 ± 15.7	97.0 ± 22.7	90.8 ± 21.3[a]	87.1 ± 17.1
Control subjects, n = 12						
Insulin (mIU/ml)	12.3 ± 2.7	11.5 ± 3.2	22.7 ± 4.7	20.9 ± 6.0	19.0 ± 6.1	18.5 ± 4.5
Glucose (mg/100ml)	76.8 ± 17.0	83.4 ± 14.2	90.3 ± 16.3	79.5 ± 16.7	81.1 ± 16.7	87.8 ± 21.6

[a] $p < .025$

Not only endocrine systems that are directly responsible for the regulation of the metabolism during the self-imposed intermittent starvation of bulimic patients are changed as a consequence of intermittent starvation in bulimia. In Chapters 2 and 3 on menstrual disturbances in bulimia, the importance of dieting for the regulation of the hypothalamic–pituitary–gonadal axis is stressed. Fifteen of the 24 patients in the present study, whose nutritional diaries were evaluated and whose endocrine response to a test meal was studied, also participated in the 12-hour blood sampling carried out for the analysis of gonadotropins (see Chapter 2). A significant correlation ($r_S = 0.58; p < .025$) was observed between T_3 values and the average FSH values in the bulimic patients. The maximal insulin values after the test meal correlated significantly with the average 12-hour FSH value ($r_S = 0.52; p < .025$). These correlations suggest that the extent of dieting determines the endocrine abnormalities.

CONCLUSIONS AND OUTLOOK

With regard to the metabolic and endocrine disturbances described in this chapter, a close similarity has been established between anorexia nervosa and bulimia (Pirke et al. 1985; Heufelder et al. 1985). In both syndromes, dieting and starvation cause a variety of metabolic and physiologic (including endocrine) abnormalities, many of which can be explained as adaptation processes to chronic and/or intermittent caloric malnutrition. Numerous endocrine observations in anorexia nervosa have been published (for a review see Pirke and Ploog 1986). Reports of many endocrine observations in bulimia can be expected in the near future. The examples given above suggest that the pathobiochemical mechanisms responsible for endocrine and other physiological alterations should be sought by analyzing the pathological behavior and its consequences (quantitative and qualitative changes in eating, hyperactivity, etc.). Analyses of this kind should be attempted before an endocrine abnormality in eating disorders is explained as the consequence of an alteration in a central nervous transmitter system, which, in turn, is considered a primary or etiologic feature of bulimia.

Our interpretation of the endocrine disturbances found in patients with eating disorders does not imply that these disturbances are merely interesting epiphenomena of abnormal eating behavior that contribute little to an understanding of the etiology of bulimia and anorexia nervosa. Rather, we believe that the metabolic and endocrine changes observed in eating disorders may affect the psychopathology, especially with respect to the affective symptoms, in these syndromes. In a recent study (Laessle et al. 1986) of 64 patients fulfilling *DSM-*

III criteria for anorexia nervosa ($n = 42$) and bulimia ($n = 22$), for example, we measured simultaneously body weight, metabolic indices of starvation, psychopathology of the eating disorder, and different aspects of depression. Multiple regression analysis yielded a significant effect of body weight and BHBA on mood and psychovegetative aspects of depression (Depression Scale, von Zerssen 1976) when the effects of diagnostic group and specific psychopathology were controlled. This means that specific depressive symptoms in eating disorders are associated with low body weight, dieting, and starvation.

It is our conviction that the simultaneous analysis of behavior, its biological consequences (including alterations of neurotransmitter systems), and psychopathology will enable us to understand the interactions between body and mind important to the pathogenesis and sustaining processes in eating disorders.

REFERENCES

American Psychiatric Association: Diagnostic and Statistical Manual of Mental Disorders (Third Edition). Washington, DC, American Psychiatric Association, 1980

Elias AN, Gwinup G: Glucose-resistant hypoglycemia in inanition. Arch Intern Med 142:743-746, 1982

Frisch RE: Food intake, fatness and reproductive ability, in Anorexia Nervosa. Edited by Vigersky RA. New York, Raven Press, 1977

Hales CN, Randle PJ: Effects of low-carbohydrate diet and diabetes mellitus on plasma concentrations of glucose, nonesterified fatty acid and insulin during oral glucose-tolerance tests. Lancet 1:790-794, 1963

Heufelder A, Warnhoff M, Pirke KM: Platelet α2-adrenoceptor and adenylate cyclase in patients with anorexia nervosa and bulimia. J Clin Endocrinol Metab 61:1053-1060, 1985

Kopin IJ, Lake RC, Ziegler M: Plasma levels of norepinephrine. Ann Inter Med 88:671-680, 1978

Laessle R, Schweiger U, Pirke KM: The effect of starvation on depressive symptoms in eating disorders. Presented at the Second International Conference on Eating Disorders, New York, April 1986

Metropolitan Life Insurance Company: New weight standards for men and women. Statistical Bulletin 40:1, 1959

Nilsson LH, Hultman E: Liver glycogen in man—the effect of total starvation or a carbohydrate-poor diet followed by carbohydrate refeeding. Scandinavian Journal of Clinical and Laboratory Investigation 32:325-330, 1974

Owen OE, Reichard KA, Boden G, et al: Interrelationships among key tissues in the utilization of metabolic substrates, in Diabetes, Obesity and Vascular Diseases, Metabolic and Molecular Interrelationships: Part 2. Advances in Modern Nutrition. Edited by Katzen H, Mahler RJ. New York, Wiley, 1978

Pahl J, Pirke KM, Schweiger U, et al: Anorectic behavior, mood, metabolic and endocrine adaptation to starvation in anorexia nervosa during inpatient treatment. Biol Psychiatry 20:874-887, 1985

Pirke KM, Ploog D: Psychobiology of anorexia nervosa, in Nutrition and the Brain (Volume 7). Edited by Wurtman RJ, Wurtman JJ. New York, Raven Press, 1986, pp 167-198

Pirke KM, Pahl J, Schweiger U, et al: Metabolic and endocrine indices of starvation in bulimia: a comparison with anorexia nervosa. Psychiatry Res 15: 33-39, 1985

Robbins TW: Peripheral mechanisms and environmental influences, in Neuroendocrinology. Edited by Lightman SL, Everitt BJ. Oxford, England, Blackwell Scientific Publications, 1986

Souci SW, Fachmann W, Kraut H: Die Zusammensetzung der Lebensmittel [The Composition of Food]. Stuttgart, Wissenschaftliche Verlagsgsellschaft, 1981

Unger RH, Eisentraut AM, Madison L: The effects of total starvation upon the levels of circulating glucagon and insulin in man. J Clin Invest 42:1031-1039, 1963

Vagenakis AG, Portnay GI, Burger A, et al: Diversion of peripheral thyroxine metabolism from activating to inactivating pathways during complete fasting. J Clin Endocrinol Metab 41:191-194, 1975

von Zerssen D, with the collaboration of Koeller DM: Klinische Selbstbeurteilungs-Skalen (KSB-S) aus dem Münchner Psychiatrischen Informationssystem [Clinical Self-Report Scales of the Munich Psychiatric Information System]. Weinheim, Beltz, 1976

Williamson DH, Mellonby J: Betahydroxybutyrat, in Methoden der Enzymatischen Analyse [Methods of Enzyme Analysis]. Edited by Bermeyer HU. Weinheim, Verlag Chemie, 1974

Young JB, Landsberg L: Suppression of sympathetic nervous system during fasting. Science 196:1473-1475, 1977

Chapter 9

Norepinephrine Regulation in Bulimia

David C. Jimerson, M.D.
David T. George, M.D.
Walter H. Kaye, M.D.
Timothy D. Brewerton, M.D.
David S. Goldstein, M.D., Ph.D.

Chapter 9

Norepinephrine Regulation in Bulimia

Studies in laboratory animals and indirect pharmacologic studies in humans suggest that dysregulation of norepinephrine activity may contribute to the symptoms of altered appetite, anxiety, depression, and fluctuations of body weight observed in patients with the syndrome of bulimia. Noradrenergic effects on appetite and mood are likely to occur predominantly in the central nervous system, while symptoms of anxiety and changes in metabolic rate may reflect changes in activity in the central and/or peripheral sympathetic nervous system. The focus of this chapter is on the possible role of altered norepinephrine regulation in the pathophysiology of bulimia; however, abnormalities in other neurotransmitter systems (for example, serotonin) and/or neuropeptides (for example, endogenous opiates) have also been implicated in preliminary studies. As with other major psychiatric syndromes, such as depression, it seems unlikely that bulimia results from an isolated excess or deficiency in any single neurochemical system.

Preliminary data indicate that norepinephrine function may be dysregulated in normal weight patients who have the syndrome of bulimia. Recent studies have shown that during the first week after hospital admission, patients with bulimia have blunted norepinephrine response to standing (Pirke et al. 1985) and increased platelet alpha$_2$-adrenoreceptor number (Heufelder et al. 1985). Resting plasma norepinephrine levels in bulimic patients were significantly reduced following three weeks of hospitalization on a clinical research unit for nutritional stabilization in the absence of bingeing and vomiting (Kaye et al. 1986a).

CLINICAL METHODOLOGY IN CATECHOLAMINE STUDIES

Changes in diet and body weight require special attention in catecholamine studies in patients with eating disorders. Thus, when studied in the early phases of treatment, low weight patients with anorexia nervosa have reduced norepinephrine activity, as reflected by concentrations of the neurotransmitter or its metabolites in plasma or urine (Halmi et al. 1978; Gross et al. 1979; Riederer et al. 1982; Luck et al. 1983; Biederman et al. 1984; Pirke et al. 1985). Recent studies have shown, however, that norepinephrine levels can actually be relatively elevated in anorexic patients studied during the first few days of hospitalization, most likely reflecting the effects of irregular food and fluid intake prior to admission, as well as stresses associated with illness and with hospital admission (Pahl et al. 1985; Lesem et al. 1987). In contrast, when studied following stabilization at goal weight for at least six months, anorexic patients were found to have reduced plasma and cerebrospinal fluid norepinephrine concentrations (Kaye et al. 1985).

Studies with bulimic patients during the first few days following hospital admission demonstrated increased plasma free fatty acids and decreased thyroid hormone levels, presumably reflecting the effects of recent dieting and/or fasting (Pirke et al. 1985). These altered eating patterns are of particular relevance because of evidence that dieting or fasting with associated weight loss is likely to reduce sympathetic nervous system activity (Landsberg and Young 1978; O'Dea et al. 1982).

Studies in other psychiatric patient populations and control groups have demonstrated a number of additional clinical variables critical to catecholamine studies in eating disorder patients (Jimerson 1984). Thus, anxiety associated with daily life stressors, the acute stress of admission to an inpatient program, and first exposure to research procedures could result in increased sympathetic nervous system activity. Conversely, extended exercise programs for physical fitness can affect resting values for pulse, blood pressure, and plasma norepinephrine concentration. Use of or withdrawal from alcohol, other substances of abuse, and psychotropic medications can influence norepinephrine activity. These and other factors (including dietary sodium intake) can be difficult to assess with psychiatric outpatients and underscore the value of a period of stabilization and observation of patients in a hospital environment when possible prior to studies of catecholamine function.

BETA-ADRENORECEPTOR FUNCTION IN BULIMIA

In recent studies by our group, pharmacologic challenge testing with intravenous infusion of isoproterenol provided a means for in vivo assessment of beta-adrenoceptor sensitivity in nutritionally and metabolically stabilized bulimic patients. Pulse and blood pressure responses were used to assess cardiovascular adrenoceptor responsivity in patients and controls. Behavioral ratings provided an indication of whether bulimic patients demonstrate exaggerated responsivity to isoproterenol similar to that previously described in some patients with anxiety disorders (Easton and Sherman 1976).

Isoproterenol-induced release of free fatty acids provided information on the question of whether decreased sensitivity to the lipolytic effects of catecholamines might contribute to the reduced resting metabolic rate and caloric requirement for weight maintenance observed in some bulimic patients (Kaye et al. 1986b; Obarzanek et al. 1987). Upregulation of beta-adrenoreceptor function in bulimia would be consistent with the hypothesis that the clinical efficacy of antidepressant treatments may be related to decreased presynaptic release of norepinephrine and/or downregulation of postsynaptic receptor activity produced by these medications (Charney et al. 1981).

As described in detail elsewhere (George et al. 1986a), catecholamine studies were conducted in 14 female bulimic patients and 11 healthy female volunteers. All subjects were admitted to a clinical research unit at the National Institute of Mental Health and gave written informed consent prior to participating in the studies. Patients met criteria from the *Diagnostic and Statistical Manual of Mental Disorders (Third Edition)* (American Psychiatric Association 1980) for bulimia, with the additional admission criterion of bingeing and purging with a frequency of at least once daily. Patients with a past history of anorexia nervosa or obesity were excluded. All patients were in good medical health, with normal serum electrolytes at the time of the studies. Control subjects were in good medical health, and were screened to exclude present symptoms or a past history of major psychiatric illness either in themselves or in first-degree relatives. All subjects were free of medication for at least three weeks at the time of the study, and followed a reduced monoamine diet for at least three days prior to testing. Patients were hospitalized in a behaviorally oriented treatment program with enforced abstinence from bingeing and vomiting for three weeks prior to study, and were asked to follow a nutritionally balanced diet with calories adjusted to maintain a stable body weight (± 1 kg). Controls were admitted to the same clinical research unit one or more days prior to the studies.

Infusion procedures were conducted after overnight fast and bedrest, with patients supine throughout the study. Behavioral ratings, pulse, blood pressure, and body temperature were obtained at baseline and at regular intervals throughout the infusion. Blood samples for neurotransmitter and hormone measurements were obtained from an intravenous catheter. Isoproterenol was administered as a continuous infusion, with doses increased at 15-minute intervals to a dose endpoint of 25 beat/min. pulse increase.

Bulimic patients and control subjects were matched for age (mean ± SD were 22.2 ± 4.3 years versus 23.4 ± 4.1 years, respectively) and body weight (92.8 ± 6.0 percent versus 95.8 ± 8.5 percent ideal weight, respectively). As reported in more detail elsewhere (George et al. in preparation), bulimic patients had significantly reduced resting pulse ($p < .005$, student's t test, two-tailed), systolic blood pressure ($p < .01$), body temperature ($p < .005$), and plasma norepinephrine ($p < .02$) compared with controls. In response to increasing doses of isoproterenol, bulimic patients showed increased sensitivity to the chronotropic effects of isoproterenol, reaching the 25 beats/min. endpoint at a significantly lower drug dose than controls ($p < .01$).

Bulimic patients had significantly higher ratings of anxiety than did the controls at the time of the preinfusion baseline on both the Spielberger Trait Anxiety Scale ($p < .0001$) and the Spielberger State Anxiety Scale ($p < .001$). Ratings on the Spielberger State Anxiety Scale showed similar increases for both patients and controls over the course of the infusion, such that the postinfusion rating was significantly higher for patients than for controls ($p < .01$).

Levels of free fatty acids were not significantly different for patients and controls at baseline. Moreover, the isoproterenol-induced release of free fatty acids was similar in both patient and control groups.

NOREPINEPHRINE FUNCTION AND SYMPTOM PROFILES IN BULIMIA

The results of studies to date have shown that following metabolic, nutritional, and behavioral stabilization in a hospital setting, female bulimic patients were significantly different from age- and weight-matched controls on behavioral ratings, cardiovascular measures, and catecholamine activity. Evidence for the degree of stabilization achieved, apart form the careful clinical observation for avoidance of bingeing, purging, and substance abuse, included stability of body weight for three weeks prior to the study, and normal baseline levels of free fatty acids at the time of the infusion.

The observation that bulimic patients had significantly lower resting pulse than did controls is consistent with the significantly reduced plasma norepinephrine levels observed in the patients, although it is possible that there could be a cholinergic component to the observed bradycardia. Results of the present studies are consistent with previous results showing reduced norepinephrine levels in bulimic patients (Pirke et al. 1985; Kaye et al. 1986a). Increased responsivity to the chronotropic effects of isoproterenol is likely to reflect up-regulation of cardiovascular beta-adrenoreceptors, possibly as a compensatory response to decreased presynaptic release of norepinephrine. The present findings are in line with our recent results from in vitro radioreceptor binding studies showing that lymphocytes from bulimic patients manifested a shift to a higher affinity beta-adrenergic agonist binding state when compared with binding parameters for lymphocytes for control subjects (Buckholtz et al. 1987).

The pathophysiology underlying reduced plasma norepinephrine levels in bulimia is uncertain. Future studies of norepinephrine turnover are needed to verify that low circulating levels of the transmitter reflect decreased presynaptic release rather than increased clearance from plasma. Future studies of high-risk populations or long-term follow-up studies of recovered bulimic patients may help clarify whether norepinephrine dysregulation is a stable physiological trait in these subjects. Alternatively, state-related changes in norepinephrine activity could contribute to self-perpetuating aspects of the syndrome (for example, see discussion of anxiety symptoms below). It has been shown in laboratory animals and healthy volunteers that restriction of caloric intake and weight loss can result in decreased sympathetic activity (Landsberg and Young 1978; O'Dea et al. 1982). These changes in sympathetic activity may be related to changes in insulin-mediated glucose metabolism in the ventromedial hypothalamus (Landsberg and Young, 1985). While the bulimic patients were not at a significantly lower weight than the controls when measured against expected weight (adjusted for height and age), it is possible that the patients may have stabilized themselves at a weight significantly lower than their individually normal physiological ("set point") weight. Future studies would benefit from use of additional measures to assess this set point weight for patients and controls.

In the setting of stabilization in a hospital treatment program, bulimic patients had higher baseline ratings of anxiety than did controls. This finding is similar to previous reports that bulimic patients had elevated levels of anxiety when assessed in a phase of active bingeing and purging. The fact that elevated levels of anxiety persist following several weeks of hospitalization suggests that these symptoms may reflect relatively stable personality characteristics or biological traits in these patients. It is also possible that in spite of their familiarity with the research setting, the patients had increased anticipatory anxiety about the upcoming infusion study in comparison with responses in the controls. The present study does not clarify whether increased sensitivity of beta-adrenoceptors could play a role in the elevated baseline anxiety ratings observed in the bulimic patients.

Demonstration of increased anxiety ratings in patients and controls during the infusion of isoproterenol, a beta-adrenergic agonist, is consistent with previous evidence that activation of peripheral beta-adrenoreceptors can produce symptoms of anxiety, and with reports that peripherally active beta-adrenergic antagonists have some anxiolytic effects (Gorman et al. 1985). The rating changes showing similar absolute increases in anxiety for patients and controls following isoproterenol infusion indicates that the bulimic patients do not characteristically show overt "hyperdynamic" behavioral responses to isoproterenol infusion previously reported in some patients with anxiety disorder (Easton and Sherman 1976). The bulimic patients did, however, reach significantly higher anxiety ratings at the end of the infusion than did the controls. It seems possible that outside of the hospital setting, such high anxiety levels could reach a threshold for severe intrapsychic distress (Margraf et al. 1986), which in turn could precipitate bulimic episodes. In a previous study, we showed that bulimic patients, in comparison to controls, had a trend toward increased vulnerability to anxiety (although without overt panic attacks) following sodium lactate infusion (George et al. in press; also see results of Roose et al. in Chapter 11). Catecholamine activation could play a role in situational anxiety experienced by bulimic patients if, in addition to increased sensitivity of adrenoreceptors, bulimic patients experienced increased sensitivity to stress-induced presynaptic release of norepinephrine. It is also important to note that while much of the preceding discussion addresses the possible role of alterations in peripheral catecholamine activity in the symptoms of anxiety experienced by bulimic patients, anxiety symptoms could also result from similar changes in presynaptic and postsynaptic norepinephrine activity in some brain regions (for example, as reflected in decreased cerebrospinal fluid norepinephrine in these patients [Kaye et al. 1986a]).

One challenge that does cause substantial increases in circulating norepinephrine in bulimic patients is bingeing and purging (Kaye et al. 1986a). It is not yet clear whether this reflects an increased sensitivity to presynaptic sympathetic activation in bulimic patients or a normal physiological response to ingestion of a large amount of food (Welle et al. 1981). Clinically, this observation raises the question whether these episodes of elevated plasma norepinephrine would be sufficient to down-regulate peripheral adrenoreceptors (Fraser et al. 1981), which might theoretically contribute to the decrease in anxiety ratings observed following binge/purge episodes (Kaye et al. 1986c). (Recent evidence is variable, however, regarding the extent and time course of down-regulation of beta-adrenoreceptors following physiological activation of the sympathetic nervous system in man [Brodde et al. 1984; deBlasi et al. 1986]). This possible cycle is illustrated in Figure 15. Moreover, since the therapeutic effects of tricyclic antidepressants in bulimic patients do not necessarily parallel antidepressant effects (Brotman et al. 1984; Walsh et al. 1984; Pope et al. 1983), it is possible that the medication-related decrease in bingeing in bulimic patients is parallel to the anxiolytic effects of antidepressants in anxiety disorder patients, an effect that has been linked to decreased noradrenergic activity (Charney and Heninger 1985).

Recent studies suggest that bulimic patients in a normal weight range have increased metabolic efficiency in the utilization of ingested calories. Thus, bulimic patients were found to require lower daily caloric intake than controls to maintain a stable body weight (Kaye et al. 1986b), and appear to have decreased resting metabolic rate as assessed by indirect calorimetry (Obarzanek et al. 1986). Since the sympathetic nervous system plays an important role in the regulation of metabolic rate, isoproterenol-induced release of free fatty acids may provide an index of sensitivity to catecholamine-mediated lipolysis. Similar increases of free fatty acids in patients and controls suggest that in contrast to adrenoreceptor sensitivity in the cardiovascular system, beta-adrenoceptors mediating lipolysis did not show increased sensitivity in the patient group. While preliminary, these

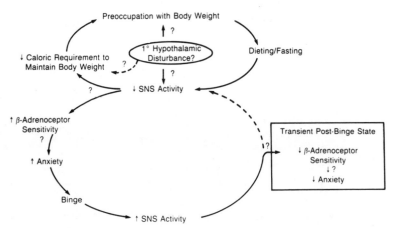

Fig. 15. Hypothetical cycle implicating altered norepinephrine function in bulimia. ? = highly speculative links. A number of other steps are supported only by very preliminary evidence. SNS = sympathetic nervous system.

results indicate that decreased presynaptic activity of the sympathetic nervous system, possibly in conjunction with decreased thyroid activity (Pirke et al. 1985; see also Chapters 4 and 8), may contribute to decreased metabolic rate in bulimic patients. Increased efficiency in the utilization of dietary calories may prompt further restriction in caloric intake, resulting in additional decreases in sympathetic nervous system activity.

SUMMARY

Recent studies have demonstrated dysregulation of norepinephrine activity in bulimic patients during a period of abstinence from bingeing and vomiting. Further studies are needed to clarify whether these alterations predate the onset of symptomatology and are reflective of neurobiologic risk factors for development of bulimia. Conversely, if noradrenergic changes occur as a consequence of the onset of the syndrome, they may contribute to the self-perpetuating character of the symptoms. Changes in sympathetic nervous system activity may contribute to increased symptoms of anxiety prior to binge episodes and to decreases in anxiety following binges. Clinical studies with selective pharmacologic probes are needed to clarify the extent to which noradrenergic effects of antidepressant treatments contribute to the efficacy of these medications in some bulimic patients.

REFERENCES

Biederman J, Herzog DB, Rivinus TM, et al: Urinary MHPG in anorexia nervosa patients with and without a concomitant major depressive disorder. J Psychiatr Res 18:149-160, 1984

Brotman AW, Herzog DB, Woods SW: Antidepressant treatment of bulimia: the relationship between bingeing and depressive symptomatology. J Clin Psychiatry 45:7-9, 1984

Brodde O-E, Daul A, O'Hara N: β-adrenoceptor changes in human lymphocytes, induced by dynamic exercise. Naunyn-Schmiedeberg's Arch Pharmacol 325:190-192, 1984

Buckholtz N, George DT, Davies AO, et al: Lymphocyte beta-adrenergic receptor modification in bulimia. Submitted for publication, 1987

Charney DS, Heninger GR: Noradrenergic function and the mechanism of action of antianxiety treatment: II. The effect of long-term imipramine treatment. Arch Gen Psychiatry 42:473-481, 1985

Charney DS, Menkes DB, Heninger GR: Receptor sensitivity and the mechanism of action of antidepressant treatment: implications for the etiology and therapy of depression. Arch Gen Psychiatry 38:1160-1180, 1981

deBlasi A, Maisel AS, Feldman RD, et al: In vivo regulation of β-adrenergic receptors on human mononuclear leukocytes: assessment of receptor number, location, and function after posture change, exercise, and isoproterenol infusion. J Clin Endocrinol Metab 63:847-853, 1986

Easton DJ, Sherman DG: Somatic anxiety attacks and propranolol. Arch Neurol 33:689-691, 1976

Fraser J, Nadeau J, Robertson D, et al: Regulation of human leukocyte beta receptors by endogenous catecholamines: relationship of leukocyte beta receptor density to the cardiac sensitivity to isoproterenol. J Clin Invest 67:1777-1784, 1981

George DT, Kaye WH, Goldstein DS, et al: Comparison of cardiovascular and behavioral responses to isoproterenol in bulimic patients and healthy controls. In preparation

George DT, Brewerton TD, Jimerson DC: Comparison of lactate-induced anxiety in bulimic patients and healthy controls. Psychiatry Res, in press

Gorman JM, Liebowitz MR, Fyer AJ, et al: Treatment of social phobia with atenolol. J Clin Psychopharmacol 5:298-301, 1985

Gross HA, Lake CR, Ebert MH, et al: Catecholamine metabolism in primary anorexia nervosa. J Clin Endocrinol Metab 49:805-809, 1979

Halmi KA, Dekirmenjian H, Davis JM, et al: Catecholamine metabolism in anorexia nervosa. Arch Gen Psychiatry 35:458-460, 1978

Heufelder A, Warnhoff M, Pirke KM: Platelet alpha-2-adrenoceptor and adenylate cyclase in patients with anorexia nervosa and bulimia. J Clin Endocrinol Metab 61:1053-1060, 1985

Jimerson DC: Neurotransmitter hypotheses of depression: research update. Psychiatr Clin North Am 7:563-573, 1984

Kaye WH, Jimerson DC, Lake CR, et al: Altered norepinephrine metabolism following long-term weight recovery in patients with anorexia nervosa. Psychiatry Res 14:333-342, 1985

Kaye WH, Gwirtsman HE, Lake CR et al: Noradrenergic disturbances in normal weight bulimia [NR27]. Presented at the 139th Annual Meeting of the American Psychiatric Association. Washington, DC, 1986a

Kaye WH, Gwirtsman HE, Obarzanek E, et al: Disturbed metabolic efficiency in eating disorders [Symposium No. 106E]. Presented at the 139th Annual Meeting of the American Psychiatric Association. Washington, DC, 1986b

Kaye WH, Gwirtsman HE, George DT, et al: Relationship of mood alterations to bingeing behavior in bulimia. Br J Psychiatry 149:479-485 1986c

Landsberg L, Young JB: Fasting, feeding and regulation of the sympathetic nervous system. New Engl J Med 298:1295-1301, 1978

Landsberg L, Young JB: Insulin-mediated glucose metabolism in the relationship between dietary intake and sympathetic nervous system activity. Int J Obes 9 [Suppl 2]:63-68, 1985

Lesem MD, George DT, Kaye WH, et al: Decrease in plasma norepinephrine following nutritional stabilization in underweight patients with anorexia nervosa. Submitted for publication, 1987

Luck P, Mikhailidis DP, Dashwood MR, et al: Platelet hyperaggregability and increased alpha-adrenoceptor density in anorexia nervosa. J Clin Endocrinol Metab 57:911-914, 1983

Margraf J, Ehlers A, Roth WT: Sodium lactate infusion and panic attacks: a review and critique. Psychosom Med 48:23-51, 1986

O'Dea K, Esler M, Leonard P, et al: Noradrenaline turnover during under- and over-eating in normal weight subjects. Metabolism 31:896-899, 1982

Obarzanek E, Lesem M, Jimerson DC: Resting metabolic rate in bulimic patients [NR 204]. Presented at the 140th Annual Meeting of the American Psychiatric Association, Chicago, 1987.

Pahl J, Pirke KM, Schweiger U, et al: Anorectic behavior, mood, and metabolic and endocrine adaptation to starvation in anorexia nervosa during inpatient treatment. Biol Psychiatry 20:874-887, 1985

Pirke KM, Pahl J, Schweiger U, et al: Metabolic and endocrine indices of starvation in bulimia: a comparison with anorexia nervosa. Psychiatry Res 15:33-39, 1985

Pope HG Jr, Hudson JI, Jonas JM, et al: Bulimia treated with imipramine: placebo-controlled double-blind study. Am J Psychiatry 140:554-558, 1983

Riederer P, Toifl K, Kruzik P: Excretion of biogenic amine metabolites in anorexia nervosa. Clin Chim Acta 123:27-32, 1982

Walsh BT, Stewart JW, Roose SP, et al: Treatment of bulimia with phenelzine: double-blind, placebo-controlled study. Arch Gen Psychiatry 41:1105-1109, 1984

Welle S, Lilavivat U, Campbell RG: Thermic effect of feeding in man: increased plasma norepinephrine levels following glucose but not protein or fat consumption. Metabolism 30:953-958, 1981

Chapter 10

Serotonin Regulation in Bulimia

Walter H. Kaye, M.D.
Harry E. Gwirtsman, M.D.
Timothy D. Brewerton, M.D.
David T. George, M.D.
David C. Jimerson, M.D.
Michael H. Ebert, M.D.

Chapter 10

Serotonin Regulation in Bulimia

B ulimia, an eating disorder that occurs most frequently in normal weight women, is often associated with alterations of mood and neuroendocrine function. Very little is known about the pathophysiology of the disturbances of appetite, mood, and neuroendocrine function found in bulimia. Converging lines of evidence from animal and human studies raise a question as to whether dysregulation of central nervous system serotoninergic activity might contribute to the pathophysiology of bulimia. Theoretically, serotoninergic dysregulation could play a part in the expression of disturbances of appetite, mood, and neuroendocrine function.

In this chapter, we will first review the evidence that serotonin pathways contribute to the modulation of appetite, mood, and hormonal secretion. We will then review the limited data suggesting that bulimic patients might have a disturbance of brain serotonin activity. Finally, we will discuss the possibility that bingeing and vomiting behavior, per se, might alter serotonin neurotransmission.

The possibility that bingeing and vomiting might contribute to changes in serotonin neurotransmission brings up an issue of great importance: If a serotoninergic disturbance is found to exist in bulimia, is it trait or state related? It is theoretically possible that disturbances of mood, neuroendocrine function, and appetite regulation could be due to an underlying disturbance of the neurotransmitter(s) in the brain known to regulate each of these systems. Alternatively, abnormalities in dietary intake could produce secondary disturbances in behavioral and physiological systems. In anorexia nervosa, it is well known that starvation contributes to psychological and neurobiological symptoms. Although bulimic patients do not suffer from great weight loss, it is quite possible that dietary influences (for example, overfeeding or intermittent starvation) also contribute to the pathophysiology of this illness (see Chapter 8).

Data suggesting serotonin abnormalities in bulimia are, for the most part, preliminary. Thus these data must be replicated and extended before such hypotheses are accepted. Second, serotonin is only one of a number of neurotransmitters known to contribute to the modulation of food, mood, and hormonal release. Thus, several other neurotransmitter systems (for example, norepinephrine or the opioids) could be similarly implicated (see Chapters 6, 7, and 9).

RELATIONSHIP BETWEEN SEROTONIN, BEHAVIOR, AND PHYSIOLOGY

Serotonin and Feeding Behavior

Our limited understanding about the pathophysiology of feeding behavior in bulimia stands in contrast to our considerable knowledge about the neurophysiology of feeding behavior in animals. A large number of neuropharmacological, neurochemical, and behavioral studies of feeding behavior in animals has clearly established that brain serotoninergic pathways modulate appetite. Treatments that increase intrasynaptic serotonin or directly activate serotonin receptors tend to reduce food consumption and are thought to decrease carbohydrate selection and spare protein intake (Wurtman and Wurtman 1979; Wurtman et al. 1985; Leibowitz and Shor-Posner 1986; Blundell 1984; Wurtman 1983; also see Chapter 14). Increased serotonin neurotransmission or activation of serotonin receptors produces a significant decrease in the size and duration of meals, as well as a reduced rate of eating. Conversely, interventions that diminish serotoninergic neurotransmissions or serotonin receptor activation reportedly increase food consumption and promote weight gain (Blundell 1984; Leibowitz and Shor-Posner 1986).

Bulimic behavior is theoretically consistent with hyposerotoninergic function. Bulimic patients appear to have increased hunger and/or decreased satiety. In addition, bulimic patients have an increase in the size and duration of meals, as well as an increased rate of eating (Kaye et al. 1986). While patients self-report frequently choosing snack or dessert foods during binges (Mitchell et al. 1981; Rosen et al. 1986) it is not clear whether they preferentially select carbohydrates or consume any sweet food, including foods with high fat content (see Chapter 8).

Serotonin and Mood Regulation

Hudson et al. (1983b) have proposed that bulimia is linked to affective disorders on the basis of findings of a high prevalence rate (49 to 73 percent) among bulimic patients of lifetime major affective disorder (Herzog 1984; Walsh et al. 1985; Lee et al. 1985). Other evidence in support of this contention lies in the therapeutic response to antidepressants of bulimic patients (Pope and Hudson 1986), shared neuroendocrine disturbances (Gwirtsman et al. 1983; see also Chapters 1 and 4), and findings of a family history of depression in bulimia (Hudson et al. 1983a).

It must be noted that other psychopathological disturbances aside from depression are common. Hudson et al. (1983b) reported a lifetime prevalence of 47 percent for anxiety disorder among bulimic patients. Bulimic patients also have been reported to exhibit social isolation, characterologic disturbances, alcohol/substance abuse, and impulse dyscontrol (Crisp et al. 1980; Herzog 1982; Johnson and Larson 1982; Strober et al. 1982; Gwirtsman et al. 1983; Weiss and Ebert 1983).

In general, however, many bulimic patients are dysphoric and impulsive, and it is possible that such disturbances could be due to serotonin disturbances. Low brain serotonin levels have been related to depression (Murphy et al. 1978; Coppen and Wood 1982) and aggressive dyscontrol in humans (Asberg et al. 1976; Brown et al. 1982) and rats (Valzelli et al. 1981).

On the other hand, alterations in mood could develop as a result of chronic bingeing and vomiting. Walsh et al. (1985) found that 75 percent of bulimic patients developed a major mood disturbance after the onset of bulimia, supporting the possibility that chronic bingeing and vomiting may cause, rather than be caused by, an affective disturbance. It is speculative at this point whether chronic bingeing and vomiting alters diet-induced synthesis of serotonin (see description below) and thus eventually effects other systems such as mood.

Serotonin and Neuroendocrine Function

A number of investigations suggest that bulimic patients have neuroendocrine disturbances including absent or irregular menstrual periods (see Chapters 2 and 3) and cortisol nonsuppression after dexamethasone administration (see Chapter 1). Several studies have reported abnormal thyroid function tests, and an abnormal thyroid-stimulating hormone response to thyrotropin-releasing hormone has also been found to a variable degree in bulimic patients (see Chapter 4). Mitchell and Bantle (1983) found three of six subjects had increased baseline prolactin levels, whereas Pirke et al. (Chapter 2) found normal prolactin levels in 15 bulimic patients. A total of six of nine bulimic patients have been reported to have an abnormal increase in growth hormone after administration of thyrotropin-releasing hormone (Mitchell and Bantle 1983; Gwirtsman et al. 1983). Mitchell and Bantle (1983) also reported that in three of six bulimic patients growth hormone was not suppressed after oral glucose administration.

The pathophysiology of neuroendocrine disturbances in bulimia remains unknown, but it is theoretically possible that a disturbance of hypothalamic serotoninergic function could be contributory. Animal studies have suggested the involvement of serotoninergic pathways in the central regulation of the secretion of cortisol, gonadotropins, prolactin, and perhaps thyroid hormones (for a review, see Smythe 1977). As with disturbances of mood, it is not known whether neuroendocrine disturbances reflect a trait-related disturbance of neurotransmitters that regulate hormonal secretion or they are state related. If hormonal disturbances are state related, it is not known whether chronic bingeing and vomiting or some other factor is responsible for the hormonal dysregulation.

THE EVIDENCE FOR A DISTURBANCE OF SEROTONIN IN BULIMIA

Antidepressant Studies

Pope et al. (1983) first reported that tricyclic antidepressants were efficacious in the treatment of bulimia. Subsequently, a number of double-blind placebo-controlled trials have been conducted on several different antidepressants in bulimia (Sabine et al. 1983; Hsu 1984; Mitchell and Groat 1984; Walsh et al. 1984; Hughes et al. 1986). Some, but not all, antidepressant trials have been reported to be therapeutically useful. These data are reviewed by Pope and Hudson (1986).

It is not certain whether antidepressant medications are effective in normal weight bulimia because of a selective antibulimic action or merely because of a nonspecific antidepressant effect. In two recent studies antidepressants were found to decrease bingeing behavior in nondepressed bulimic patients (Walsh et al. 1984; Hughes et al. 1986). It is possible that antidepressants, by means of their actions on brain serotoninergic systems, may work in bulimia to enhance satiety and thereby suppress the desire to binge and purge.

Physiological Indices of Serotonin Activity in Bulimia

Cerebrospinal Fluid Studies.   One method of assessing central nervous system serotonin activity in humans is to measure its major metabolite, 5-hydroxyindoleacetic acid (5-HIAA), in cerebrospinal fluid (CSF). To our knowledge, no such studies have been reported in normal weight bulimia. Cerebrospinal fluid 5-HIAA levels have been reported in anorexia nervosa, however. We will briefly review the 5-HIAA data in anorexia nervosa for two reasons. First, it appears that very malnourished anorectic patients have reduced levels of CSF

5-HIAA that normalize after weight recovery. This suggests that the state of nutrition does have an influence on brain serotonin activity. Second, we have reported that after weight recovery nonbulimic anorectic patients have higher concentrations of CSF 5-HIAA (after administration of probenecid) than do bulimic anorectic individuals. These data are consistent with a relationship between bingeing behavior and reduced brain serotonin function.

Cerebrospinal Fluid 5-HIAA in Underweight Anorectic Patients. Concentrations of CSF 5-HIAA in underweight anorectic patients have been compared with those of controls in several studies. We found (Kaye et al. 1984a) that CSF 5-HIAA concentrations were significantly lower in eight underweight anorectic patients compared with the same patients after weight restoration (see Figure 16) and that CSF 5-HIAA levels for the underweight patients, as well as the same patients after weight correction, were similar to those of healthy control women. Gillberg (1983) reported that two underweight anorectic patients had CSF 5-HIAA levels that were below the range of age-matched controls. In contrast, Gerner et al. (1984) found that underweight anorectic patients had normal basal CSF 5-HIAA levels.

Since our earlier study with eight patients, we have measured CSF 5-HIAA in another 14 anorectic patients. In total we have found that the 22 underweight anorectic patients had CSF 5-HIAA levels of 10.6 ± 5.8 ng/ml, significantly less ($t = 3.06, p < .01$, Student's t-test, two-tailed) than those of all the control women (16.5 ± 6.1 ng/ml, $n = 17$). Underweight anorectic patients had a significant increase in CSF 5-HIAA ($t = 4.30, p < .001$) when restudied after short-term weight restoration (14.2 ± 7.2 ng/ml, $n = 18$). Short-term weight-restored anorectic patients had levels that were similar to those of control subjects.

The difference between our data and that of Gerner et al. may be due to several factors. First Gerner's underweight subjects were at a substantially higher mean body weight. Second, our patients were studied before weight gain commenced, whereas Gerner et al.'s subjects were studied after some degree of refeeding and weight gain. Thus it is likely that underweight, malnourished anorectic patients have reduced CSF 5-HIAA levels. It should be noted (given the data cited below) that bulimic and nonbulimic anorectic patients do not appear to have differences in *basal* CSF 5-HIAA levels.

Cerebrospinal Fluid 5-HIAA in Bulimic vs Nonbulimic Anorectic Patients. Patients with anorexia nervosa can be subdivided on the basis of appetite-related behavior into two groups: those who fast and those who binge (Beaumont et al. 1976; Russell 1979; Garfinkel et al. 1980; Casper et al. 1980). We reasoned that differences in appetitive behavior could be due to differences in the activity of neurotransmitters, such as serotonin, that contribute to the modulation of feeding behavior. To test this hypothesis, we measured CSF 5-HIAA in 16 anorexic patients who were separated by style of appetite-related behavior into two groups (Kaye et al. 1984b). Five patients had lost weight by restricting caloric intake (nonbulimic anorectic patients) and never binged. Eleven patients engaged in binge eating (bulimic anorectic patients), and these patients all vomited and/or used laxatives afterward. The range of binge eating was from a few times a month to more than once daily.

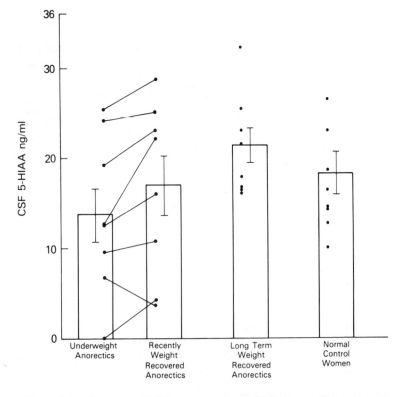

Figure 16. Mean (± SEM) concentrations of 5-hydroxyindoleacetic acid (5-HIAA) in cerebrospinal fluid (CSF) for each group of anorectic patients and normal controls.

Several points about this study should be emphasized. First, we found a difference in CSF 5-HIAA only in anorectic patients studied after weight restoration. Eight were short-term weight restored (studied three to four weeks after correction of weight loss), and eight were long-term weight restored (weight recovered for a mean of 20 months). Second, this difference was found only after the intravenous administration of probenecid. Probenecid is a compound that blocks 5-HIAA from leaving the CSF compartment and entering the peripheral circulation. Probenecid administration is thought to produce an accumulation of 5-HIAA in CSF that may reflect serotonin turnover. Some controversy exists as to the usefulness of probenecid-induced accumulations of 5-HIAA (Faull et al. 1981; Cowdry et al. 1983). This controversy is that the amount of probenecid that can be given to humans does not result in a complete block of 5-HIAA and that the means of adjusting for CSF probenecid levels are not certain.

We found that nonbulimic anorectic patients had higher levels of the accumulation of CSF 5-HIAA (the post-probenecid CSF 5-HIAA level minus the pre-probenecid CSF 5-HIAA level) than did bulimic anorectic patients. Interestingly, bulimic anorectic patients had less of an accumulation of CSF 5-HIAA than did control subjects (see Figure 17). When CSF 5-HIAA accumulation was corrected for CSF probenecid concentration (in this case by dividing the 5-HIAA accumulation by the CSF probenecid level), we found that nonbulimic anorectic patients continued to have higher levels of 5-HIAA than did bulimic anorectic patients. However, after this adjustment, 5-HIAA levels were similar between bulimic patients and control subjects.

These data suggest that after weight recovery, nonbulimic anorectic patients have increased brain serotonin metabolism compared with that of bulimic anorectic patients. This difference in serotonin metabolism is apparent only after Probenecid administration. It is not certain, however, whether weight-recovered bulimic anorectic patients and control subjects have differences in brain serotoninergic activity.

Probes of Serotonin Activity.   Other tools have been developed to aid in the clinical assessment of central nervous system serotoninergic activity in humans, for example, the administration of a pharmacological agent that increases brain serotonin neurotransmission or acts on a serotonin receptor. Such probes produce changes in behavior or hormonal secretion that are thought to reflect brain serotoninergic functional activity.

Brewerton, Jimerson, and co-workers at the National Institute of

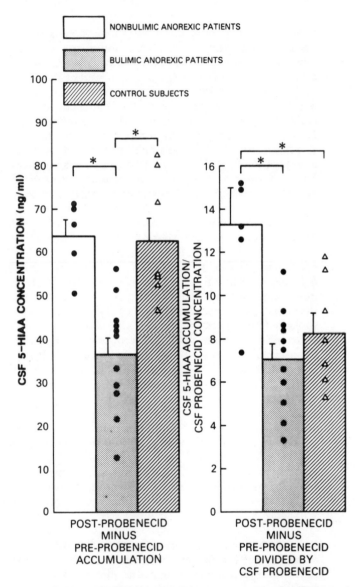

Figure 17. Comparison of post-probenecid accumulations of cerebrospinal fluid (CSF) 5-hydroxyindoleacetic acid (5-HIAA) in nonbulimic and bulimic anorectic patients and controls. *Significant ($p < .05$) difference between groups by one-way analysis of variance and Scheffé post-hoc test.

Mental Health are currently using several such tools to study normal weight bulimic patients. One probe uses intravenous infusion of the serotonin precursor L-tryptophan (100 mg/kg), which is thought to increase serotonin neurotransmission. Another probe uses the oral administration of the serotonin postsynaptic receptor agonist m-chlorophenylpiperazine (m-CPP) (0.5 mg/kg p.o.) to bulimic patients. Both studies have demonstrated a blunted prolactin response in bulimic patients compared with healthy volunteers (Brewerton et al. 1986a, 1986b). These data support the possibility that bulimic patients have hyposerotoninergic activity.

Brewerton et al. (1986c) have also reported an increase of migraine headaches in bulimic patients after the administration of m-CPP. They reported that 10 of 16 normal weight bulimic patients and 5 of 7 bulimic anorectic patients had severe migraine-like headaches. These headaches typically commenced 6 to 8 hours after drug administration and peaked from 10 to 12 hours postchallenge. This was in marked contrast to the absence of migraine-like headaches in 21 control subjects. It was notable that 10 of the 15 patients who developed m-CPP induced migrainous headache had a family history of migraine, which was not found in other patients or controls. These results are of particular interest because of the serotonin alterations that have been reported in migraine patients (Eadie and Tyrer 1985). These data also suggest that bulimics may have a vulnerability to serotoninergic dysfunction that is genetically transmitted.

Does Bingeing Increase Brain Serotonin?

Not only do serotonin pathways modulate appetite, but the converse also appears to be true. Food consumption, depending on the proportion of carbohydrate and protein in the food eaten, can enhance brain serotonin release (Fernstrom and Wurtman 1971, 1972), thereby affecting appetite regulation. In brief, carbohydrate consumption causes an insulin-mediated fall in plasma levels of the large neutral amino acids (LNAA; tyrosine, phenylalanine, valine, leucine, isoleucine), which compete with tryptophan for uptake into the brain. This elevates the plasma tryptophan/LNAA (TRP/LNAA ratio) ratio and thus brain tryptophan, which rapidly accelerates brain serotonin synthesis and release. Dietary proteins tend to block these effects by contributing large amounts of the LNAA to the blood stream.

No experimental methods are available for the direct assessment of brain serotonin release in bulimic subjects. However, one factor affecting serotonin release, the availability of tryptophan, can be assessed indirectly by measuring the plasma TRP/LNAA ratio and determining its response, if any, to bingeing and vomiting behavior.

We (Kaye et al. in press) have measured this ratio in bulimic subjects when they were allowed to binge and vomit. In addition, we measured plasma prolactin as a possible indication of central serotoninergic neurotransmission (MacIndoe and Turkington 1973).

We found that there were two distinct patterns of plasma TRP/LNAA response during bingeing and vomiting and that these corresponded to two distinct patterns of satiety (see Figure 18). The bulimic patients (subjects 1 to 6) who voluntarily self-terminated bingeing and vomiting after one to three cycles exhibited early increases in their plasma TRP/LNAA ratios compared with their baseline plasma TRP/LNAA ratios. In contrast, those bulimic patients (subjects 7 to 9) who binged and vomited four times, and who stopped bingeing and vomiting only after we requested that they do so, did not exhibit increases in their plasma TRP/LNAA ratios over baseline plasma TRP/LNAA value. These patients reported at the end of the fourth vomit that they continued to feel unsatisfied; subjects 8 and 9 volunteered that they would have continued to binge and vomit had they been allowed.

Whether the difference in satiety between the two groups of patients is due to tryptophan-induced synthesis of serotonin cannot be clearly established since there is no method for directly determining whether increased plasma TRP/LNAA actually did increase brain serotoninergic turnover in our subjects. The fact that the patients with increased plasma TRP/LNAA ratios all exhibited greater increases in plasma prolactin tends to support the hypothesis that serotoninergic neurotransmission had been enhanced in this group of bulimic patients.

Several factors are known to contribute to the plasma TRP/LNAA ratio. Insulin facilitates the uptake of LNAA, thus lowering LNAA plasma levels but not those of tryptophan, thereby increasing the plasma TRP/LNAA ratio (Martin-Du Pan et al. 1982). Protein consumption tends to decrease the TRP/LNAA ratio, since TRP is scarce in proteins while abundant in other LNAA (Fernstrom et al. 1979). It remains uncertain whether these differences are related to protein consumption or insulin secretion.

In conclusion, these results suggest that satiety and termination of bulimic episodes may be associated with an increase in brain serotonin levels and that those subjects who fail to get such a rise in brain serotonin do not become satiated. Whether bulimic patients binge and vomit in order to raise brain serotonin levels because they have an underlying serotoninergic dysfunction is a question that is raised but cannot be answered by these data. It is possible that such

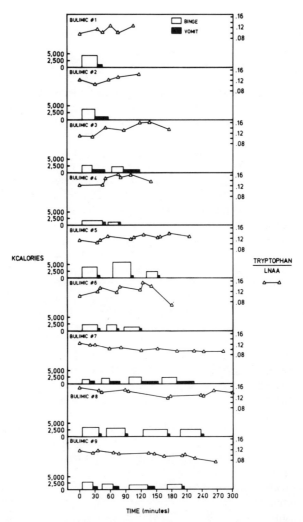

Figure 18. Plasma tryptophan (TRP)/large neutral amino acid (LNAA) levels (triangles connected by lines) during cycles of bingeing and vomiting in nine bulimic subjects. The right-hand *y* axis indicates the plasma TRP/LNAA ratio. The left-hand *y* axis indicates caloric consumption during bingeing. Time spent in bingeing and vomiting is shown on the *x* axis. The duration and caloric content of the binge are indicated by the open rectangle. The duration of vomiting is shown by the solid rectangle.

a trait-related deficit in serotoninergic function exists in bulimia and that it contributes to an increased appetite or a resistance to achieve satiety by normal food intake.

SUMMARY

The data suggesting that bulimic individuals have a disturbance of brain serotonin are intriguing, but very preliminary in nature. Much work needs to be done before this hypothesis is proven. Still, such hypotheses offer a possible explanation for neurobiological disturbances in bulimia that can be clinically tested.

One working hypothesis to be tested is that behavioral and physiological disturbances in bulimia could be related to both a primary central neurotransmitter dysfunction and feeding-related alterations in neurotransmitter activity. For example, the disturbance of appetite regulation (bingeing due to diminished satiety) seen in bulimia could be a consequence of hyposerotoninergic activity. Dietary intake, through an increase in serotonin neurotransmission, appears to send the brain information about the amount of food ingested. Bingeing may exaggerate diet-induced serotonin synthesis as a means of overcompensating for hyposerotoninergic function. In this scenario, mood and neuroendocrine disturbances could either be due to the primary disturbance of serotonin or be secondary to binge-induced effects.

We are only now beginning to develop the tools by which to study the neurobiological implications of anorexia nervosa and bulimia. Although evidence along these lines is still preliminary, it has raised many provocative questions and has indicated directions for further research. Neurobiological research by no means minimizes the significance of psychosocial factors related to eating disorders. Rather, it seeks to broaden our total understanding of these disorders in both their psychological and physiological dimensions.

REFERENCES

Asberg M, Traskman L, Thoren P: Is 5-HIAA in the cerebrospinal fluid a biochemical suicide predictor? Arch Gen Psychiatry 33:1193, 1976

Beaumont PVJ, George GCW, Smart DE: 'Dieters' and 'vomiters and purgers' in anorexia nervosa. Psychol Med 6:617-622, 1976

Blundell JE: Serotonin and appetite. Neuropharmacology 23:1537-1551, 1984

Brewerton TD, George DT, Jimerson DC: Neuroendocrine response to L-tryptophan in bulimia. Presented at the annual meeting of the American Psychiatric Association, Washington, DC, May 1986a

Brewerton TD, Mueller E, George T, et al: Blunted prolactin response to the serotonin agonist m-chlorophenylpiperazine (m-CPP) in bulimia. Presented at the Collegium Internationale Neuro-Psychopharmacologicum, Puerto Rico, December 1986b

Brewerton TD, Mueller EA, George DT, et al: Serotonin, bulimia, and migraine: results with m-CPP [NR22]. Presented at the annual meeting of the American Psychiatric Association, Washington, DC, May 1986c

Brown GL, Ebert MH, Goyer PF, et al: Aggression, suicide, and serotonin: relationships to CSF amine metabolites. Am J Psychiatry 139:741-746, 1982

Casper RC, Eckert ED, Halmi KA, et al: Bulimia: its incidence and clinical importance in patients with anorexia nervosa. Arch Gen Psychiatry 37:1030-1035, 1980

Coppen A, Wood K: 5-Hydroxytryptamine in the pathogenesis of affective disorders, in Serotonin in Biological Psychiatry. Edited by Ho BT, Schoolar JC, Usdin E. New York, Raven Press, 1982

Cowdry RW, Ebert MH, van Kammen DP, et al: Cerebrospinal fluid probenecid studies: a reinterpretation. Biol Psychiatry 18:1287-1299, 1983

Crisp AH, Hsu LKG, Harding B: The starving hoarder and voracious spender—stealing in anorexia nervosa. J Psychosom Res 24:225-231, 1980

Eadie MJ, Tyrer JH (eds): Biochemical changes which appear part of the migraine mechanism, in The Biochemistry of Migraine. Lancaster, MTP Press, 1985

Faull KF, Kraemer HC, Barchas DJ, et al: Clinical application of the probenecid test for the measurement of monoamine turnover in the CNS. Biol Psychiatry 16:879-899, 1981

Fernstrom JD, Wurtman RJ: Brain serotonin content: increase following ingestion of carbohydrate diet. Science 174:1023-1025, 1971

Fernstrom JD, Wurtman RJ: Brain serotonin content: physiological regulation by plasma neutral amino acids. Science 178:414-416, 1972

Fernstrom JD, Wurtman RJ, Hammarstrom-Wiklund B, et al: Dirunal variations in plasma concentrations of tryptophan, tyrosine, and other neutral amino acids: effect of dietary protein intake. Am J Clin Nutr 32:1912-1922, 1979

Garfinkel PE, Moldofsky, Garner DM: The heterogeneity of anorexia nervosa. Arch Gen Psychiatry 37:1036-1040, 1980

Gerner RH, Cohen DJ, Fairbanks L, et al: CSF neurochemistry of women with anorexia nervosa and normal women. Am J Psychiatry 141:1441-1444, 1984

Gillberg C: Low dopamine and serotonin levels in anorexia nervosa (letter). Am J Psychiatry 140:948-949, 1983

Gwirtsman HE, Roy-Byrne P, Yager J, et al: Neuroendocrine abnormalities in bulimia. Am J Psychiatry 140:559-563, 1983

Herzog DB: Bulimia: the secretive syndrome. Psychosom 23:481-487, 1982

Herzog DB: Are anorexic and bulimic patients depressed? Am J Psychiatry 141:1594-1597, 1984

Hsu LKG: Treatment of bulimia with lithium. Am J Psychiatry 141:1260-1262, 1984

Hudson JI, Pope HG Jr, Jonas JM, et al: Family history study of anorexia nervosa and bulimia. Br J Psychiatry 142:133-139, 1983a

Hudson JI, Pope HG Jr, Jonas JM, et al: Phenomenologic relationship of eating disorders to major affective disorder. Psychiatry Res 9:345-354, 1983b

Hughes PL, Wells LA, Cunningham CJ, et al: Treating bulimia with desipramine: a double-blind, placebo-controlled study. Arch Gen Psychiatry 43:182-186, 1986

Johnson C, Larson R: Bulimia: an analysis of moods and behavior. Psychol Med 44:341-351, 1982

Kaye WH, Ebert MH, Raleigh M: Abnormalities in CNS monoamine metabolism in anorexia nervosa. Arch Gen Psychiatry 41:350-355, 1984a

Kaye WH, Ebert MH, Gwirtsman HE, et al: Differences in brain serotonergic metabolism between nonbulimic and bulimic patients with anorexia nervosa. Am J Psychiatry 141:1598-1601, 1984b

Kaye WH, Gwirtsman HE, George DT, et al: Relationship of mood alterations to bingeing behaviour in bulimia. Br J Psychiatry, 149:479-485, 1986

Kaye WH, Gwirtsman HE, Brewerton TD, et al: Bingeing behavior and plasma amino acids: a possible involvement of brain serotonin in bulimia. Psychiatry Res, in press

Lee FL, Rush AJ, Mitchell JE: Bulimia and depression. J Affective Disord 9:231-238, 1985

Leibowitz SF, Shor-Posner G: Brain serotonin and eating behavior. Appetite 7:1-13, 1986

MacIndoe JH, Turkington RW: Stimulation of human prolactin secretion by intravenous infusion of l-tryptophan. J Clin Invest 52:1972-1978, 1973

Martin-Du Pan R, Mauron C, Glaeser B, et al: Effect of various oral glucose doses on plasma neutral amino acid levels. Metabolism 31:937-942, 1982

Mitchell JE, Bantle JP: Metabolic and endocrine investigations in women of normal weight with bulimia syndrome. Biol Psychiatry 18:355-365, 1983

Mitchell JE, Groat R: A placebo-controlled double-blind trial of amitriptyline in bulimia. J Clin Psychopharmacol 4:186-193, 1984

Mitchell JE, Pyle RL, Eckert ED: Frequency and duration of binge-eating episodes in patients with bulimia. Am J Psychiatry 138:835-836, 1981

Murphy DL, Campell I, Costa JL: Current status of the indoleamine hypothesis of affective disorders, in Psychopharmacology: A Generation of Progress. Edited by Lipton MA, DiMascio A, Killam KF. New York, Raven Press, 1978

Pope HG Jr, Hudson JI: Antidepressant drug therapy for bulimia: current status. J Clin Psychiatry 47:339-345, 1986

Pope HG Jr, Hudson JI, Jonas JM, et al: Bulimia treated with imipramine: a placebo-controlled double-blind study. Am J Psychiatry 140:554-558, 1983

Rosen JC, Leitenberg J, Fisher C, et al: Binge-eating episodes in bulimia nervosa: the amount and type of food consumed. International Journal of Eating Disorders 5:255-267, 1986

Russell G: Bulimia nervosa: an ominous variant of anorexia nervosa. Psychol Med 9:429-448, 1979

Sabine EJ, Yonace A, Farrington AJ: Bulimia nervosa: A placebo-controlled double-blind therapeutic trial of mianserin. Br J Clin Pharmacol 15:195S-202S, 1983

Smythe GA: The role of serotonin and dopamine in hypothalamic–pituitary function. Clin Endocrinol 7:325-341, 1977

Strober M, Salkin B, Burroughs J, et al: Validity of the bulimia-restrictor distinction in anorexia nervosa: parental personality characteristics and family psychiatric morbidity. J Nerv Ment Dis 170:345-351, 1982

Valzelli L. Bernasconi S, Dalessandro M: Effect of tryptophan administration on spontaneous and p-PCA-reduced muricidal aggression in laboratory rats. Pharmacol Res Commun 9:891-897, 1981

Walsh BT, Stewart JW, Roose SP, et al: Treatment of bulimia with phenelzine: a double-blind, placebo-controlled study. Arch Gen Psychiatry 41:1105-1109, 1984

Walsh BT, Roose SP, Glassman AH, et al: Bulimia and depression. Psychosom Med 47:123-131, 1985

Weiss SR, Ebert MH: Psychological and behavior characteristics of normal-weight bulimics and normal-weight controls. Psychol Med 45:293-303, 1983

Wurtman JJ, Wurtman RJ: Drugs that enhance central serotoninergic transmission diminish elective carbohydrate consumption by rats. Life Sci 24:895-903, 1979

Wurtman JJ, Wurtman RJ, Mark S, et al: d-Fenfluramine selectively suppresses carbohydrate snacking by obese subjects. International Journal of Eating Disorders 4:89-99, 1985

Wurtman RJ: Behavioral effects of nutrients. Lancet 1:1145-1147, 1983

Chapter 11

Biological Probes of Anxiety in Bulimia

Steven P. Roose, M.D.
B. Timothy Walsh, M.D.
David C. Lindy, M.D.
Madeline Gladis, M.A.
Alexander H. Glassman, M.D.

Chapter 11

Biological Probes of Anxiety in Bulimia

In this chapter we shall present data on the response of normal weight bulimic patients and controls to lactate infusion and the oral administration of yohimbine. The idea for this study arose from clinical observations of bulimic patients. Originally, we were very impressed with the data drawing an association between bulimia and affective disorder. Many authors, using a variety of rating scales, have noted a high frequency of depressed mood among bulimic patients (Abraham and Beumont 1982; Fairburn and Cooper 1984; Johnson and Larson 1982; Weiss and Ebert 1983). In addition to the symptom of depression, several investigators have used structured interviews to determine how many patients with bulimia meet criteria for distinct affective syndromes (Herzog 1984; Hudson et al. 1983b; Piran et al. 1985; Walsh et al. 1985b). In these studies, the frequency of current major depression ranged from 20 to 70 percent and lifetime frequency for major depression appeared to be more than 50 percent. However, the depressive syndrome that occurred in bulimic patients was predominately of the nonendogenous type and was characterized by a reactive mood and a significant degree of anxiety (Walsh et al. 1985b).

The diagnosing of major depression in bulimic patients has naturally prompted investigators to see if first-degree relatives of bulimics have a higher rate of affective disorder than do relatives of control subjects. To date, two controlled studies have focused on this subject, and their findings have been essentially contradictory (Hudson et al. 1983a; Stern et al. 1984). Thus, though there is the suggestion of a higher than expected frequency of affective disorder in the families of patients with bulimia, this issue is far from settled.

Biological measures, though originally suggestive, have recently been more equivocal in suggesting an association between bulimia and affective disorder. Several studies of normal weight bulimic patients have shown a higher than expected frequency of nonsuppression to the dexamethasone suppression test (DST) (Gwirtsman et al. 1983; Hudson et al. 1983c; Lindy et al. 1985; see also Chapter 1), although an abnormal DST can, at this point, hardly be considered a specific diagnostic test. In recent studies on electroencephalographic sleep measures in patients with bulimia, three investigators did not find abnormalities in bulimic individuals similar to those in patients with major affective disorder (Levy et al. 1987; Walsh et al. 1985a; Hudson et al. 1987; also see Chapter 12).

Perhaps the most persuasive evidence in the case for a link between bulimia and affective disorder has been the striking response of bulimic patients to antidepressant medication. It has been well established in double-blind, placebo-controlled studies that bulimic patients have a marked reduction in their binge frequency when treated with tricyclic antidepressants, imipramine or desipramine (Hughes et al. 1986; Pope et al. 1983) or monoamine oxidase inhibitors (Kennedy et al. 1986; Walsh et al. 1984). With this response to antidepressant medication as the cornerstone, and the data cited in previous paragraphs stacked atop, a case has been made that bulimia is, at a minimum, strongly associated with affective disorder and perhaps a form of depression.

However, we have also been impressed with the prevalence of anxiety in our bulimic patients and particularly with the cycle that a number of bulimic patients would describe in which increasing anxiety was relieved by a binge only to be followed by purging and a dysphoric mood. Furthermore, in the studies cited above in which both current symptomatology of bulimic patients and whether they met criteria for specific affective disorders were examined, there was a persistent finding of marked symptoms of anxiety. In fact, two groups have found that about one-half of the patients with bulimia met the *Diagnostic and Statistical Manual of Mental Disorders (Third Edition) (DSM-III;* American Psychiatric Association 1980) criteria for panic disorder (Hudson et al. 1983a; Piran et al. 1985).

With respect to the bulimic patient's response to antidepressant medication, it has been demonstrated that the decrease in binge frequency is not dependent on the presence of a depressed mood at initiation of treatment (Walsh et al. 1984; Hughes et al. 1986). Furthermore, theoretically, it can be misleading to infer a diagnosis on the basis of a response to treatment. After all, the tricyclic antidepressants are also Type I antiarrhythmics, and obviously one would not equate ventricular arrhythmias to affective disorder simply on the basis that a single drug is efficacious in both conditions.

Thus, though cognizant of the data drawing an association between bulimic and affective disorder, we were equally impressed with the possible relationship between anxiety disorders and bulimia and were interested in pursuing this connection. One approach would be to see if the biological characteristics of patients with an anxiety disorder can be observed in normal weight bulimics. Perhaps the most consistently demonstrated characteristic is that patients with panic disorder have a greater responsivity to lactate infusion and oral administration of yohimbine than do normal controls: Approximately 50 percent of patients with panic disorder have a panic attack induced by lactate infusion and/or yohimbine (Gorman et al. 1985; Charney et al. 1984). Thus, our hypothesis was that if bulimia were closely related to panic disorder, bulimic patients would also have a higher rate of panic attack than would normal subjects when given sodium lactate infusion or yohimbine. Furthermore, there may be other dimensions in which bulimic patients would be more sensitive to these biological probes than would normal controls; for example, even if bulimics do not have a panic attack induced by lactate or yohimbine, they may become increasingly anxious and, perhaps, have an increased desire to binge in response to these pharmacological probes.

METHODS

To be included in this study, subjects had to be female, meet *DSM-III* criteria for bulimia, have been bulimic for at least one year, be bingeing at least three times weekly, be of normal weight, and be between 18 and 40 years old. Subjects were excluded if they were on current psychoactive medications, had current alcohol or drug abuse, or had any significant medical illness. Control subjects were recruited from the Medical Center and University campus, and applicants were excluded if there was a history of eating disorder or any other psychiatric diagnosis apparent on clinical interview.

Subjects were tested on three separate days, receiving either lactate infusion first, followed by yohimbine/placebo test, or the reverse order. There was a minimum separation of three days between each test.

LACTATE INFUSION

We followed the protocol of Gorman et al. (1985): A needle was intravenously inserted, normal saline was infused for 30 minutes, followed by 10 ml/kg of 0.5 normal sodium lactate over 20 minutes, then 10 more minutes of normal saline. The Acute Panic Inventory, a standard rating measure for this type of study, was administered every 20 minutes. The infusion itself was videotaped and the decision on whether a subject panicked or not was made by a rater who was blind to diagnosis.

Demographic data of patients and controls are shown in Table 13. Four of 18 bulimic patients panicked during lactate infusion compared with 0 of 11 controls (see Table 14), a nonsignificant difference by Fisher's exact test. In a series of 37 patients with panic disorder, Gorman et al. (1985) reported that 51 percent had a panic attack during lactate infusion. Comparison of the rate of panic attack in bulimics versus that of patients with panic disorder showed that patients with panic disorder panicked during lactate infusion significantly more frequently than did bulimic patients ($p < .05$). Thus, the first part of our hypothesis was not borne out; bulimic patients do not panic at the same rate as panic attack patients during sodium lactate infusion, nor are they significantly different from normal controls.

In terms of other dimensions of sensitivity to lactate, the blind rater of the videotapes also scored the data for two other dimensions: emotional reactivity and somatic symptoms that are considered to

Table 13. Characteristics of Bulimic Patients and Controls

	Bulimic Subjects ($n = 18$)		Control Subjects ($n = 11$)	
	Mean	SD	Mean	SD
Age (years)	25.3 ±	5.2	25.8 ±	3.9
Height (inches)	63.9 ±	2.1	64.6 ±	2.5
Weight (lbs)	116.8 ±	15.3	130.1 ±	15.0
Years of illness	7.9 ±	4.6	—	
Binges per week	13.8 ±	8.1	—	

Table 14. Frequency of Blindly Rated Panic During Lactate Infusion

Panic	Bulimic Patients	Control Subjects	Panic Disorder Patients	Control Subjects
Yes	4 (22%)[a]	0	19 (51%)	1 (12%)[a]
No	14	11	18	7

[a] $p < .05$ versus panic disorder patients.

be other indicators of sensitivity to sodium lactate that can be quantified even if the subject does not have a panic attack during the infusion. Ten of the 18 bulimic patients were rated as experiencing moderate or severe emotional reactivity or somatic symptoms, whereas none of the 11 controls did ($p = .05$ by Fisher's exact test) (see Table 15). Thus, although the bulimic patients were not different than controls in their rate of panic on sodium lactate, they appeared to be more sensitive than normal controls to other effects of sodium lactate.

YOHIMBINE STUDIES

The yohimbine protocol was modeled after that used by Charney et al. at Yale (1984) so that we could compare our data in bulimic patients to their data in panic attack patients. After remaining NPO (taking nothing by mouth) after 10:00 P.M. the previous evening, patients came to the study unit; they had a catheter placed in the forearm that was kept open by a slow normal saline infusion and from which blood samples for cortisol, norepinephrine, 3-methoxy-4-hydroxyphenylethylene glycol (MHPG), and yohimbine levels were drawn every 30 minutes. In addition, the Acute Panic Inventory and blood pressure measurements were made every 30 minutes. After 60 minutes of baseline measurements, either 22 mg of yohimbine or placebo was given. The entire testing period lasted 5 hours with rating scale and biological measures performed every 30 minutes. Three days later the procedure was repeated.

In patients with panic disorder, there is a 50 percent rate of panic after yohimbine administration, and in addition, those patients who do not panic have significantly more anxiety induced by the drug than do normal controls (Charney et al. 1984). Therefore, we com-

Table 15. Blind Ratings of Emotional Reactivity and Somatic Symptoms During Lactate Infusion

Number of subjects with:	Bulimic patients ($n = 18$)	Controls ($n = 11$)
Panic	4	0
Emotional reactivity score >2	7[a]	0
Somatic symptom score >2	10[b]	2

[a]$p < .05$ versus control subjects.
[a]$p = .05$ versus control subjects.

pared 1) the rate of panic of bulimic patients versus that of controls when given yohimbine and 2) the effect of yohimbine on bulimic patients versus controls on other parameters such as anxiety and the desire to binge.

During this experiment, 3 of 14 bulimic patients panicked, 2 when given yohimbine and 1 when given placebo. One of 11 normal controls panicked when given yohimbine. Thus, when given yohimbine bulimic patients 1) did not panic at the same rate as panic disorder patients and 2) did not panic at a greater rate than normals. Furthermore, in all the other dimensions measured, for example, anxiety, blood pressure, restlessness, and depression, there was no significant difference between the bulimic patients and controls during yohimbine administration. Although it was not reflected in the rating scales, a number of bulimic patients, when they did become anxious, reported that it was the kind of feeling state that would often precede a binge. We are confused as to why this effect was not reflected by the scale scores, and at this point consider it an unproved albeit intriguing possible effect of the drug.

Yohimbine levels were measured every 30 minutes for both control and bulimic subjects. Despite the fact that the weight range of these groups was very narrow, and thus all subjects received essentially the same mg per kg dose of yohimbine, there was a striking interindividual difference in the maximum yohimbine plasma level achieved. Ninety minutes after drug administration, plasma levels ranged from 27 ng/ml to over 900 ng/ml. Thus, the great variability in plasma concentration of yohimbine warrants caution in the conclusions that one can draw from this study. After all, the intention is to compare the response of bulimic patients to normal controls when both groups are at comparable plasma concentrations of drug, and this is far from what happened. It serves as a reminder that when we use pharmacological agents as a research probe, we have to be mindful of the pharmacokinetic parameters involved.

CONCLUSION

In summary, bulimic patients did not panic with the same frequency as did panic disorder patients in response to sodium lactate infusion. However, bulimics did have a greater response to sodium lactate in the dimensions of emotional reactivity and somatic symptoms than did normal controls. With respect to yohimbine, bulimic subjects did not panic at the same rate as did panic disorder patients, nor were there responses that significantly distinguished the bulimic subjects from the controls.

Thus, the strategy of applying lactate infusion and yohimbine administration as a method of establishing a relationship between bulimia and anxiety disorders appears to be unrewarding. However, it is important to recall that baseline measures of anxiety on three separate days, that is, prior to lactate infusion and yohimbine/placebo administration, showed that the bulimic patients were consistently more anxious than the normal controls. Thus we continue to be impressed with the symptoms of anxiety in bulimic patients and are back at the drawing board developing new strategies to explore the relationship between anxiety and eating disorders.

REFERENCES

Abraham SF, Beumont PJV: How patients describe bulimia or binge eating. Psychol Med 12:625-635, 1982

Charney DS, Heninger GR, Breier A: Noradrenergic function in panic anxiety. Arch Gen Psychiatry 41:751-763, 1984

Fairburn CG. Cooper PJ: The clinical features of bulimia nervosa. Br J Psychiatry 144:238-246, 1984

Gorman JM, Dillon D, Fyer AJ, et al: The lactate infusion model. Psychopharmacol Bull 21:428-433, 1985

Gwirtsman HE, Roy-Byrne P, Yager J, et al: Neuroendocrine abnormalities in bulimia. Am J Psychiatry 140:559-563, 1983

Herzog DB: Are anorexic and bulimic patients depressed? Am J Psychiatry 141:1594-1597, 1984

Hudson JI, Pope HG Jr, Jonas JM, et al: Family history study of anorexia nervosa and bulimia. Br J Psychiatry, 142:133-138, 1983a

Hudson JI, Pope HG Jr, Jonas JM, et al: Phenomenologic relationship between eating disorders and major affective disorder. Psychiatry Res 9:345-354, 1983b

Hudson JI, Pope HG Jr, Jonas JM, et al: Hypothalamic–pituitary–adrenal axis hyperactivity in bulimia. Psychiatry Res 8:111-117, 1983c

Hudson JI, Pope HG Jr, Jonas JM, et al: Sleep EEG in bulimia. Biol Psychiatry, 22:820-828, 1987

Hughes PL, Wells LA, Cunningham CJ, et al: Treating bulimia with desipramine. Arch Gen Psychiatry 43:182-184, 1986

Johnson C, Larson R: Bulimia: an analysis of moods and behavior. Psychosom Med 44:341-351, 1982

Kennedy S, Piran N, Garfinkel PE: Isocarboxazid in treatment of bulimia. Am J Psychiatry 143: 1495-1496, 1986

Levy AB, Dixon KN, Schmidt HS: REM and delta sleep in anorexia nervosa and bulimia. Psychiatry Res 20:189-197, 1987

Disorder Lindy DC, Walsh BT, Roose SP, et al: The dexamethasone suppression test in bulimia. Am J Psychiatry 142:1375-1376, 1985

Piran N, Kennedy S, Garfinkel PE: Affective disturbance in eating disorders. J Nerv Ment Dis 173:359-400, 1985

Pope HG Jr, Hudson JI, Jonas JM, et al: Bulimia treated with imipramine: a placebo-controlled, double-blind study. Am J Psychiatry 140:554-558, 1983

Stern SL, Dixon KN, Nemzer E, et al: Affective disorder in the families of women with normal weight bulimia. Am J Psychiatry 141:1224-1227, 1984

Walsh BT, Stewart JW, Roose SP, et al: Treatment of bulimia with phenelzine. A double-blind placebo-controlled study. Arch Gen Psychiatry 41:1105-1109, 1984

Walsh BT, Goetz RR, Roose SP, et al: EEG-monitored sleep in anorexia nervosa and bulimia. Biol Psychiatry 20:947-956, 1985a

Walsh BT, Roose SP, Glassman AH, et al: Bulimia and depression. Psychosom Med 47:123-131, 1985b

Weiss SR, Ebert MH: Psychological and behavioral characteristics of normal-weight bulimics and normal-weight controls. Psychosom Med 45:293-303, 1983

Chapter 12

Electroencephalographic Sleep in Bulimia

James I. Hudson, M.D.
Harrison G. Pope, Jr., M.D.
Jeffrey M. Jonas, M.D.
Joseph F. Lipinski, M.D.
David J. Kupfer, M.D.

Chapter 12

Electroencephalographic Sleep in Bulimia

Although the etiology of bulimia is unknown, evidence from studies of phenomenology (Hudson et al. 1983c, in press-b; Herzog 1984; Walsh et al. 1985b; Hudson and Pope, 1987a), family history (Hudson et al. 1983a, in press-a; Hudson and Pope 1987a), response to neuroendocrine tests (Gwirtsman et al. 1983; Hudson et al. 1983b; Hudson and Hudson 1984; Lindy et al. 1985; Mitchell et al. 1985; Hughes et al. 1986a; Kiriike et al. 1986; also see Chapters 1 and 4), and response to thymoleptic medications (Pope et al. 1983; Mitchell and Groat 1984; Walsh et al. 1984; Hughes et al. 1986b; Kennedy et al. 1986; Pope and Hudson 1986; Hudson and Pope 1987b) suggests that bulimia may be related to major affective disorder.

Since patients with major depression have been consistently reported to display abnormalities of electroencephalographic (EEG) sleep (Kupfer et al. 1976, 1978, 1985; Gillin et al. 1979, 1981; Akiskal et al. 1982; Feinberg et al. 1982; Reynolds et al. 1982; Rush et al. 1982; Mendlewicz et al. 1984), it would be of interest to study the EEG sleep in patients with bulimia to determine whether such patients display abnormalities similar to those found in patients with major depression. Previous studies of the EEG sleep in bulimic patients have yielded conflicting findings. Katz et al. (1984) reported shortened rapid eye movement (REM) latency, similar to that observed in major depression, in a series of 20 patients with anorexia nervosa, 17 of whom displayed bulimic symptoms. By contrast, Weilberg et al. (1985) studied two normal weight patients with bulimia and found long REM latencies, but noted "REM-like periods" occurring much earlier than normal for the onset of REM. Finally, Walsh et al. (1985a) and Levy et al. (1987) performed sleep EEGs on 14 and 10 normal weight bulimic patients, respectively, and found no significant differences between bulimic patients and control subjects with respect to any sleep EEG variables.

To investigate further sleep EEG characteristics in bulimia, we performed all-night sleep EEG recordings in 11 patients with bulimia. Further details of this study can be found elsewhere (Hudson et al. 1987b).

METHOD

Subjects

Eleven women meeting *Diagnostic and Statistical Manual of Mental Disorders (Third Edition) (DSM-III;* American Psychiatric Association, 1980) criteria for bulimia were recruited from among outpatients referred to two of the investigators at McLean Hospital (JIH and HGP) for evaluation. (One patient, referred from out of state, was hospitalized during the evaluation period.) The demographic and clinical characteristics of the subjects are shown in Table 16. The mean age of the bulimic subjects was 25.2 years (SD = 5.6, range = 18 to 37). All subjects were between 80 and 120 percent of ideal body weight by height and age (Society of Actuaries and Association of Life Insurance Medical Directors of America 1980). No subject had taken any medication except for occasional aspirin or acetaminophen in the two weeks prior to study; only one subject, treated with imipramine one year previously, had received any psychotropic medication other than occasional benzodiazepines.

All subjects were given the Diagnostic Interview Schedule (DIS) (Robins et al. 1980), to assess current and past diagnoses by *DSM-III* criteria; the Atypical Depression Diagnostic Schedule (ADDS) (Liebowitz et al. 1984), to assess the presence of atypical depression; and the 17-item Hamilton Rating Scale for Depression (HRSD) (Hamilton 1967). Five subjects displayed current major depression, but none met criteria for atypical depression. One subject had a current diagnosis of bipolar disorder, manic. The mean HRSD score was 13.0 (SD = 6.8).

Electroencephalographic Sleep Procedure for Bulimic Subjects

All-night sleep EEG recordings were performed at Massachusetts General Hospital Sleep EEG Laboratory (10 subjects) and at McLean Hospital Sleep EEG Research Laboratory (1 subject). Ten subjects were studied on two consecutive nights, and one subject was studied on only one night.

Comparison Groups

Comparison groups for the EEG sleep studies consisted of women age 37 years and younger studied at the Sleep Evaluation Center, Western Psychiatric Institute and Clinic (WPIC) in the following

Table 16. Clinical Characteristics of 11 Women With Bulimia

Subject No.	Age in Years	% of Ideal Body Weight	Duration of Illness, In Years	Binges Per Week	History of Anorexia Nervosa	HRSD Score	First-Degree Relative With Major Affective Disorder
Without Concurrent Major Affective Disorder							
1.	23	101	2	5	No	12	Yes
2.	27	112	6	2	No	7	No
3.	27	99	9	3	No	3	No
4.	21	112	3	7	No	9	No
5.	37	92	18	8	No	5	No
With Concurrent Major Depression							
6.	23	109	4	3	Yes	15	No
7.	18	99	5	7	Yes	14	Yes
8.	23	102	2	21	No	17	Yes
9.	33	120	19	7	No	17	Yes
10.	21	80	6	10	Yes	17	Yes
With Concurrent Bipolar Disorder, Manic							
11.	24	120	10	14	No	27	Yes
Mean	25.2	104.2	7.6	7.9		13.0	
SD	5.6	12.0	6.0	5.5		6.8	

Note: HRSD = Hamilton Rating Scale for Depression.

categories: a) healthy normal controls (n = 20), selected according to procedures described by Kupfer et al. (1985) (mean age = 28.4 years, SD = 5.6, range 20 to 37); and b) outpatients with depression meeting Research Diagnostic Criteria (RDC) (Spitzer et al. 1978) for primary affective disorder (n = 44), enrolled in a study of recurrent depression, as described elsewhere (Frank and Kupfer 1985) (mean age = 31.5 years, SD = 4.0, range = 24 to 37). There was no significant difference in age between the bulimic and normal control subjects. However, the depressed subjects were significantly older than both the bulimic (p < .001, Wilcoxon rank sum test, two-tailed) and normal control (p < .05) subjects. The mean 17-item HRSD score for 43 of the 44 outpatients with depression was 22.7 (SD = 3.8, range 16-31); HRSD data for one patient were not available.

Electroencephalographic Sleep Records and Analysis

Electroencephalographic sleep studies monitored the EEG, electromyogram (EMG), and electrooculogram (EOG). Records were scored at the WPIC according to standard methods (Taska and Kupfer 1982).

For analysis of the EEG sleep data, results from night 1 and night 2 were first compared within each study group, using the Wilcoxon rank sum test, two tailed. No significant intragroup differences emerged between the two nights of sleep on any variable, and hence we used the mean of the two nights of sleep for subsequent analyses. Intergroup comparisons of sleep variables were performed using the Wilcoxon rank sum test, two tailed. Correlation coefficients were generated using the Spearman rank correlation test.

RESULTS

Intragroup Variation Among Bulimic Subjects

The bulimic subjects showed little intragroup variation in EEG sleep characteristics (see Tables 17 and 18). There were no significant differences on any sleep EEG variable between bulimic subjects with and those without current affective disorder. The one subject with a current manic episode showed EEG characteristics similar to those of the other subjects, and the significance level of all intragroup and intergroup comparisons remains unchanged if this subject is excluded from analysis.

Sleep Continuity

The bulimic subjects exhibited no difference in sleep continuity variables compared with normal controls, but did display a number of

Table 17. Sleep Continuity and Sleep Architecture Measures in 11 Bulimic Subjects

Subject No.	Total Recording Period, in min.	Sleep Latency, in min.	Minutes Spent Asleep	Sleep Efficiency %	Sleep Maintenance %	% of Stage 1	% of Stage 2	% of Delta (Stages 3 and 4) Sleep	% of Stage 1 REM Sleep	% of Stage 2 REM Sleep
Without Concurrent Major Affective Disorder										
1.	433	52	371	86.7	97.3	3.2	53.4	23.7	19.6	0.1
2.	315	10	300	95.2	98.3	7.0	70.0	8.7	14.3	0
3.	509	5	499	98.1	99.1	4.6	62.7	14.2	18.5	0
4.	440	12	405	92.0	94.6	5.9	64.0	0.5	29.4	0.2
5.	383	9	360	94.0	96.5	5.5	61.1	13.5	20.0	0
With Concurrent Major Depression										
6.	399	6	390	97.6	99.1	6.4	60.9	15.2	17.6	0
7.	392	20	370	96.8	99.2	0.4	51.4	32.9	15.3	0
8.	443	15	418	94.5	97.0	7.2	59.8	8.5	24.4	0.1
9.	412	14	389	94.5	97.8	9.2	57.6	11.9	21.5	0
10.	362	30	320	88.5	96.5	6.4	29.0	32.0	32.7	0
With Concurrent Bipolar Disorder, Manic										
11.	408	12	384	94.3	97.0	2.9	52.6	24.8	19.8	0

Note: Values are means of two nights of sleep, except for subject nos. 2 and 4, respectively, for which values are for second night only and for first night only.

Table 18. Rapid Eye Movement Measures in 11 Bulimic Subjects

Subject No.	REM Latency, in min.	Units of REM Activity	REM Density[a]					REM Intensity[b]	No. of REM Periods
			1st period	2nd period	3rd period	4th period	Total		
Without Concurrent Major Affective Disorder									
1.	81.5	69	.81	.86	1.14	1.06	.96	.19	4.0
2.	85.0	50	1.09	1.25	1.08	—	1.16	.17	3.0
3.	49.5	81	.94	.93	.83	.80	.89	.17	4.5
4.	69.0	113	.77	.81	.90	1.28	.95	.28	4.0
5.	64.5	72	.86	.91	1.13	1.01	1.01	.20	4.0
With Concurrent Major Depression									
6.	64.0	66	.74	.87	1.02	1.06	.96	.17	4.5
7.	144.0	65	.83	.92	.89	—	1.10	.17	3.0
8.	61.5	79	.69	.66	.88	.71	.77	.19	4.0
9.	74.0	95	.95	1.18	1.21	1.17	1.13	.25	4.0
10.	74.0	120	.86	1.24	—	—	1.13	.38	2.0
With Concurrent Bipolar Disorder, Manic									
11.	68.0	89	.90	1.01	1.33	.91	1.17	.23	5.0

Note: Values are means of two nights of sleep, except for subject nos. 2 and 4, respectively, for which values are for second night only and for first night only.
[a] REM activity/time spent in REM sleep period
[b] REM activity/time spent asleep

differences compared with the patients with major depression: The depressed subjects exhibited significantly increased sleep latency, decreased sleep efficiency, and decreased sleep maintenance, as compared with both the bulimic and control groups (see Table 19). The depressed subjects also exhibited significantly less time spent asleep than did the control group, but did not differ significantly from the bulimic group on this measure.

Sleep Architecture

Sleep architecture was similar among all groups on most variables (see Table 19). The only significant differences occurred in percentage of stage 1 sleep, with bulimic and depressed subjects both showing a decreased percentage of stage 1 sleep as compared with normal controls.

Rapid Eye Movement Measures

On REM measures, the bulimic patients showed no significant differences as compared with normal controls. However, the REM density of the first REM period was greater in the bulimic versus control subjects (see Table 19), but this difference only approached statistical significance ($p < .1$). Comparisons within the bulimic group revealed no significant differences in REM latencies or REM densities between subjects with major depression and those without affective disorder, and between subjects with a family history of major affective disorder and those without; nor was there any significant correlation between REM latency and HRSD score or percentage of ideal body weight.

There were no significant differences in REM latency between the study groups, although the depressed subjects exhibited a trend toward shortened REM latency compared with control subjects (see Table 19). The depressed subjects showed significantly increased total REM density, as well as increased REM density for each individual REM period, compared with bulimic and control subjects. REM intensity was significantly increased in depressed versus control subjects, but did not differ significantly in depressed versus bulimic subjects.

DISCUSSION

Comparison With Previous Studies

In 11 normal weight women with bulimia, we observed all-night sleep EEGs that were largely indistinguishable from those of normal women. These findings are similar to those of Walsh et al. (1985a)

Table 19. Electroencephalographic Sleep Measures in Bulimic, Depressed, and Control Subjects

Measure	Bulimia N = 11		Major Depression N = 44		Normal Controls N = 20	
	Mean	(SD)	Mean	(SD)	Mean	(SD)
Sleep Continuity						
Total recording period, in min.	409	(50)	413	(49)	426	(24)
Sleep latency, in min.	17	(14)[a]	28	(20)	15	(7.7)[b]
Minutes spent asleep	382	(52)	362	(51)	399	(27)[b]
Sleep efficiency, %	94	(3.6)[c]	87	(6.1)	94	(3.8)[c]
Sleep maintenance, %	98	(1.4)[a]	94	(5.1)	97	(3.1)[b]
Sleep Architecture						
% of stage 1 sleep	5.3	(2.4)[d]	5.5	(2.5)	7.9	(3.0)[b]
% of stage 2 sleep	56.6	(10.7)	61.0	(9.1)	59.3	(7.3)
% of delta (stages 3 and 4) sleep	16.9	(10.2)	12.0	(8.3)	11.9	(8.5)
% of stage 1 REM sleep	21.2	(5.6)	21.3	(4.6)	20.9	(3.7)
% of stage 2 REM sleep	0.04	(0.7)	0.30	(1.6)	0.03	(0.8)
Rapid Eye Movement						
REM latency, in min.	75.9	(25)	68.8	(22)[e]	77.0	(16)
Units of REM Activity	81.7	(21)	102.9	(49)[f]	80.7	(28)
REM Density						
1st period	0.85	(0.13)[fh]	1.00	(0.29)[c]	0.68	(0.32)
2nd period	0.97	(0.19)[a]	1.22	(0.43)[c]	0.84	(0.30)
3rd period	1.05	(0.17)[h]	1.34	(0.48)[c]	0.98	(0.38)
4th period	1.00	(0.19)[c]	1.57	(0.63)[c]	1.01	(0.38)
Total	1.02	(0.13)[a]	1.28	(0.37)	0.97	(0.30)[b]
REM intensity	0.22	(0.07)	0.28	(0.12)	0.20	(0.08)[b]
No. of REM periods	3.8	(0.84)	3.6	(0.77)	3.9	(0.54)

[a] $p < .05$ vs. major depression
[b] $p < .01$ vs. major depression
[c] $p < .001$ vs. major depression
[d] $p < .05$ vs. normal controls
[e] $p = .1$ vs. normal controls
[f] $p < .1$ vs. normal controls
[g] REM activity/time spent asleep
[h] $p < .1$ vs. major depression
[i] REM activity/time spent in REM sleep period

and Levy et al. (1987), who reported normal all-night sleep EEGs in samples of normal weight bulimic women. Also, like Walsh et al. (1985a), we did not consistently observe a pattern of increased REM latency described in two patients with bulimia by Weilberg et al. (1985). However, in one subject with bulimia and concurrent major depression, prolonged REM latency was observed on both nights of sleep (120 min. and 173 min. on nights 1 and 2, respectively). In the study of Walsh et al. (1985a), three of the 14 subjects displayed increased REM latencies (means of 155, 158, and 176 min. for two nights).

In contrast to studies of normal weight bulimic patients, reports of bulimic patients with anorexia nervosa appear less consistent. Katz et al. (1984) reported shortened REM latencies in patients with anorexia nervosa (most of whom were at least partially weight recovered), particularly those who exhibited bulimic symptoms. However, Walsh et al. (1985a) studied eight anorexic patients, four of whom had bulimic symptoms, and found no significant difference in REM latencies between the anorexic patients and normal controls. None of the patients in our study was currently anorexic, although three subjects had a past history of anorexia nervosa.

Rapid Eye Movement Density in Bulimia

We observed a trend toward increased REM density in the first REM period among the bulimic subjects compared with the control subjects. Increased REM density—particularly in the first REM period—has been reported consistently in depressed patients (Gillin et al. 1981; Lahmeyer et al. 1983; Mendlewicz et al. 1984; Kupfer et al. 1985). Further, Cashman et al. (1986) recently found increased REM density in the first REM period among a group of depressed adolescents who displayed normal REM latencies. Thus, it is possible that bulimia, which affects mainly younger individuals, may show EEG sleep characteristics similar to adolescent patients with depression. Further studies of bulimic patients will be necessary to test this hypothesis. Since automated analysis may highlight differences in REM activity, REM density, and REM intensity between groups that may not be apparent by traditional hand scoring (Kupfer et al. 1985), it would be of particular interest to use automated scoring in subsequent studies of bulimic patients.

Electroencephalographic Sleep in Bulimia Compared to Major Depression

Bulimic subjects in the present study differed from outpatients with major depression on several sleep measures. The most robust differences were found in sleep continuity, with bulimic patients show-ing significantly lower sleep latencies, and significantly higher sleep efficiency and sleep maintenance, compared with the depressed out-patients. Sleep architecture failed to reveal any significant differences between bulimic and depressed subjects. With regard to REM meas-ures, the bulimic subjects differed significantly from the depressed subjects on only one variable, total REM density. However, the REM densities of the first and second REM periods in the bulimic subjects were not significantly different from those found in the patients with depression. Comparison data from other centers are unavailable, since no previous study has compared bulimic patients directly with pa-tients with depression.

Interestingly, the five bulimic subjects with concurrent depression were similar to the five without affective disorder on all sleep vari-ables, with none of the differences showing even a trend toward significance ($p < .2$ for all comparisons). In addition, there was no correlation between REM latency or REM density of the first REM period and HRSD scores. The finding of little difference between depressed and nondepressed bulimic subjects is similar to that re-ported by Walsh et al. (1985a) among normal weight bulimic pa-tients. However, Katz et al. (1984) found a significant negative correlation between HRSD scores and REM latency in a sample of anorexic patients, most of whom also had bulimic symptoms. It might be argued that the failure to find differences between depressed bulimic subjects and normal controls may be due to differences in the type of depression seen in bulimia compared with major affective disorder (Cooper and Fairburn 1986; Hudson and Pope 1987a). However, none of the bulimic subjects with major depression ex-hibited atypical depression, as defined by Liebowitz et al. (1984), and the phenomenology of the depression in these bulimic subjects did not differ significantly from that seen in an age-matched group of depressed women evaluated at our center (Hudson et al. in press-b). Thus, the failure to find differences between depressed and non-depressed bulimic subjects does not appear to be due to differences in the type of depression seen in conjunction with bulimia, as com-pared to the type of depression found in patients with major depres-sion alone.

In addition, it should be noted that 24-hour urinary free cortisol levels (UFC) levels and response to the 1 mg dexamethasone suppres-sion test (DST) were assessed in 6 of the 11 subjects in this study (Hudson et al. 1987a). In all instances, normal urinary free cortisol levels and DST responses were found. Given that previous studies of the DST have suggested that nonsuppressed DST responses are common in bulimia (Gwirtsman et al. 1983; Hudson et al. 1983b; Hudson and Hudson 1984; Lindy et al. 1985; Mitchell et al. 1984; Hughes et al. 1986a; Kiriike et al. 1986; also see Chapter 1) and major affective disorder (see Hudson and Hudson 1984), these observations suggest that our sample of bulimic patients (with and without current major affective disorder) may have been somewhat atypical, in that none of the patients exhibited abnormalities of hypothalamic–pituitary–adrenal axis function. Furthermore, given that several studies (Rush et al. 1982; Mendlewicz et al. 1984; Shipley et al. 1986) have reported an association between shortened REM latency and nonsuppressed DST responses in major depression, it is possible that shortened REM latencies, and possibly other EEG sleep abnormalities, might be found more commonly in bulimic patients showing nonsuppressed responses to the DST. Further studies of bulimic patients, comparing those exhibiting nonsuppressed versus suppressed responses to the DST, would be useful to evaluate this issue.

The outpatients with major depression studied in the present investigation exhibited some, but not all, of the sleep EEG abnormalities generally found in patients with major depression as compared with normal individuals (Kupfer et al. 1976, 1978, 1985; Gillin et al. 1979, 1981; Akiskal et al. 1982; Feinberg et al. 1982; Reynolds et al. 1982; Rush et al. 1982; Mendlewicz et al. 1984). For example, marked disturbances of sleep continuity were found. However, other studies of younger outpatients with depression have failed to find such sleep continuity disturbances (Taub et al. 1978; Puig-Antich et al. 1982; Lahmeyer et al. 1983; Hawkins et al. 1985; Cashman et al. 1986)

With respect to sleep architecture, many previous studies have found decreased delta (slow wave) sleep in depression (Gillin et al. 1979, 1981; Reynolds et al. 1982; Kupfer et al. 1985). However, some studies, particularly of younger patients with depression, have failed to find this abnormality (Puig-Antich et al. 1982; Lahmeyer et al. 1983; Goetz et al. 1987).

Turning to REM measures, the depressed outpatients failed to show significantly shortened REM latency compared with normal controls, although there was a trend in this direction ($p = .10$). The lack of a robust difference in REM latencies between these groups is at variance with most studies of depression in older inpatients and outpatients (Kupfer et al. 1976, 1978; Gillin et al. 1979, 1981; Akiskal et al. 1982; Feinberg et al. 1982; Reynolds et al. 1982; Rush et al. 1982), younger inpatients (Gillin et al. 1981; Kupfer et al. 1985), as well as one study in younger outpatients (Lahmeyer et al.

1983). However, other studies of depression in younger outpatients (Taub et al. 1978; Puig-Antich et al. 1982; Hawkins et al. 1985; Cashman et al. 1986; Goetz et al. 1987) have found no difference in REM latencies as compared with normal controls.

In agreement with other studies of depressed patients (Gillin et al. 1981; Lahmeyer et al. 1983; Kupfer et al. 1985), REM density and REM activity were increased in the depressed versus the normal control subjects, although the difference for the latter comparison only approached statistical signficance. Thus, of the three abnormalities of REM sleep commonly reported in major depression—shortened REM latency, increased REM density, and increased REM activity—the depressed outpatients displayed unequivocally increased REM density and trends towards shortened REM latency and increased REM activity.

It should also be noted that the depressed subjects were somewhat older than the bulimic and normal control subjects. However, the difference in mean age between the depressed subjects and the latter groups was only 6.2 and 3.1 years, respectively. Since an age difference of at least a decade is required before significant differences in EEG sleep characteristics emerge (Kupfer et al. 1985, 1986), the small differences in age observed among groups in this study would be expected to generate only minimal intergroup variation due to the effects of age. However, in all instances, the increased age of the depressed subjects would be expected to exaggerate the significance of the comparisons between depressed patients and other subject groups.

Implications for the Relationship Between Bulimia and Major Affective Disorder

In conclusion, we found essentially normal EEG sleep characteristics in patients with bulimia. What can be inferred from this finding about the relationship between bulimia and major affective disorder? On the one hand, bulimic patients in this and other studies do not appear to show the EEG sleep abnormalities characteristically found in older patients with depression; hence, bulimia may be dissimilar to major affective disorder on this biological test. On the other hand, EEG sleep abnormalities are often not present, or present only to a modest degree, in younger outpatients with depression; hence, the EEG sleep of bulimic patients may be similar to that of younger depressed outpatients. Further studies of the EEG sleep of patients with bulimia, as well as of younger outpatients with major depression, are needed to resolve this issue. Since automated analysis of EEG sleep records may highlight disturbances of slow-wave sleep and

REM measures not detectable by traditional hand-scoring methods, it would be particularly useful to apply this technique to the scoring of EEG sleep records in subsequent studies of these populations. Our results raise a larger issue, namely, that it is difficult to assess the possible relationship between bulimia and major affective disorder on the basis of EEG sleep and neuroendocrine studies. The low sensitivity of these tests for major affective disorder in younger patients with mild to moderately severe disorders (see Hudson and Pope 1987a), and the low specificity of neuroendocrine tests for major affective disorder (Hudson and Hudson 1984; also see Chapters 1 and 4) argue that it may be premature to use the results of available biological tests as a basis for speculation about the nosologic status of bulimia.

REFERENCES

Akiskal HS, Lemmi H, Yerevanian B, et al: The utility of the REM latency test in psychiatric diagnosis: a study of 81 depressed outpatients. Psychiatry Res 7:101-110, 1982

American Psychiatric Association: Diagnostic and Statistical Manual of Mental Disorders (Third Edition). Washington, DC, American Psychiatric Association, 1980

Cashman MA, Coble P, McCann BS, et al: Sleep markers for major depressive disorder in adolescent patients. Sleep Res 15: Abs. 91, 1986

Cooper PJ, Fairburn CG: The depressive symptoms of bulimia nervosa. Br J Psychiatry 148:268-274, 1986

Feinberg M, Gillin JC, Carroll BJ, et al: EEG studies of sleep in the diagnosis of depression. Biol Psychiatry 17:305-316, 1982

Frank E, Kupfer DJ: Maintenance treatment of recurrent unipolar depression: pharmacology and psychotherapy, in Chronic Treatment in Neuropsychiatry. Edited by Kemali D, Racagni G. New York, Raven Press, 1985

Gillin JC, Duncan W, Pettigrew KD, et al: Successful separation of depressed, normal, and insomniac subjects by EEG sleep data. Arch Gen Psychiatry 36:85-90, 1979

Gillin JC, Duncan WC, Murphy DL, et al: Age-related changes in sleep in depressed and normal subjects. Psychiatry Res 4:73-78, 1981

Goetz RR, Puig-Antich J, Ryan N, et al: Electroencephalographic sleep of adolescents with major depression and normal controls. Arch Gen Psychiatry 44:61-68, 1987

Gwirtsman HE, Roy-Byrne P, Yager J, et al: Neuroendocrine abnormalities in bulimia. Am J Psychiatry 140:599-563, 1983

Hamilton M: Development of a rating scale for primary depressive illness. Br J Soc Clin Psychol 6:278-296, 1967

Hawkins DR, Taub JM, Van de Castle RL: Extended sleep (hypersomnia) in young depressed patients. Am J Psychiatry 142:905-910, 1985

Herzog DB: Are anorectics and bulimics depressed? Am J Psychiatry 141:1594-1597, 1984

Hudson JI, Hudson MS: Endocrine dysfunction in anorexia nervosa and bulimia: comparison with abnormalities in other psychiatric disorders and distrubances due to metabolic factors. Psychiatr Develop 4:237-272, 1984

Hudson JI, Pope HG Jr: Depression and eating disorders, in Presentations of Depression. Edited by Cameron OG. New York, John Wiley & Sons, 1987a

Hudson JI, Pope HG Jr: Newer antidepressants in the treatment of bulimia nervosa. Psychopharmacol Bull 23:52-57, 1987b

Hudson JI, Pope HG Jr, Jonas JM, et al: Family history study of anorexia nervosa and bulimia. Br J Psychiatry 142:133-138, 1983a

Hudson JI, Pope HG Jr, Jonas JM, et al: Hypothalamic–pituitary–adrenal axis hyperactivity in bulimia. Psychiatry Res 8:111-118, 1983b

Hudson JI, Pope HG Jr, Jonas JM, et al: Phenomenologic relationship between eating disorders and major affective disorder. Psychiatry Res 9:345-354, 1983c

Hudson JI, Katz DL, Pope HG Jr, et al: Urinary free cortisol and response to the dexamethasone suppression test in bulimia: a pilot study. Int J Eating Disorders 6:191-198, 1987a

Hudson JI, Pope HG Jr, Jonas JM, et al: Sleep EEG in bulimia. Biol Psychiatry, 22:820-828, 1987b

Hudson JI, Pope HG Jr, Jonas JM, et al: A controlled family history study of bulimia. Psychol Med, in press-a

Hudson JI, Pope HG Jr, Yurgelun-Todd D, et al: Lifetime prevalence of affective and other psychiatric disorders in bulimic outpatients: a controlled study. Am J Psychiatry, in press-b

Hughes PL, Wells LA, Cunningham CJ: The dexamethasone suppression test in bulimia before and after successful treatment with desipramine. J Clin Psychiatry 47:515-517, 1986a

Hughes PL, Wells LA, Cunningham CJ, et al: Treating bulimia with desipramine: a double-blind, placebo-controlled study. Arch Gen Psychiatry 43:182-186, 1986b

Katz JL, Kuperberg A, Pollack CP, et al: Is there a relationship between eating disorder and affective disorder? New evidence from sleep recordings. Am J Psychiatry 141:753-759, 1984

Kennedy S, Piran N, Garfinkel PE: Isocarboxazid in the treatment of bulimia. Am J Psychiatry 143:1495-1496, 1986

Kiriike N, Nishiwaki S, Izumiya Y, et al: Dexamethasone suppression test in bulimia. Biol Psychiatry 21:325-328, 1986

Kupfer DJ, Foster F, Reich L, et al: EEG sleep changes as predictors in depression. Am J Psychiatry 138:429-434, 1976

Kupfer DJ, Spiker DG, Coble PA, et al: The application of EEG sleep for the differential diagnosis of affective disorders. Am J Psychiatry 135:69-74, 1978

Kupfer DJ, Ulrich RF, Coble PA, et al: EEG sleep of younger depressives: comparison to normals. Arch Gen Psychiatry 42:806-810, 1985

Kupfer DJ, Reynolds CF, Ulrich RF, et al: Comparison of automated REM and slow-wave sleep analysis in young and middle-aged depressed subjects. Biol Psychiatry 21:189-200, 1986

Lahmeyer HW, Poznanski EO, Bellur SN: EEG sleep in depressed adolescents. Am J Psychiatry 140:1150-1153, 1983

Levy AB, Dixon KN, Schmidt HS: REM and delta sleep in anorexia nervosa and bulimia. Psychiatry Res 20:189-197, 1987

Liebowitz MR, Quitkin FM, Stewart JW, et al: Phenelzine v imipramine in atypical depression: a preliminary report. Arch Gen Psychiatry 41:669-677, 1984

Lindy DC, Walsh BT, Roose SP, et al: The dexamethasone suppression test in bulimia. Am J Psychiatry 142:1375-1376, 1985

Mendlewicz J, Kerkhofs M, Hoffman G, et al: Dexamethasone suppression test and REM sleep in patients with major depressive disorder. Br J Psychiatry 145:383-388, 1984

Mitchell JE, Groat R: A placebo-controlled, double-blind trial of amitriptyline in bulimia. J Clin Psychopharmacol 4:186-193, 1984

Mitchell JE, Pyle RL, Hatsukami D, et al: The dexamethasone suppression test in patients with bulimia. J Clin Psychiatry 45:508-511, 1985

Pope HG Jr, Hudson JI: Antidepressant drug therapy for bulimia: current status. J Clin Psychiatry 47:339-345, 1986

Pope HG Jr, Hudson JI, Jonas JM, et al: Bulimia treated with imipramine: a placebo-controlled double-blind study. Am J Psychiatry 140:554-558, 1983

Puig-Antich J, Goetz R, Hanlon C, et al: Sleep architecture and REM sleep measures in prepubertal children with major depression. Arch Gen Psychiatry 39:932-939, 1982

Reynolds CF, Newton TF, Shaw DH, et al: Electroencephalographic sleep findings in outpatients with primary depression. Psychiatry Res 6:65-72, 1982

Robins LN, Helzer JI, Croughan J, et al: NIMH Diagnostic Interview Schedule (2nd edition). Rockville, MD, National Institute of Mental Health, 1980

Rush AJ, Giles DE, Roffwarg HP, et al: Sleep EEG and dexamethasone suppression test findings in outpatients with unipolar major depressive disorder. Biol Psychiatry 17:327-341, 1982

Shipley JE, Kumar A, Eiser A, et al: Clinical, EEG sleep, and DST correlates of sleep onset REM periods. Sleep Res 15: Abs. 97, 1986

Society of Actuaries and Associates of Life Insurance Medical Directors of America: 1979 Build Study. Chicago, Author, 1980

Spitzer R, Endicott J, Robins E: Research diagnostic criteria. Arch Gen Psychiatry 34:773-782, 1978

Taska LS, Kupfer DJ: Sleep Scoring Manual. Pittsburgh, Western Psychiatric Institute and Clinic, 1982

Taub JM, Hawkins DR, Van de Castle RL: Electrographic analysis of the sleep cycle in young depressed patients. Biol Psychol 7:203-214, 1978

Walsh BT, Stewart JW, Roose SP, et al: Treatment of bulimia with phenelzine: a double-blind, placebo-controlled study. Arch Gen Psychiatry 41:1105-1109, 1984

Walsh BT, Goetz R, Roose SP, et al: EEG-monitored sleep in anorexia nervosa and bulimia. Biol Psychiatry 20:947-956, 1985a

Walsh BT, Roose SP, Glassman AH, et al: Bulimia and depression. Psychosom Med 47:123-131, 1985b

Weilberg JB, Stakes JW, Brotman A, et al: Sleep architecture in bulimia: a pilot study. Biol Psychiatry 30:225-228, 1985

Chapter 13

Seasonal Affective Disorder and Its Relevance for the Understanding and Treatment of Bulimia

Norman E. Rosenthal, M.D.
Michael Genhart, B.S.
David A. Sack, M.D.
Robert G. Skwerer, M.D.
Thomas A. Wehr, M.D.

Chapter 13

Seasonal Affective Disorder and Its Relevance for the Understanding and Treatment of Bulimia

Seasonal affective disorder (SAD) is a condition characterized by regular fall and winter depressions alterating with nondepressed periods in the spring and summer (Rosenthal et al. 1984). During depressions patients experience a variety of symptoms, but changes in eating patterns are a major part of the clinical picture. Most patients with SAD crave carbohydrates and overeat during their winter depressions. Binge eating and weight gain are common. Considering the prominence of disturbances of appetitive behavior in SAD, the condition could be considered as a type of eating disorder. A major problem confronting the researcher in studying the evolution of eating disorders is that by the time the patient presents, the eating disorder is already well established. In SAD the changes in eating behavior are recurrent and predictable. It is therefore possible to study patients prospectively and follow them through the various stages of eating behavior. Of equal interest to the way in which the disturbances in eating behavior develop in the fall and winter is how they resolve the following spring. Perhaps the mechanisms that underlie these alterations in eating behavior could be applied to the study of the eating disorders in general.

By now it has been firmly established that the depressive symptoms of SAD, including those concerning eating behavior, can be reversed by exposing the patient to bright artificial light. Thus SAD constitutes not only a spontaneously remitting form of eating disorder, but one that can be reversed by nonpharmacological manipulations of the environment.

What, then, are the similarities and differences between SAD and bulimia? How can information from the one area of study be applied to the other? What basic underlying systems might be disturbed in both conditions? These are some of the questions we attempt to answer in the present chapter.

SEASONAL AFFECTIVE DISORDER AS AN EATING DISORDER

As the days become shorter, patients with SAD begin to complain of their fall–winter symptoms. In the Washington, D.C. area this usually occurs in October or November. In the early stages patients

Table 20. Symptoms of Depression in Seasonal Affective Disorders (n = 220)

	Percentage
1. Decreased activity	94
2. Changes in affect	
Sadness	95
Irritability	86
Anxiety	88
3. Changes in appetite	
Increased	70
Decreased	19
Mixed or no change	11
Carbohydrate craving	71
4. Changes in weight	
Increased	75
Decreased	11
Mixed or no change	14
5. Changes in sleep	
Earlier onset	70
Increased duration	83
Changes in quality	66
Daytime drowsiness (n = 167)	71
6. Decreased libido	55
7. Difficulties at work	87
8. Interpersonal difficulties	94
9. Depression milder nearer equator (n = 90)	88
10. Menstrual difficulties (n = 132)	57

report lethargy, a need to sleep more, a shift in their food preferences (from the leaner foods and vegetables of summer to high-carbohydrate, high-calorie foods). For example, one man who was uninterested in high-carbohydrate foods in the summer developed a marked craving for ice cream in the winter. Predictably, these changes in eating pattern, together with the reduced energy level, are followed by weight gain. The affective symptoms of sadness, irritability, and anxiety often follow these early vegetative symptoms, and difficulty concentrating and social withdrawal occur. Depressions are usually mild to moderate in severity but may be severe, with patients presenting as a suicidal risk and requiring hospitalization.

Although the majority of patients with SAD report overeating and weight gain, a sizable minority report eating less and losing weight during their winter depressions, as shown in Table 20. Other clinical and demographic features are shown in Table 21. There is a

Table 21. Clinical and Demographic Features of Seasonal Affective Disorder ($n = 220$)

1. Sex ratio	
Females	182
Males	38
2. Age (years)	37.5 ± 10.9
3. Age of onset (years)	21.9 ± 9.4
4. Length of depression (months)	5.1 ± 1.4
5. Diagnosis	
Bipolar II	83%
Bipolar I	6%
Unipolar	11%
6. Family history (At least one affected first degree relative)	
Major affective disorder	55%
Alcohol abuse	34%
7. Previous treatment history	
No treatment	25%
Antidepressants	41%
Lithium	17%
Thyroid	10%
Hospitalization	6%
Electroconvulsive therapy	1%

strong preponderance of women in the population (83 percent), a ratio more typical of the eating disorders than of the other affective disorders. It appears that this sex ratio is not merely an artifact of our recruitment procedures (most patients have been recruited via newspaper articles), since it has remained constant over the years and has also been noted by other authors (Yerevanian et al. 1986; Wirz-Justice et al. 1986a). In the D.C. metropolitan area, depressions of SAD patients last an average of 5.1 months. Most patients have a lifetime diagnosis of bipolar II affective disorder, with hypomanic episodes occurring in the spring and summer. Less commonly, patients experience manic episodes or have a recurrent unipolar history. There is a high family incidence of affective disorders and alcohol-related problems.

An outstanding feature of this condition, besides its seasonality, is the responsiveness of patients to alterations in climate, latitude, and environmental light. The majority of patients who have travelled during the winter months report an exacerbation of symptoms when they travel north and relief of symptoms when they travel south. In addition, patients complain that anything that causes a decrease in environmental light intensity frequently results in deterioration in mood. Thus, a spell of cloudy weather may produce mood problems, even if it occurs in the summer, as may a move into a poorly lit office or home.

DIFFERENTIAL DIAGNOSIS OF SEASONAL AFFECTIVE DISORDER

Because of the atypical vegetative symptoms, which frequently dominate the clinical picture and often precede the affective symptoms, patients with SAD often present to general medical practitioners. Differential diagnoses include other conditions that produce sustained decreases in energy and increased intake of carbohydrates. Thus, patients have frequently been evaluated for hypothyroidism, hypoglycemia, and infectious mononucleosis, generally with negative results.

The patient's subjective experience of his or her eating being out of control resembles the feelings of the bulimic patient. Frequently, patients with SAD do binge, that is, they eat large amounts of food in a relatively short space of time. However, purging behavior is unusual. In addition, SAD patients appear to prefer to binge on high-carbohydrate foods. This has been reported by a substantial percentage of our subjects, and recently Wurtman et al. (1986) documented the phenomenon prospectively by measuring food choices in eight SAD patients in the spring and fall. They noted that the patients chose many more carbohydrate-rich snacks during the fall. Their carbohydrate intake during meals also increased but to a more modest degree than in their snacking behavior. Although there was an overall increase in caloric intake during the fall, protein intake did not increase. Bulimic patients, on the other hand, have been reported to generally not preferentially select different food constituents in their binges (Mitchell et al. 1981; Abraham and Beaumont 1982; Kaye et al. 1986) although Pirke et al. (see Chapter 8) found increased consumption of fat during binges. Notwithstanding these differences, it is clear that in the overeating and bingeing seen in SAD, we have a type of behavior that is quite similar to that seen in bulimia.

ANIMAL MODELS OF SEASONAL AFFECTIVE DISORDER

The student of SAD has access to many naturally occurring animal models of the condition, since seasonal rhythms of behavior abound in nature (Gwinner 1981). The cold temperatures and scarcity of food that prevail in the winter months in boreal and temperate zones pose a major adaptational challenge to the organism. Different species respond to this challenge in different ways. Some, such as hamsters, increase their body fat stores, whereas others, such as voles, conserve energy by decreasing their body mass, which allows them to continue to forage actively through the winter. They compensate for the loss of body mass by growing a longer pelage that has the same insulating capacity as the lost fat (Dark and Zucker 1985). Somehow the information that the climate is changing must be conveyed to the organism so as to cause these behavioral changes to occur. Day length, or photoperiod, has been shown to be the most widely important seasonal time cue among a variety of animal species (Immelman 1973). It is teleologically understandable that this should be the case since day length is the climatic variable that changes most predictably from year to year. In one model of seasonal weight change, namely, obesity among golden hamsters, experimental shortening of the photoperiod has been shown to induce weight increases similar to those seen during the winter (Wade and Bartness 1984). However, other factors, such as a decrease in the environmental temperature, interact with the shortened photoperiod to induce these changes (Hoffman et al. 1982).

Various investigators have studied mechanisms by which environmental changes may lead to changes in behavior. The secretion of melatonin by the pineal gland has been shown to be a major mechanism responsible for mediating the effects of the changing seasons on behavior (Tamarkin et al. 1985; Lincoln 1983; also see Chapter 5). Pineal melatonin is secreted nocturnally on a circadian basis, a rhythm generated by the suprachiasmatic nuclei of the hypothalamus. Environmental light impinges on the retina, from which the photic information is conveyed to the suprachiasmatic nuclei via the retinohypothalamic tracts, and from there, by a series of neurons, to the pineal gland (Hoffman 1981). Environmental light is capable of modifying pineal melatonin secretion both by having a rapid suppressant effect if exposure occurs at night, and by influencing the timing of nocturnal secretion (entraining the rhythm) in relation to the light–dark cycle (Lewy et al. 1985). Secretion of melatonin by the pineal normally occurs in response to stimulation of beta-adrenergic receptors on the surface of the pineal gland. Studies of seasonal rhythms of energy utilization have shown that factors other than the pineal gland may influence the timing of seasonal rhythms of energy utilization in animals (Hoffman et al. 1982).

Seasonal rhythms of energy conservation may prove to be a heuristic animal model for SAD and, perhaps, for other types of affective disorders. Many of the symptoms of SAD, such as increased intake of high-carbohydrate foods, increased appetite and weight, decreased activity and libido, and social withdrawal, can be considered energy-conserving behaviors. Conversely, the hypomanic symptoms of spring can be regarded as energy-dissipating behaviors. The changing seasons, which are associated with changing energy requirements and food availability, are naturally occurring stimuli for these different sets of behaviors. Insofar as the symptoms of the eating disorders overlap with those of the affective disorders, seasonal changes in eating- and weight-regulating behavior in animals may also be useful models for the eating disorders. It is possible that these seasonal changes in eating may have been adaptive at some time in the past, when humans had less control over their physical environment and food supply than they do now. Perhaps those members of society who needed to conserve energy most (for childbearing and lactation), but who were not required to be as active and energetic in their ability to pursue goal-directed activities (such as hunting) all year round, were most likely to evolve these adaptive mechanisms. This may explain the high female-to-male ratio in patients with SAD. However, if these behaviors were indeed adaptive in the past, this is no longer the case in a society that places little value on efficient energy utilization but requires people to work and intereact with others all year round.

SEASONALITY AS A DIMENSION IN NORMAL AND BULIMIC INDIVIDUALS

Kraepelin (1921) first noted that the changes in mood and behavior seen in seasonally occurring cases of manic-depression resemble those "changes which come over even healthy individuals at the changes of the seasons" (p. 139). This raised the question of whether most individuals are subject to seasonal changes in behavior and whether, perhaps, patients with SAD simply represent the extreme end of the spectrum. Preliminary evidence based on a retrospective questionnaire we have used for some years (see Appendix 1), but have not as yet thoroughly validated, suggests that Kraepelin's suggestion is probably true (see Figures 19 and 20). Although SAD patients, by definition, experience far more marked winter changes than do normal subjects, the pattern of seasonal changes in mood reported by normal subjects resembles in distribution those reported by patients with SAD. Similarly, normal individuals resemble SAD patients in their reported distribution of seasonal changes in appetite and weight, sleep, activity level, and energy. These observations are supported by population studies that showed a tendency for people to gain weight in fall and winter and lose weight in spring and summer (Attarzadeh 1983). Similarly, a food choice study performed at the National Institute of Health cafeteria showed that there was an increase in purchases of starchy foods in the winter months (Zifferblatt et al. 1980).

Thus it appears that there are certain seasonally changing environmental variables that cause acceptable changes in mood, activity, energy, and sleep in many normal people. In vulnerable individuals, these changes may reach symptomatic levels. It would be interesting to know whether bulimic patients are vulnerable to seasonal fluctuations in their bingeing behavior. Anecdotally, we have encountered a few patients with eating disorders who have developed bulimic symptoms predominantly in the winter. This question is certainly worthy of further study, especially since SAD has been shown to be reversible by exposure to bright environmental light, and the possibility exists that certain bulimic patients may also benefit from this form of treatment.

PHOTOTHERAPY FOR SEASONAL AFFECTIVE DISORDER

Experimental Studies

The idea to use bright environmental light in the treatment of SAD was inspired by the finding of Lewy et al. (1980) that human nocturnal melatonin secretion could be suppressed by bright artificial light but not by light of the intensity generally found with regular indoor lighting. Following an initial successful treatment of a patient with seasonally recurring mood cycles by extending his day with six hours of bright environmental light (Lewy et al. 1982), several controlled studies of phototherapy were conducted. In three separate studies, Rosenthal et al. (1984, 1985a; James et al., 1985) showed that bright full-spectrum fluorescent light had antidepressant effects in patients with SAD whereas dimmer light did not. Subsequently, Wirz-Justice et al. (1986a) and Checkley et al. (1986) have also shown

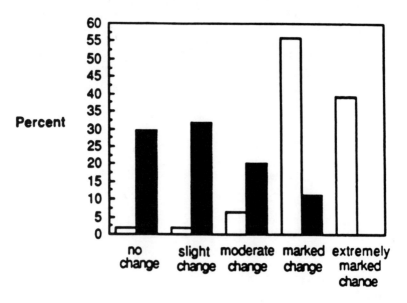

Figure 19. The degree of self-reported seasonal mood variation is shown for 44 patients with SAD (clear bar) and 23 normal controls (black bar). As one would predict, SAD patients report a far greater degree of mood variability. However, almost a third of the normal subjects report moderate to marked seasonal mood changes (see Appendix 1, question 12C).

bright light to be superior to dim light in the treatment of this condition.

Lewy et al. (1985) and Lewy and Sack (1986) have claimed that the timing of phototherapy is critical for its efficacy and have shown in eight SAD patients that two hours of light treatment in the morning was superior to two hours of treatment in the evening. This finding has been replicated by Terman et al. (1986). It thus seems likely that the morning hours are an especially sensitive time for eliciting a response to phototherapy in patients with SAD. However, they do not appear to be a critical time since numerous studies have now shown that bright light treatment at other times of the day, including the evening (James et al. 1985; Hellekson et al. 1986,

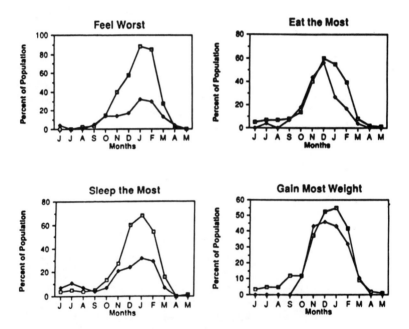

Figure 20. The patterns of self-reported seasonal changes in mood, eating, sleeping and weight gain, are shown for the same 44 SAD patients (clear-blocked line) and 23 normal controls (black-blocked line) depicted in Figure 19. Although the patterns of seasonal changes in mood and behavior are more clearly defined in the patients, the timing of the peaks and shapes of the curves are similar in normals and patients (see Appendix 1, questions 13H, E, J, and B).

Wehr et al. 1986a) and daytime hours (Wehr et al. 1986b; Thompson et al. 1986) may be effective.

There appears to be a relationship between duration of treatments and efficacy of phototherapy (Terman et al. 1986; Wirz-Justice et al. 1986b), though one study by Lewy et al. (1986) in which the investigators failed to find a difference between 30 minutes and two hours of bright light treatment in the morning would tend to disagree with these other findings. Our clinical impressions support the idea of a duration–response curve to phototherapy, since we have frequently seen patients who fail to respond to treatment until they use the requisite number of hours per day. Conversely, we have seen many cases who responded initially to phototherapy, but relapsed after the duration of treatment fell below the necessary threshold.

The efficacy of phototherapy seems somewhat specific for SAD. Kripke et al., who have performed several studies on the effects of bright light in nonseasonal depressives, have reported a very weak antidepressant effect (1985). Yerevanian et al. (1986) treated eight patients with SAD and nine nonseasonal depressives with bright environmental light and found that whereas light treatment was quite effective for patients with SAD, it had no effect on the nonseasonal depressives. The latter study is the only one, to our knowledge, in which incandescent lights were used. It thus appears that phototherapy does not require full-spectrum light in order to be effective.

Practical Aspects of Phototherapy

The following is a description of how phototherapy has been given most frequently in the six years since it was first used. We recognize that this is not the only possible way to administer it, nor even necessarily the best. However, it is well tested and has proven to be effective and safe in approximately 80 percent of the 112 patients treated at the NIMH and in a high percentage of cases treated at other centers as well.

The light source most frequently used has been full-spectrum fluorescent (Vitalite®). Six or eight 40-watt tubes have been inserted into a rectangular metal fixture, two × four feet, with a reflecting surface behind them and a plastic diffusing screen in front. Patients have been asked to place the box at eye level, either horizontally on a desk or table or vertically on the ground. They have been asked to sit approximately three feet away from the lights and to stare at them for a few seconds each minute. The intensity of light measured at three feet from this light source is 2500 lux, the amount of light to which one would be exposed by looking out of a window on a spring day. This is 5 to 10 times brighter than ordinary room lighting. We do not know whether it is necessary for patients to glance directly at the lights intermittently, as we have asked them to do, since we do not know where the relevant photoreceptors are in the retina. If they are the rods on the periphery of the retina, it may be unnecessary for patients to glance at the lights at all. Indeed, it is only recently that we found out that the effects of phototherapy are probably mediated by the eye and not the skin (Wehr et al. in press).

In treating a patient with SAD, the initial suggestion for timing and duration of treatment is a matter of clinical judgment; the convenience and available time of the patient are relevant considerations in this regard. Since it does not appear that timing is crucial, it seems reasonable initially to recommend times that are convenient for the patient. It is often advantageous to establish in the first week whether the patient is a responder to phototherapy or not. Therefore we generally begin by recommending at least four hours of treatment per day. If this is successful, the patient can reduce the duration later. Another approach would be to begin with two hours of treatment in the morning, a regimen that has been found to be effective in a high percentage of patients (Lewy and Sack 1986; Lewy et al. 1986; Terman et al. 1986). When a response occurs, it is almost always apparent within the first four days (Rosenthal et al. 1985a). If no response occurs within the first week, one can either increase the duration or alter the timing. Treatment may be given in conjunction with antidepressant medications. This may enable the patient to be treated with a lower dosage of medication.

Although side-effects are uncommon, patients sometimes complain of irritability (of the kind seen in hypomania), eye strain, headaches or insomnia. The latter is seen especially when patients use lights late at night. Side-effects can generally be reversed easily by decreasing the duration of treatments or suggesting that patients sit further from the light source. In one case, however, we had to discontinue treatment altogether because of severe eye irritation. Although we have seen several cases of hypomanic responses, we have seen no cases of florid mania following phototherapy in any typical SAD patients. We did observe mania in one atypical case, who had a history of both anorexia and bulimia. Fortunately we have not to date encountered any cases of long-term side-effects with phototherapy.

The Effects of Phototherapy on Eating Behavior

In attempting to measure the severity of symptoms in SAD, it soon became apparent to us that the standard 21-item Hamilton Rating Scale for Depression (HRSD) (Hamilton 1967) was inadequate for documenting the symptoms of SAD. The HRSD was designed specifically for measuring the severity of endogenous depression and does not inquire about several atypical symptoms that are characteristic of SAD. In fact, improvement in some of the symptoms of SAD, for example weight loss, would be registered as points on the HRSD, suggesting a deterioration in function. We have thus made use of a group of supplementary symptoms (see Appendix 2), which we have found to be useful in our studies of SAD.

Table 22 shows the effects of one week phototherapy on the various symptoms of SAD. It is apparent that there is an improvement in the symptoms involving eating behavior. Of the three symptoms measured by the supplementary items to the HRSD, carbohydrate craving shows the greatest improvement (49 percent decrease), followed by weight gain (38 percent decrease) and increased appetite (11 percent decrease). This suggests that phototherapy has a specific effect on the regulation of appetite for carbohydrates that is greater than its effect on appetite in general.

Mechanism of Action of Phototherapy

The mechanism of action of phototherapy is unknown at this time. Two main theories have been proposed, neither of which satisfactorily explains the phenomenon. These two theories have been termed the melatonin hypothesis and the phase-shift hypothesis. The melatonin hypothesis, advanced by Rosenthal et al. (1985c), states that the symptoms of SAD are due to abnormal melatonin secretion or to an abnormal reaction of the brain to melatonin. According to this theory, light exerts its antidepressant effects by modifying melatonin secretion. The phase-shift hypothesis, proposed by Lewy et al. (1985) holds that the symptoms of SAD are due to abnormal circadian rhythms and that light exerts its antidepressant effects by normalizing the timing of these rhythms.

The melatonin hypothesis was based on the importance of this substance in regulating seasonal rhythms in animals (Tamarkin et al. 1985; Lincoln 1983) and on the observation that light that was bright enough to suppress melatonin secretion had significant antidepressant effects, whereas light that was too dim to suppress melatonin secretion was ineffective as an antidepressant. Rosenthal et al. (1985c) investigated the melatonin hypothesis in several ways:

1. By measuring plasma melatonin levels in SAD patients and normals in summer and winter and in SAD patients before and after effective phototherapy;
2. By administering melatonin orally to SAD patients while they were being treated with phototherapy, to which they had already

responded, to see whether this would reinduce the symptoms of SAD;

3. By administering the beta-adrenergic blocking agent atenolol, which is known to suppress nocturnal melatonin secretion, in an attempt to mimic the effects of light pharmacologically; and

4. By administering pulses of light in the early morning and late at night, thereby extending the length of the day and suppressing

Table 22. Effect of Bright Light on Mood in Seasonal Affective Disorder as Measured by 21-item HRSD and Supplementary Items ($N = 47$)

Symptoms	Baseline Mean ± SEM	Rx Mean ± SEM	t	p	% reduction
HRSD					
Depressed mood	2.20 ± .15	0.85 ± .15	−7.21	.0001	61
Guilt	1.40 ± .13	0.60 ± .12	−4.05	.0002	57
Suicide	1.00 ± .16	0.40 ± .12	−4.59	.0001	60
Early insomnia	0.85 ± .13	0.81 ± .13	−0.60	ns	5
Middle insomnia	1.20 ± .14	0.91 ± .14	7.55	.0001	24
Late insomnia	0.81 ± .14	0.57 ± .10	−1.66	ns	27
Work functioning	2.90 ± .14	1.30 ± .19	−7.03	.0001	55
Retardation	1.30 ± .10	0.64 ± .12	−4.82	.0001	51
Agitation	0.97 ± .12	1.10 ± .13	0.40	ns	−4
Anxiety psychic	2.10 ± .15	1.10 ± .15	−4.73	.0001	48
Anxiety somatic	1.40 ± .18	0.68 ± .15	−3.48	.001	51
G.I. somatic	0.72 ± .11	0.34 ± .09	−3.49	.001	53
General somatic	1.60 ± .08	1.00 ± .12	−3.96	.0003	38
Sex drive	1.30 ± .12	0.60 ± .11	−5.05	.0001	54
Hypochondriasis	0.74 ± .13	0.53 ± .13	−2.48	.02	28
Weight loss	0.47 ± .13	0.53 ± .12	0.28	ns	−13
Insight	0.00 ± .00	0.03 ± .03	1.00	ns	
Diurnal variation	1.40 ± .09	1.20 ± .12	−1.46	ns	14
Diurnal severity	1.70 ± .09	1.30 ± .11	−2.38	.02	23
Depersonalization	0.53 ± .12	0.25 ± .10	−2.00	.01	53
Paranoia	0.48 ± .10	0.21 ± .07	−2.23	.03	56
Obsessive-compulsive	0.55 ± .10	0.35 ± .09	−1.95	ns	36
Supplementary					
Increased appetite	0.81 ± .14	0.72 ± .13	−0.52	ns	11
Carbohydrate craving	1.60 ± .18	0.81 ± .16	−4.02	.0002	49
Weight gain	0.79 ± .14	0.49 ± .12	−1.71	ns	38
Hypersomnia	1.30 ± .21	0.43 ± .11	−3.78	.0005	67
Fatigue	3.10 ± .14	1.50 ± .21	−6.17	.0001	52
Social withdrawal	2.70 ± .15	1.10 ± .20	−7.63	.0001	59

Note: HRSD = Hamilton Rating Scale for Depression.

melatonin secretion, and comparing this treatment with the administration of pulses of light during the day in such a way as not to suppress melatonin secretion (Wehr et al. 1986).

For a more detailed discussion of the methodological considerations in these studies and the specific details of the findings, the interested reader is referred to Rosenthal et al. (1985c) and Wehr et al. (1986). In summary, findings of these studies were the following:

1. Seasonal affective disorder patients did not show any significant differences in plasma melatonin profiles from summer to winter or before and after light treatment. Furthermore, there were no systematic differences between patients and normal controls.
2. The administration of melatonin did not reinduce symptoms of SAD, as measured by the 21-item HRSD. However, there was a significant exacerbation of the supplementary symptoms (overeating, oversleeping, weight gain, carbohydrate craving, fatigue and social withdrawal).
3. The administration of atenolol was not statistically superior to placebo in 19 SAD patients. However, 3 of the 19 patients reported repeated and sustained responses to atenolol and relapsed when atenolol was withdrawn.
4. Pulses of light administered early and late in the day suppressed melatonin, whereas those administered towards the center of the day did not. However, both treatment conditions were equally and significantly effective as antidepressants (Wehr et al., 1986).

Thus, while there was some suggestion that melatonin secretion may play a role in the development of depressive symptoms in SAD and the modification of melatonin secretion may be involved in the effects of phototherapy, at least in certain cases it does not seem as though melatonin secretion has the same pivotal role in these processes as it does in mediation seasonal rhythms of behavior in animals (Tamarkin et al., 1985; Lincoln, 1983).

The phase-shift hypothesis was inspired by the observation of Lewy et al. that the onset of melatonin secretion during dim light is shifted later in the winter than in the summer (Lewy et al. 1985). On the basis of the animal literature on the phase-shifting capacity of light (de Coursey, 1960; Hoban and Sulzman, 1985) and the observation that bright light was necessary to suppress human melatonin (Lewy et al. 1980), Lewy et al. postulated that bright light exposure at different times of the day would shift rhythms in different directions and to different degrees. The seasonal phase changes he observed in the timing of the onset of melatonin secretion suggested to these authors that rhythms needed to be advanced in order to be returned to their summer phase position and that light, by inducing such phase advances, was capable of reversing the winter depressive symptoms. This hypothesis was supported by their observation in eight patients with SAD that two hours of light treatment in the morning was significantly more effective than two hours in the evening (Lewy et al. 1986). Further support for this hypothesis came from Terman et al. (1986), who replicated this finding.

However, there are several studies that would weigh against this hypothesis. First, there are studies that show that light treatment may be effective at other times of the day than the morning, for example, in the evening (James et al. 1985; Hellekson et al. 1986; Wehr et al. in press) or during the day (Wehr et al. 1986; Jacobsen et al. in press; Thompson et al. 1986). On the basis of results of animal studies, one would not expect that light treatments during the day would have any significant effect on the timing of circadian rhythms. Second, in our studies of sleep architecture, circadian temperature, and plasma cortisol, melatonin, and prolactin measurements, we did not find any evidence that these rhythms were phase delayed in patients with SAD, nor did we find that a combination of morning and evening phototherapy, which was effective in reversing the winter symptoms of SAD, was associated with any change in circadian phase (Rosenthal et al., unpublished observation, 1986). Thus we do not believe at this time that phase shift *per se* is responsible for the symptomatic improvement seen after phototherapy.

Since neither of these two theories provides a satisfactory explanation for the efficacy of phototherapy, we shall have to look elsewhere for the mechanism(s). We know that light probably operates by stimulating receptors in the eye (Wehr et al. in press) as opposed to working via the skin. While some effect of therapy may be felt after the first treatment, it generally takes two to four days before a stable improvement is observed. Thus light impinges on the retina, where it is converted into neural impulses, which are transmitted to the brain, probably along the retino–hypothalamic tract. This presumably causes certain chemical changes to occur in the brain, reversing the neurochemical abnormalities found in SAD and thereby reversing the symptoms of the condition. Such a theory begs the question of what these neurochemical changes may be and what neurotransmitter or neuromodulator systems may be involved.

The growing complexity of our knowledge about neurotransmitter and neuromodulatory systems makes a simple hypothesis, a one-neurotransmitter theory, seem increasingly less likely. However, certain neurotransmitter systems seem particularly promising. Of these, the serotonin system is of special interest. Deficient serotonergic transmission in the central nervous system has for some time been postulated as a potential cause of depression (Murphy et al. 1978). Carlsson et al. (1980), in a postmortem study of people who died from nonneurological, nonpsychiatric conditions, found that hypothalamic serotonin concentration decreased from fall into winter, when it reached its nadir. Finally, Wurtman et al. (1984, 1985; also see Chapter 14) have data from both animal and human studies suggesting that dietary carbohydrate increases serotonin synthesis and serotonergic transmission. Thus the carbohydrate craving seen in patients with SAD may represent a complex behavioral–biochemical feedback loop, the outcome of which is to replenish depleted brain serotonin levels (see also Chapter 10). Clearly there are many other possible neurochemical candidates apart from serotonin that may be involved in the seasonal behavior changes, a complete discussion of which is beyond the scope of this chapter.

EFFECTS OF CARBOHYDRATE ON MOOD AND BEHAVIOR

Given that patients with SAD crave carbohydrates in the winter, it is reasonable to wonder whether carbohydrates produce some positive internal state that serves to reinforce the behavior. Spring et al. (1983) have shown that carbohydrate meals appear to produce sleepiness in women and calmness in men. More recently, Lieberman et al. (1986) have shown that obese carbohydrate cravers react differently to dietary carbohydrates than do those obese subjects without carbohydrate craving. Following experimental carbohydrate-rich meals, the latter group reported increased depression, fatigue and sleepiness, whereas the carbohydrate cravers reported decreased depression and little change in fatigue and sleepiness (see also Chapter 14).

To study the effects of carbohydrates in SAD patients during the winter, we administered isocaloric high-carbohydrate and high-protein lunches to 16 SAD patients and 16 normal controls in a random-ordered crossover design (Rosenthal et al., unpublished observations, 1986). We measured plasma amino acids at regular intervals over a four-hour period and administered psychometric tests, including the Profile of Mood States (POMS), Stanford Sleepiness Scale, visual analog scales, and letter cancellation tasks. We found powerful ordering effects, and it appeared as though high levels of tension and anxiety seen just before the first treatment condition, which decreased during the study, made it difficult to detect the effects of the first meals. However, during the second treatment condition, it was possible to detect specific effects of the different foods: The normal volunteers reported increased fatigue during the first hour after ingestion of carbohydrates, whereas SAD patients reported decreased fatigue following carbohydrate intake.

This finding is compatible with that of Lieberman et al. (1986) in their population of obese carbohydrate cravers and suggests that SAD patients, who complain of reduced energy levels during the winter, may actually energize themselves with the help of carbohydrate-rich foods. This type of addiction model has also been proposed for bulimia. It has similarly been suggested that bulimics may binge in order to alleviate some dysphoric internal state (Johnson and Larson 1982; Abraham and Beaumont 1982). The emotional responses to having a binge appear to be diverse, ranging from relief from anxiety to feelings of increased guilt, shame, and anger. Kaye et al. (1986) have studied emotional changes experienced by bulimics over the course of bingeing and purging and have found that while diverse changes were reported, some patients did report relief of anxiety following either bingeing or purging.

CONCLUSION

Eating disturbances are prominent in the winter depressive phase of SAD. The increased appetite and bingeing reported by many patients resemble the symptoms of bulimia. However, most patients report carbohydrate craving, which has not been documented to be a key feature in bulimia. Furthermore, the purging behavior frequently seen in bulimics is relatively uncommon in SAD.

Seasonality of mood and behavior appears to be a dimension affecting many different people, including normal individuals and those with conditions other than SAD. It is quite possible that some bulimics have seasonal exacerbations or perhaps in some cases are only symptomatic in the fall and winter months. This question has not yet been researched but is eminently worth studying, especially since it has treatment implications.

The depressive symptoms of SAD, including those involving eating behavior, can be reversed by treatment with bright artificial light. Carbohydrate craving appears to be particularly responsive to this form of treatment. Whether phototherapy may be beneficial to a subset of patients with bulimia, presumably those with seasonal exacerbations, has yet to be tested.

The biological mechanisms underlying the seasonal changes in behavior in SAD are not as yet known. Two factors make research in this area seem particularly promising. First, winter depression symptoms can be readily reversed and allowed to recur by non-pharmacological interventions, namely exposure to or removal of bright light; and second, numerous relevant animal models of light-responsive seasonal rhythms are available for study. Given the similarities between eating disorders and affective disorders, which may represent different manifestations of a common underlying vulnerability (see Rosenthal and Heffernan 1986; Hudson and Pope 1987), it would be useful to use the insights obtained from the study of SAD for the understanding and treatment of bulimia.

REFERENCES

Abraham SF, Beaumont PJV: How patients describe bulimia or binge eating. Psychol Med 12:625-635, 1982

Attarzadeh F: Seasonal variation in stature and body weight. Int J Orthod 21(4):3-12, 1983

Carlsson A, Svennerholm L, Winblad B: Seasonal and circadian monoamine variations in human brains examined post-mortem. Acta Psychiatr Scand 61(Suppl 280):75-85, 1980

Checkley S, Winton F, Franey C, et al: Antidepressant effects of light in seasonal affective disorder. Presented at the Royal College of Psychiatry, Southampton, England, June 1986

Dark J, Zucker I: Seasonal cycles in energy balance: regulation by light, in The Medical and Biological Effects of Light. Edited by Wurtman RJ, Baum MJ, Potts JT Jr. Annals of the New York Academy of Sciences 453:170-181, 1985

de Coursey P: Daily light sensitivity in a rodent. Science 131:33-35, 1960

Gwinner E: Circannual systems, in Handbook of Behavioral Neurobiology [Volume 4]. Edited by Aschoff J. New York, Plenum Press, 1981, pp 382-389

Hamilton M: Development of a rating scale for primary depressive illness. Br J Soc Clin Psychol 6:278-296, 1967

Hellekson CJ, Kline JA, Rosenthal NE: Phototherapy for seasonal affective disorder in Alaska. Am J Psychiatry 143:1035-1037, 1986

Hoban TM, Sulzman FM: Light effects on circadian timing system of a diurnal primate, the squirrel monkey. Am J Physiol 249:R274-280, 1985

Hoffman K: Photoperiodism in vertebrates, in Handbook of Behavioral Neurobiology [Volume 4]. Edited by Aschoff J. New York, Plenum Press, 1981

Hoffman RA, Davidson K, Steinberg K: Influence of photoperiod and temperature on weight gain, food consumption, fat pads and thyroxine in male golden hamsters. Growth 46:150-162, 1982

Hudson JI, Pope HG Jr: Depression and eating disorders, in Presentations of Depression. Edited by Cameron OG. New York, Wiley, 1987

Immelman K: The role of the environment in reproduction as a source of "predictive" information, in Breeding Biology of Birds. Edited by Farner DS, Washington, DC, National Academy of Sciences, 1973

Jacobsen FM, Wehr TA, Skwerer RA, et al: Morning versus midday phototherapy of seasonal affective disorder. Am J Psychiatry, in press.

James SP, Wehr TA, Sack DA, et al: Treatment of seasonal affective disorder with light in the evening. Br J Psychiatry 147:424-428, 1985

Johnson C, Larsen R: Bulimia: an analysis of moods and behavior. Psychosom Med 44:341-350, 1982

Kaye WH, Gwirtsman HE, George T, et al: Relationship of mood alterations to bingeing behavior in bulimia. Br J Psychiatry 149:479-485, 1986

Kraepelin E: Manic-depressive illness and paranoia, in Insanity. Edited by Robertson GM, Livingstone E, Livingstone M. Translated by Barclay RM. Edinburgh, E & S Livingstone, 1921

Kripke DF: Therapeutic effects of bright light in depression, in The Medical and Biological Effects of Light. Edited by Wurtman RJ, Baum MJ, Potts JT. Annals of the New York Academy of Sciences, 453:270-281, 1985

Lewy AJ, Wehr TA, Goodwin FK, et al: Light suppresses melatonin secretion in humans. Science 210:1267-1269, 1980

Lewy AJ, Kern HA, Rosenthal NE, et al: Bright artificial light treatment of a manic-depressive patient with a seasonal mood cycle. Am J Psychiatry 139:1496-1498, 1982

Lewy AJ, Sack RL, Singer CM: Melatonin, light and chronobiological disorders, in Photoperiodism, Melatonin and the Pineal. Edited by Evered D, Clark S. London, Pitman, 1985

Lewy AJ, Sack RL: Minireview: light therapy and psychiatry. Proc Soc Exp Biol Med 183:11-18, 1986

Lewy AJ, Sack RL, Miller LS, et al: Superiority of A.M. Light in Winter Depression. Presented at the 139th Annual Meeting of the American Psychiatric Association. Washington, DC, May 1986

Lieberman HR, Wurtman JJ, Chew B: Changes in mood after carbohydrate consumption among obese individuals. Am J Clin Nutr 44:772-778, 1986

Lincoln G: Photoperiodism: melatonin as a seasonal time-cue: a commercial story. Nature 302:755, 1983

Mitchell JE, Pyle RL, Eckert ED: Frequency and duration of binge-eating episodes in patients with bulimia. Am J Psychiatry 138:835-836, 1981

Murphy DL, Campbell I, Costa JL: Current status of the inodolamine hypothesis of affective disorders, in Psychopharmacology: A Generation of Progress. Edited by DiMascio MA, Killam A. New York, Raven Press, 1978

Rosenthal NE, Sack DA, Gillin JC, et al: Seasonal affective disorder: a description of the syndrome and preliminary findings with light therapy. Arch Gen Psychiatry 41:72-80, 1984

Rosenthal NE, Sack DA, Carpenter CJ, et al: Antidepressant effects of light in seasonal affective disorder. Am J Psychiatry 142:163-170, 1985a

Rosenthal NE, Sack DA, James SP, et al: Seasonal affective disorder and phototherapy, in The Medical and Biological Effects of Light. Edited by Wurtman RJ, Baum MJ, Potts JT. Annals of the New York Academy of Sciences 453:260-269, 1985b

Rosenthal NE, Sack DA, Jacobsen FM, et al: The role of melatonin in seasonal affective disorder (SAD) and phototherapy, in Melatonin in Humans. Edited by Wurtman RJ, Waldhauser F. Cambridge, MA, Center for Brain Sciences and Metabolism Charitable Trust, 1985c

Rosenthal NE, Heffernan MM: Bulimia, carbohydrate craving and depression: a central connection? in Nutrition and Brain. Edited by Wurtman RJ, Wurtman J. New York, Raven Press, 1986

Spring BJ, Maller O, Wurtman JJ, et al: Effects of protein and carbohydrate meals on mood and performance: interactions with sex and age. Psychiatr Res 17(2):155-167, 1983

Tamarkin L, Baird CJ, Almeida OFX: Melatonin: a coordinating signal for mammalian reproduction? Science 227:714-720, 1985

Terman M, Quitkin FM, Terman JS: Light therapy for SAD: dosing regimens [NR 121]. Presented at the 139th Annual Meeting of the American Psychiatric Association, Washington, DC, 1986

Thompson C, Isaacs G, Miles A: Seasonal affective disorder, phototherapy and salivary melatonin (Abstract 136b). Proceedings of the Centennial Celebration, Psychiatrische Universitatsklinik, Basel, June 1986

Wade GN, Bartness TJ: Seasonal obesity in Syrian hamsters: effects of age, diet, photoperiod, and melatonin. Am J Physiol 16:R328-334, 1984

Wehr TA, Skwerer RJ, Jacobsen FM, et al: Eye- versus skin-phototherapy of seasonal affective disorder. Am J Psychiatry, in press

Wehr TA, Jacobsen FM, Sack DA, et al: Phototherapy in seasonal affective disorder: time of day and suppression of melatonin are not critical for antidepressant effects. Arch Gen Psychiatry 43:870-875, 1986

Wirz-Justice A, Buchelli C, Graw P, et al: Light treatment of seasonal affective disorder in Switzerland. Acta Psychiatr Scand 74:193-204, 1986a

Wirz-Justice A, Buchelli C, Graw P, et al: How much light is antidepressant? Psychiatry Res 17:75-77, 1986b

Wurtman RJ, Wurtman JJ: Nutritional control of central neurotransmitters, in The Psychobiology of Anorexia Nervosa. Edited by Pirke KM, Ploog D. Berlin, Springer-Verlag, 1984

Wurtman JJ, Wurtman RJ, Mark S, et al: d-fenfluramine selectively suppresses carbohydrate snacking by obese subjects. International Journal of Eating Disorders 4:89-99, 1985

Wurtmann JJ, O'Rouke DA, Wurtman RJ: Disorders of food intake: excessive carbohydrate intake among a class of obese people. Presented at the New York Academy of Sciences Conference on Obesity, New York, June 1986

Yerevanian BI, Anderson JL, Grota LJ, et al: Effects of bright incandescent light on seasonal and non-seasonal major depressive disorder. Psychiatry Res 18:355-364, 1986

Zifferblatt SM, Curtis CS, Pinsky JL: Understanding food habits. Am Diet Assoc 76:9-14, 1980

APPENDIX 1
Seasonal Pattern Assessment Questionnaire

■ **Seasonal Pattern Assessment Questionnaire**　　　■■　　　(SPAQ)

1. Name: _____

2. Address:
_____
_____
_____

3. Place of birth:
City & State _____
Country _____

4. TODAY'S DATE			5. AGE (in years)	6. CURRENT WEIGHT (in lbs.)
Month	Day	Yr.		
Jan				
Feb				
Mar	⓪⓪ 82		⓪⓪	⓪⓪⓪
Apr	①① 83		①①	①①①
May	②② 84		②②	②②②
Jun	③③ 85		③③	③③③
Jul	④ 86		④④	④④④
Aug	⑤ 87		⑤⑤	⑤⑤⑤
Sep	⑥ 88		⑥⑥	⑥⑥⑥
Oct	⑦ 89		⑦⑦	⑦⑦⑦
Nov	⑧ 90		⑧⑧	⑧⑧⑧
Dec	⑨ 91		⑨⑨	⑨⑨⑨

7. Years of education:

Less than 4 years
of high school............. ◯

High school only .... ◯

1–3 years post high
school.................... ◯

4 or more years
post high school .... ◯

8. Sex:

Male ◯

Female ◯

9. Marital status:

Single ◯
Married ◯
Sep./Divorced ◯
Widowed ◯

10. Occupation . . .
_____

Enter number of years →

11. How many years have you lived in this climatic area?

Example:
For one year fill in

0	1
●	⓪
①	②

The purpose of this form is to find out how your mood and behavior change over time. Please fill in all the relevant circles. Note: We are interested in <u>your</u> experience; <u>not others</u> you may have observed.

12. To what degree do the following change <u>with the seasons</u>?
(ONE CIRCLE ONLY FOR EACH QUESTION)

	NO CHANGE	SLIGHT CHANGE	MODERATE CHANGE	MARKED CHANGE	EXTREMELY MARKED CHANGE
A. Sleep length	◯	◯	◯	◯	◯
B. Social activity	◯	◯	◯	◯	◯
C. Mood (overall feeling of well being)	◯	◯	◯	◯	◯
D. Weight	◯	◯	◯	◯	◯
E. Appetite	◯	◯	◯	◯	◯
F. Energy level	◯	◯	◯	◯	◯

Be sure to fill in the questions on back of sheet

Norman E. Rosenthal, Gary H. Bradt and Thomas A. Wehr　　　NCS Trans-Optic* EB01-20707:321　　A6700

13. In the following questions, fill in circles for all applicable months. This may be a single month ●, a cluster of months, E.G., ●●●, or any other grouping.
   At what time of year do you . . .

```
                        J F M A M J J A S O N D
A. Feel best            O O O O O O O O O O O O    O
B. Tend to gain most weight  O O O O O O O O O O O O    O
C. Socialize most       O O O O O O O O O O O O    O
D. Sleep least          O O O O O O O O O O O O    O                  No particular month(s)
E. Eat most             O O O O O O O O O O O O  OR  O               stand out as extreme
F. Lose most weight     O O O O O O O O O O O O    O                  on a regular basis
G. Socialize least      O O O O O O O O O O O O    O
H. Feel worst           O O O O O O O O O O O O    O
I. Eat least            O O O O O O O O O O O O    O
J. Sleep most           O O O O O O O O O O O O    O
```

14. Using the scale below, indicate how the following weather changes make you feel. (ONE CIRCLE ONLY FOR EACH QUESTION)

   −3 = In very low spirits or markedly slowed down
   −2 = Moderately low/slowed down
   −1 = Mildly low/slowed down
    0 = No effect
   +1 = Slightly improves your mood or energy level
   +2 = Moderately improves your mood or energy level
   +3 = Markedly improves your mood or energy level

```
                        −3 −2 −1 0 +1 +2 +3    DON'T KNOW
A. Cold weather          O O O O O O O            O
B. Hot weather           O O O O O O O            O
C. Humid weather         O O O O O O O            O
D. Sunny days            O O O O O O O            O
E. Dry days              O O O O O O O    OR      O         DO NOT WRITE
F. Grey cloudy days      O O O O O O O            O
G. Long days             O O O O O O O            O         IN THIS SPACE
H. High pollen count     O O O O O O O            O
I. Foggy, smoggy days    O O O O O O O            O
J. Short days            O O O O O O O            O
```

15. By how much does your weight fluctuate during the course of the year?
   O 0–3 lbs.
   O 4–7 lbs.
   O 8–11 lbs.
   O 12–15 lbs.
   O 16–20 lbs.
   O Over 20 lbs.

16. Approximately how many hours of each 24-hour day do you sleep during each season? (Include naps)

```
                                    Hours slept per day                        OVER 18 HOURS
WINTER (Dec 21–Mar 20)   0 1 2 3 4 5 6 7 8 9 10 11 12 13 14 15 16 17 18 .         O
SPRING (Mar 21–June 20)  0 1 2 3 4 5 6 7 8 9 10 11 12 13 14 15 16 17 18           O
SUMMER (June 21–Sept 20) 0 1 2 3 4 5 6 7 8 9 10 11 12 13 14 15 16 17 18           O
FALL (Sept 21–Dec 20)    0 1 2 3 4 5 6 7 8 9 10 11 12 13 14 15 16 17 18           O
```

17. Do you notice a change in food preference during the different seasons? .... O No   O Yes →

   Please specify:
   _____

18. If you experience changes with the seasons, do you feel that these are a problem for you? .... O No   O Yes

```
                                    MILD   MODERATE   MARKED   SEVERE   DISABLING
If yes, is this problem .............. O       O          O        O          O
```

Thank you for completing this questionnaire.

APPENDIX 2

Supplementary Items to Hamilton Depression Rating Scale

1. Fatigability (or low energy level, or feelings of being heavy, leaden, weighted down)

   0 = Does not feel more fatigued than usual
   1 = Feels more fatigued than usual but this has not impaired function significantly; less frequent than in (2)
   2 = More fatigued than usual; 1 hr/day, 3 day/week
   3 = Fatigued much of the time most days
   4 = Fatigued almost all the time

2. Social Withdrawal

   0 = Interacts with other people as usual
   1 = Less interested in socializing with others but continues to do so.
   2 = Interacting less with other people in social (optional) situations
   3 = Interacting less with other people in work or family situations (i.e. where this is necessary)

3. Appetite Increase

   0 = No increase in appetite
   1 = Wants to eat a little more than usual
   2 = Wants to eat somewhat more than usual
   3 = Wants to each much more than usual

4. Increased Eating

   0 = Is not eating more than usual
   1 = Is eating a little more than usual
   2 = Is eating somewhat more than usual
   3 = Is eating much more than normal

5. Carbohydrate Craving (in relation to total amount of food desired or eaten)

   0 = No change in food preference
   1 = Eating somewhat more carbohydrates (starches and sugars) than usual
   2 = Eating much more carbohydrates than usual
   3 = Irresistible cravings for carbohydrates

6. Weight Gain

   0 = No weight gain
   1 = Probable weight gain associated with present illness
   2 = Definite weight gain (according to patient)

7. Hypersomnia (use euthymic sleep length for comparison)

   0 = No increase in sleep length
   1 = At least 1 hr increase in sleep length
   2 = 2 + hrs increase　　"
   3 = 3 + hrs increase　　"
   4 = 4 + hrs increase　　"

Chapter 14

Carbohydrate Craving: A Disorder of Food Intake and Mood

Judith J. Wurtman, Ph.D.

Chapter 14

Carbohydrate Craving: A Disorder of Food Intake and Mood

U ntil recently, it has been assumed that the excessive amounts of calories ingested by obese individuals were caused by their inability to adjust their calorie intake to meet, but not exceed, their energy needs. Their overeating was characterized as chronic, in that every time these individuals ate, they ate too much for their energy needs, or sporadic, possibly in response to environmental cues such as an overabundance of food (for example, buffets, cruises), or proximity of easily accessible foods (for example, ice cream or cookie shops). Or, they were simply characterized as reluctant to limit their calorie intake to their energy needs when the food available was particularly desirable (for example, at gourmet restaurants).

In any event, such individuals were regarded as overeating indiscriminately, and their inability or unwillingness to limit calorie intake was thought to be the fault of some yet unidentified mechanism regulating energy balance. Following these assumptions was the belief that teaching such people about the caloric value of food and how to select foods to meet nutritional needs but not to exceed caloric requirements would produce successful weight loss and maintenance of a medically optimal weight. The failure of most weight loss programs to achieve these objectives indicates that the problem is more complex than the appropriate selection of calorically correct foods and use of will power.

This relatively simple and uninformed view of the etiology of obesity has been held because few studies have actually examined in quantitative ways the patterns of food intake among the obese when their weight is steady and, especially, when they are actually gaining weight. Although food records have been used to describe the caloric intake of the obese, they rarely represent typical food intake patterns, since food consumption often improves while records of it are being kept and snack consumption is usually underestimated, underreported, or temporarily eliminated while the food records are being kept. (Indeed, the dietician at our Clinical Research Center at the Massachusetts Institute of Technology asked obese subjects to keep food records for three days and then checked their last day's food record by asking them the following day to recall what they had consumed on the previous day. They tended to underreport their calorie intake by as much as 600 to 800 calories when their verbal recall was checked against their food records.)

We have developed a method of monitoring 24-hour patterns of calorie, protein, and carbohydrate consumption from both meals and snacks among obese individuals during a period of weight stability and among both normal and obese subjects during periods of rapid weight gain. We have found from such studies that a subgroup of obese individuals whose weight is excessive but stable consumes moderate amounts of calories from meals. In fact, their mealtime food intake is insufficient to sustain their weight. However, their total daily calorie intake is augmented by their snack intake: They consume an additional 800 calories or more each day in the form of carbohydrate-rich, protein-poor snack foods. Such snack intake is not random but occurs at a time of day, usually in the afternoon or evening, that is specific for each person. Moreover, the consumption of these snack foods is associated not with the desire to relieve hunger but with the desire to produce positive changes in mood (Wurtman 1984; Wurtman et al. 1981, 1985; Lieberman et al. 1986).

A similar pattern of excessive carbohydrate intake has also been observed among individuals who undergo an annual period of rapid weight gain. Their overeating occurs in association with a depression whose onset is triggered by the short days and long nights of the fall and early winter and relieved by the longer days of spring and summer (Rosenthal et al. 1984; also see Chapter 13). People suffering from this depression, which has been called seasonal affective disorder, are characterized not only by changes in mood, sleep, and energy levels, but also by an intense desire to consume large amounts of carbohydrate-rich foods. We have monitored the patterns of food intake among such individuals while they were depressed and subsequently when they were in remission (O'Rourke et al. 1986). These individuals exhibited a significant increase in carbohydrate intake both from meals and from snacks during the fall and winter, when they were depressed, and a similarly significant reduction in such food intake during the spring, when their mood and energy levels had returned to normal. These subjects, as with the carbohydrate snackers, report positive mood changes following the consumption of carbohydrate-rich foods.

It appears, therefore, that many individuals who are either obese or rapidly gaining weight choose to eat excessive amounts of carbohydrate-rich foods as a means of "self-medication," that is, to bring about desirable changes in their mood. For this subgroup of obese individuals, the etiology of their excess weight is not simply an inability to regulate calorie intake but a disorder in the regulation of carbohydrate consumption that appears linked to a possible disorder in mood regulation.

Our interest in regulation of carbohydrate consumption and whether such regulation was aberrant in certain types of eating disturbances was generated by observations made several years ago that carbohydrate intake is regulated independently of calorie intake (Wurtman and Wurtman 1977). The synthesis and activity of the brain neurotransmitter serotonin were thought to be enhanced following the consumption of a calorie-rich, protein-poor meal because of the increased uptake into the brain of serotonin's precursor, tryptophan. Conversely, the consumption of protein or a combination of proteins and carbohydrates prevented this increase in serotonin synthesis, since the amino acids that normally competed with tryptophan for uptake into the brain were increased following protein consumption.

Since carbohydrate consumption was so directly related to serotonin synthesis, we became interested in whether brain serotonin was involved in regulating the consumption of carbohydrate intake. We carried out a series of animal experiments that demonstrated a separate regulation for energy intake and carbohydrate intake: When animals were treated with drugs that increased serotonergic neurotransmission, they decreased their intake only of high-carbohydrate foods (Wurtman and Wurtman 1980). Moreover, when animals were given a meal sufficiently high in carbohydrate to increase serotonin synthesis, they consumed, in a subsequent meal, significantly more protein and less carbohydrate than did animals prefed a meal containing both protein and carbohydrate (Wurtman et al. 1983).

We followed these animal studies with a series of clinical investigations to determine whether an appetite for carbohydrates in people could also be demonstrated and whether such an appetite was also controlled in part by brain serotonin. Since serotonin's synthesis and release are affected when carbohydrate-rich, protein-poor foods are eaten but are unchanged when protein is consumed alone or along with carbohydrate, we monitored the eating patterns among normal and obese individuals to see whether their patterns of food intake were such as to result in increased serotonin synthesis and release. Did these individuals ever consume carbohydrate-rich foods without protein?

Since in our culture, the opportunity for selection and consumption of carbohydrate-rich foods occurs most frequently as snack rather than meal intake, we developed methods for monitoring food intake that occurred between or after meals. In a pilot study carried out on an outpatient basis with normal volunteers who claimed to have a tendency to snack, we found that more than 60 percent of their snack choices consisted of carbohydrate-rich foods; indeed, most of the volunteers consumed only carbohydrate-rich foods as snacks (Wurtman and Wurtman 1981).

To see if serotonin was involved in regulating the intake of these largely carbohydrate foods, we treated the subjects with d,l-fenfluramine, a drug known to increase serotoninergic neurotransmission (Wurtman and Wurtman 1981). The drug reduced significantly subjects' intake of carbohydrate snack foods compared with their intake of these foods while on placebo. Since our observations suggested that brain serotonin might be linked with the appetite for carbohydrate-rich foods in people as well as animals, we were interested in whether a possible abnormal regulation of carbohydrate intake by serotonin might be involved in the excessive carbohydrate intake reported by many obese individuals. To this end, we carried out a series of inpatient studies designed to monitor patterns of food intake among obese individuals, focusing initially on obese individuals who claimed to have an excessive appetite for carbohydrate-rich snack foods.

One of our objectives in this study was to learn whether the appetite for and consumption of carbohydrate snack foods claimed by many obese individuals was indeed related to abnormal regulation of carbohydrate intake by serotonin or, as widely assumed, was simply because carbohydrate-rich snack foods are abundant in our culture. To distinguish between these two possibilities, we developed a method of dispensing snacks that made protein-rich and carbohydrate-rich foods equally accessible any time our subjects wished to snack. A refrigerated vending machine located in a private area of our Clinical Research Center, where the studies were carried out, was stocked with 10 snack foods. All contained the same number of calories— an important consideration since many obese people attempt to avoid consuming too many calories when they *first* give into the desire to snack. Five of the snack foods in the machine were high in carbohydrate, and five were high in protein. All the snacks contained the same amount of fat; thus, the basis of snack choice was neither their calorie or fat contents.

Subjects gained access to the vending machine by typing their personal code onto a keypad attached to the door. The vending machine interfaced with a microcomputer that recorded the identity of the subject, the time a snack was removed from the vending machine, and the type of snack taken. In the first of these studies, subjects did not have a choice of meal foods but had instead to consume a study diet that met their daily nutrient needs and contained about 1000 calories. In subsequent studies, subjects were able to choose the foods they preferred for meals as well as for snacks. However, the snack choices exhibited in all three studies were similar; thus, choice of foods at meals had no effect on choice of snacks (Wurtman 1984; Wurtman et al. 1985, in press).

We found in all three studies that despite the similar accessibility of both protein snacks and carbohydrate snacks, few protein snacks were consumed on a regular basis. Subjects consumed on average five carbohydrate snacks a day in the first study and seven carbohydrate snacks a day in the second and third studies. (This difference was probably due to the slightly lower carbohydrate and calorie contents of the snacks offered in the subsequent studies.) In none of these studies was protein snack intake notable. Subjects tended to eat fewer than one protein snack a day (mean = 0.9), and the majority of subjects never consumed any protein snacks (Wurtman 1984; Wurtman et al. 1981, 1985, in press). What was also of interest was the pattern of snack intake exhibited by the subjects. Although the group as a whole tended to snack in the afternoon and evening, each individual was most likely to snack at only one of those times. Thus, snacking did not occur randomly but seemed to be somehow programmed into a pattern of eating that characterized each individual.

We found evidence of serotonin involvement in this need for and consumption of carbohydrate-rich foods. In the first inpatient study, obese subjects who were treated with d,l-fenfluramine decreased their carbohydrate snack intake by 40 percent as compared with placebo-treated individuals. In two subsequent studies, obese subjects were treated with d-Fenfluramine, and we observed similar effects on carbohydrate snack intake, that is a reduction by 40 to 41 percent (Wurtman 1984; Wurtman et al. 1985, in press).

We also extended our observations to measurements of both calorie and nutrient choice from meals. We wanted to determine whether the excessive appetite for carbohydrate-rich foods was confined to snacks or might also be demonstrated in the nutrient choices made at meals. In two separate studies, subjects were allowed to choose their meal foods from a variety of isocaloric items that were either high in carbohydrate (rice, mashed potatoes, muffins) or high in protein (seafood salad, baked chicken, cottage cheese). We found in both studies that the calorie intake from meals was moderate (about 2000 calories), as was consumption of both protein and carbohydrate foods from meals. d-Fenfluramine treatment had less of an effect on meal intake than it did on snack intake. In contrast to the 40 percent decrease in carbohydrate snack consumption, carbohydrate intake from meals was decreased by 22 percent, and protein intake was not decreased in the first study and was decreased by about 14 to 16 percent in the second.

These results suggest that this subgroup of obese individuals, whom we termed "carbohydrate cravers," tended to consume excessive amounts of carbohydrate-rich foods alone, without protein, at times of day or evening specific for each individual and that such over-consumption of carbohydrate might involve an abnormal regulation of carbohydrate intake by the brain neurotransmitter serotonin. The amelioration of this excessive carbohydrate appetite by d-Fenfluramine also suggested that the drug might be mimicking the effect of carbohydrate intake itself on brain serotonin, that is, increasing its activity and thus eliminating the appetite for these foods.

Anecdotal reports from our subjects on their mood changes prior to and following their carbohydrate snacking led us to investigate whether such snacking behavior might be associated with serotonin-mediated mood changes that might be produced following the ingestion of carbohydrates. Serotonin has been implicated in a variety of mood states, including feelings of calmness, lethargy, sleepiness, and decrease in pain perception (Young 1986). Many antidepressants work by enhancing serotonin neurotransmitter activity (van Praag and Lemus 1986). Thus it was possible that the carbohydrate cravers were consuming large amounts of carbohydrate at specific times of day or evening to bring about specific mood changes.

To see whether the carbohydrate cravers experienced any changes in serotonin-mediated mood states after consumption of carbohydrate, we gave them a high-carbohydrate meal (104 g of CHO) and measured their moods immediately prior to the meal and two hours after its completion with standardized mood surveys. Their responses were compared with those of another subgroup of obese subjects who also tended to consume an excessive number of their daily calories as snack foods (Lieberman et al. 1986), but whose snack choices almost always included protein as well as carbohydrate foods. (Such snack choices would prevent changes in serotonin synthesis and release and presumably any changes in serotonin-mediated mood states.) We found significant differences in the mood responses of those two groups of obese snackers. The carbohydrate cravers felt more vigorous, alert, less tired, and less depressed after the carbohydrate meal than did the subjects who did not desire solely carbohydrates. This remarkable difference in moods seen after carbohydrate intake among these two groups of obese snackers suggested that preference for or avoidance of specific snack foods might be associated with subsequent mood states. The overeating of carbohydrate among the carbohydrate cravers was thus not simply the result of an abnormal regulation of energy intake. Rather, the disorder in food intake seemed closely linked to a possible abnormal regulation of mood. These individuals were overeating carbohydrate as a way of altering their mood, and because the foods they ate contributed too many calories to their total daily intake, they gained and then sustained excess weight.

Some of the most compelling evidence that weight gain might be associated with serotonin-mediated mood disorders has been provided recently by the studies on seasonal affective disorder (see Chapter 13). We measured patterns of calorie and nutrient intakes among individuals suffering from seasonal affective disorder during the fall and the following spring and treated such individuals with d-fenfluramine to see whether it would have an effect on both the mood and eating disorders associated with this depression. Calorie and carbohydrate intakes from meals and snacks were significantly lower in the spring when the subjects were in remission than in the fall when they were depressed (O'Rourke et al. 1986). The most marked change was seen with snack intake. Over 1000 calories a day were consumed as carbohydrate-rich snacks during the fall measurement period and this decreased to less than 500 calories during the spring measurement period.

We were interested in whether the excessive intake of carbohydrate that characterized these subjects might involve, as with our obese carbohydrate cravers, serotonin. In a pilot study (O'Rourke et al. 1986) we treated a small number of subjects with d-fenfluramine and measured changes in food intake and mood. Drug treatment reduced food intake to levels observed in the spring when eating was normal among six out of the eight subjects treated; five of these subjects also experienced a total remission of their depression.

These results indicate that the recurring weight gain seen among individuals suffering from seasonal affective disorder might also involve serotonin. Moreover, the on–off nature of this disorder of food intake indicates that their overeating and weight gain is not due to an inability to regulate energy intake, inability to control overeating when faced with environmental temptations, or lack of information about the caloric value of foods. The close association between depression, overeating, and weight gain in the fall and winter, and normal mood, reduced food intake, and weight loss in the spring and summer certainly suggests that a disorder in the regulation of mood might underlie disorders in the regulation of food intake. It is anticipated that more such studies will eventually result in both dietary and pharmacological therapies that affect both disorders. Moreover, if these disorders of mood and associated overeating occur on a predictable basis, such as in seasonal affective disorder, such treatments may have to be used yearly in order to prevent weight gain and to sustain the weight loss that occurred during the previous seasons.

REFERENCES

Lieberman H, Wurtman J, Chew B: Changes in mood after carbohydrate consumption among obese individuals. Am J Clin Nutr 45:772-778, 1986

O'Rourke D, Wurtman J, Abou-Nader T, et al: Treatment of Seasonal Affective Disorder With d-Fenfluramine. Presented at the Conference on Human Obesity, American Academy of Science, New York, June 1986

Rosenthal N, Sack D, Gillin, J, et al: Seasonal affective disorder: a description of the syndrome and preliminary findings with light therapy. Arch Gen Psychiatry 41:72-80, 1984

van Praag HM, Lemus C: Monoamine precursors in the treatment of psychiatric disorders, in Nutrition and the Brain (Volume 7). Edited by Wurtman R, Wurtman J, New York, Raven Press, 1986

Wurtman J: The involvement of brain serotonin in excessive carbohydrate snacking by obese carbohydrate cravers. J Amer Diet Assoc 84:1004-1007, 1984

Wurtman J, Wurtman R: Fenfluramine and fluoxetine spare protein consumption while suppressing calorie intake by rats. Science 198:1178-1180, 1977

Wurtman J, Wurtman R: Drugs that enhance central serotoninergic transmission diminish elective carbohydrate consumption by rats. Life Sci 24:823-826, 1980

Wurtman J, Wurtman R: Suppression of carbohydrate intake from snacks and meals by d-fenfluramine in tryptophan, in Anorectic Drugs: Mechanisms of Action and Tolerance. Edited by Garrattini S. New York, Raven Press, 1981

Wurtman J, Wurtman R, Growdon J, et al: Carbohydrate craving in obese people: suppression by treatments affecting serotoninergic transmission. International Journal of Eating Disorders 1:2-11, 1981

Wurtman J, Moses P, Wurtman R: Prior carbohydrate consumption affects the amount of carbohydrate rats choose to eat. J Nutr 113:70-78, 1983

Wurtman J, Wurtman R, Mark S, et al: d-Fenfluramine selectively suppresses carbohydrate snacking by obese subjects. International Journal of Eating Disorders 4:89-99, 1985

Wurtman J, Wurtman R, Reynolds S, et al: d-Fenfluramine suppresses snack intake among carbohydrate cravers but not among noncarbohydrate cravers. International Journal of Eating Disorders, in press

Young SN: Psychopharmacology of tryptophan, in Nutrition and the Brain (Volume 7). Edited by Wurtman R, Wurtman J. New York, Raven Press, 1986

Commentary

Neurobiological Research in Bulimia

Michael H. Ebert, M.D.

Commentary

Neurobiological Research in Bulimia

There has been a tremendous increase in research on the eating disorders anorexia nervosa and bulimia in the past 10 years. Much of this research has explored neurobiological hypotheses about eating disorders or neurobiological mechanisms involved in the chronic phase of anorexia nervosa or bulimia. This volume surveys a variety of studies in progress on bulimia. These investigations on eating disorders have followed a similar pattern to biological research on affective disorders and schizophrenia. Neuroendocrine studies, neurotransmitter function and metabolism, electroencephalographic (EEG) sleep, and neuroendocrine challenge studies have all played a prominent role, and are documented in this volume. It is fair to say that these initial neurobiological studies of bulimia are at a survey stage or a descriptive stage, and that few unifying hypotheses of the disorder are driving research design.

Diagnostic considerations are of strategic importance in designing research studies on the mechanisms and etiology of bulimia. The diagnosis of anorexia nervosa and bulimia are primarily phenomenological diagnoses—setting objective criteria for the abnormal patterns of eating behavior and associated cognitive mood changes. However, we know that there are major linkages between eating disorders and other major psychiatric syndromes, such as affective disorders and alcoholism. Is the current diagnostic scheme, as defined in the *Diagnostic and Statistical Manual of Mental Disorders (Third Edition) (DSM-III*; American Psychiatric Association 1980), the best approach for clinical research on anorexia nervosa and bulimia? Is bulimia an addictive disorder? Do individuals with bulimia who also have an addiction to alcohol or other drugs suffer from a syndrome distinct and different from that of other bulimic patients? Patients with extreme forms of anorexia nervosa and bulimia have changes in thought processes that essentially constitute monosymptomatic delusions. Do these patients belong in the same diagnostic category as less severely ill patients? Do they have neurobiological changes characteristic of other psychoses?

Two papers in this monograph focus on the diagnostic interface issues in bulimia: Dr. Norman Rosenthal and his colleagues discuss the relevance of seasonal affective disorder (SAD) to bulimia, and Dr. Steven Roose and his associates investigate the relationship between pharmacological markers of anxiety disorders to bulimia. Eating disturbances, particularly carbohydrate craving, are prominent in the winter depressive phase of the recently described SAD. However, purging behavior is uncommon in the winter depressive phase. Carbohydrate craving, when seen in association with the depressive symptoms of SAD, is quite responsive to phototherapy. Dr. Rosenthal and his colleagues propose that seasonal changes in mood and behavior should be studied prospectively in bulimia. This is one of a number of recent observations documenting the broad interconnections between affective disorders and eating disorders.

Dr. Roose and his colleagues used the strategy of lactate infusion and yohimbine administration to identify individuals who are susceptible to panic attacks. In comparison to a group of panic disorder patients and normal controls, a group of bulimic patients did not show a significant response to lactate or yohimbine with regard to panic attacks. However, the bulimic patients were more emotionally reactive than were normals during lactate infusion. Anxiety symptoms are prominent in many bulimic patients, but bulimic patients are not similar to panic disorder patients with regard to their response to pharmacological challenge.

Electroencephalographic sleep was an early and useful physiological strategy to investigate neurobiological mechanisms in affective disorders. The study by Dr. James Hudson and his associates, which they describe in Chapter 12, was an application of this strategy to bulimia. About half of the sample of patients in their study met DSM-III diagnostic criteria for major depression. The study is remarkable for finding no disruption of sleep continuity, sleep architecture, or rapid eye movement (REM) measures. None of the studies of sleep physiology of anorexia nervosa or bulimia to date have shown distinctive changes characteristic of these disorders. However, two studies have shown that EEG sleep may offer one way of differentiating patients with anorexia nervosa who have major depression from those who do not. Of particular interest is the study of Sitaram et al. (1981), in which use of the arecoline REM induction test showed cholinergic sensitivity to correlate to the presence of either symptoms of affective disorder or to family history of major affective disorder. In addition, Katz et al. (1984) found that shortened REM latency and higher urinary free cortisol levels were associated with with increased levels of depressive symptoms in anorexia patients. Some of the most fascinating hypotheses regarding the strongly reinforcing behaviors of bulimia and the addictive quality of the disorder involve various brain neurotransmitter systems. Of particular interest to investigators in this area are the neurotransmitter systems that regulate feeding and appetitive behavior in animals, that are putatively involved in the neurobiology of affective disorders, and that play a role in the mechanism of action of antidepressant and addictive drugs.

Dr. James Mitchell and Dr. John Morley offer a sophisticated review of the role of endogenous opioid peptides in the regulation of feeding behavior in Chapter 6. They describe two peptide systems linked to feeding control: a peripheral satiety system, illustrated by cholecystokinin, and a central system, illustrated by the opioid peptides and neuropeptide Y. They conclude from a review of clinical trials on the use of opiate antagonists to induce weight loss in obese individuals that naltrexone does not appear to be an effective agent. However, they note that the kappa opioid receptor plays an important role in the stimulation of appetite and that more specific kappa antagonists have not been available for clinical trials. They present data from a pilot study of naloxone in bulimia in which reduction in frequency of binges and purging was noted.

Experience in an open therapeutic trial of naltrexone in 25 individuals with normal weight bulimia is reported by Dr. Jeffrey Jonas and Dr. Mark Gold. Naltrexone produced significant reductions in bingeing, purging, and duration of binge episodes. In both Chapters 6 and 7 are warnings of the potential hepatotoxicity of high doses of naltrexone, although liver function abnormalities were not observed in the study by Drs. Jonas and Gold. It is clear from these two chapters that double-blind placebo-controlled studies of opiate antagonist drugs should be conducted in bulimia. Clinical trials of specific kappa antagonists would also be of great interest.

In Chapter 9, Dr. David Jimerson and his colleagues present evidence of altered noradrenergic function and sympathetic nervous system function in bulimic patients who are in a behavioral treatment program and who have been abstinent from bingeing and vomiting for several weeks. Bulimic patients had significantly reduced resting pulse, systolic blood pressure, body temperature, and plasma norepinephrine. In response to increasing doses of isoproterenol, bulimic patients showed increased sensitivity to the chronotropic effects and had higher ratings of anxiety compared with normal controls. Isoproterenol-induced release of free fatty acids was similar in patient and control groups. Several of these findings suggest up-regulation of beta-adrenoreceptors as a compensatory response to decreased presynaptic release of norepinephrine. The authors note recent evidence that resting metabolic rate is decreased in normal weight bulimia. Decreased presynaptic activity of the sympathetic nervous system, perhaps in combination with changes in the thyroid axis, may contribute to a decreased metabolic rate in bulimic patients, leading to a vicious cycle of increasingly extreme attempts to lose weight.

In Chapter 10, by Dr. Walter Kaye and a related research group, data are presented on changes in brain serotonin metabolism in bulimia. Accumulation of cerebrospinal fluid 5-hydroxyindoleacetic acid after probenecid administration is lower in patients with anorexia nervosa who have bulimic symptoms than in those who do not. Intravenous infusion of L-tryptophan (a serotonin precursor) or m-chlorophenylpiperazine (a serotonin postsynaptic receptor agonist), both produce a blunted prolactin response compared with that of normal subjects, suggesting a hyposerotonergic state. The data suggest that individuals who binge regularly may produce a hyposerotonergic state in the central nervous system that may affect satiety, appetite regulation, and perhaps metabolic efficiency.

Dr. Judith Wurtman in Chapter 14 presents an elegant combination of the behavioral pharmacology in humans with the basic neurochemistry of appetite regulation. Her clinical research stems from basic animal studies that demonstrate the regulatory effect of brain serotonin systems on carbohydrate intake. In clinical studies of subjects who have a tendency to snack, d,l-fenfluramine significantly reduced the intake of carbohydrate snack foods. In inpatient obese subjects, fenfluramine had a similar effect. Mood ratings of the carbohydrate-craving obese subjects indicated elevated mood following carbohydrate snacks. Dr. Wurtman hypothesizes that choice of high-carbohydrate foods may be related to mood state and may be mediated by brain serotonin systems.

Taken together, these studies involving neurotransmitter physiology and function suggest a series of neurobiological mechanisms that may come into play in chronic eating disorders—mechanisms that may be induced by the initial aberrations in eating behavior. Serotonin and the regulation of carbohydrate intake, norepinephrine and the tone of the sympathetic nervous system, and endogenous opioid systems all have a high probability of being involved. We still lack a unifying hypothesis that interrelates these systems in eating disorders. The past decade of work on the neurochemistry of appetite regulation and feeding behavior in animals demonstrates complex and redundant regulatory mechanisms, with multiple feedback loops.

Thus we should not be discouraged that a unifying hypothesis of the neurochemistry of human eating disorders does not exist at this point.

Neuroendocrine studies have been applied widely in psychiatric research, particularly in affective disorders, as a "window" into brain function. It is logical to apply these techniques in eating disorders, particularly since neuroendocrine abnormalities are some of the core findings in severe anorexia nervosa with cachexia. However, if neuroendocrine strategies are a window into neural mechanisms of bulimia, it is an opaque window at this time.

Dr. B. Timothy Walsh and his colleagues present data in Chapter 1 on periodic sampling of plasma cortisol over 24 hours in normal weight bulimia. Unlike patients with anorexia nervosa, who have elevated plasma cortisol levels at virtually all times during the 24-hour period, patients with bulimia have a 24-hour pattern of cortisol secretion that is identical to that of normal controls. The investigators have offered an explanation for the high incidence of abnormal dexamethasone suppression tests in bulimia by demonstrating that dexamethasone levels are frequently low in these patients and predictably the dexamethasone levels correlate with degree of suppression of plasma cortisol.

A careful review of existing studies on thyroid function in bulimia is presented by Dr. Allan Kaplan in Chapter 4, and he adds survey data of his own on thyroid function tests in 40 bulimic patients. He concludes that there are no characteristic abnormalities seen in thyroid function tests in bulimia. Bulimic patients demonstrate a blunted response of thyroid-stimulating hormone to thyrotropin-releasing hormone at a rate below that seen in depressed patients but above the rate seen in normal controls.

Dr. Paul Copeland and Dr. David Herzog review the incidence and possible etiology of amenorrhea in normal weight bulimia in Chapter 3. Reported to occur in 40 to 95 percent of these patients, this amenorrhea is likely to be caused by disruptions in secretion of gonadotropin-releasing hormone from the hypothalamus, which in turn may be affected by episodic starvation, weight fluctuations, excessive exercise, stress, and depression. The various possible neuroendocrine mediators of decreased gonadotropin-releasing hormone are reviewed.

The chapter on the hypothalamic–pituitary–ovarian axis by Dr. Karl Pirke and his associates elucidates the mechanisms of amenorrhea in bulimia. Some of the patients they studied had a grossly defective luteal phase. When the menstrual cycle was evaluated by endocrine parameters, only 1 out of 15 bulimic patients had a normal cycle.

Dr. Pirke and his colleagues demonstrate by serial sampling of plasma gonadal hormones that the average 12-hour follicle-stimulating hormone (FSH) values are significantly lower in bulimic patients than controls—even though the frequencies of FSH and luteinizing hormone peaks were unaltered. In contrast to Dr. Kaplan's findings, Dr. Pirke's group observed low triiodothyronine values in about half of these patients, and these low values correlated with decreased FSH values. In a separate study, Dr. Pirke's group has shown that short-term dieting in normal women also produces disturbed gonadal hormone secretion in about half of the individuals. The study offers strong evidence for the profound effect of intermittent starvation and dieting on menstrual function in bulimic patients who maintain normal weight.

The phasic secretion of melatonin has been a useful means of studying circadian rhythm disturbances in affective disorders, and indirectly studying alpha-2 and beta-1 adrenoreceptor function. A carefully controlled group of 12 bulimic patients studied by Dr. Sidney Kennedy and his associates and reported in Chapter 5 did not show significant differences in melatonin levels or an earlier peak in secretion compatible with phase advance. Thus, bulimic patients are not similar to patients with affective disorders who show evidence of disrupted circadian rhythms.

Taken as a whole, the studies described in this monograph indicate the movement of psychiatric research into the mainstream of biomedical research. Although a unifying hypothesis of the neurobiology and psychobiology of bulimia is not yet agreed upon or even clearly formulated, an impressive amount of useful phenomenological research is underway that will lead to more coherent hypotheses in the near future. Some of the most promising lines of investigation involve primary or secondary adaptive changes in several neurotransmitter systems (noradrenergic, serotonergic, opioid) that are putatively involved in affective state, appetite regulation, food consumption, and neuroendocrine function. If these investigations proceed in a hypothesis-generating manner, in tandem with sophisticated psychological methods, it may be possible to elucidate the etiology and pathophysiology of this major psychosomatic disorder.

REFERENCES

American Psychiatric Association: Diagnostic and Statistical Manual of Mental Disorders (Third Edition). Washington, DC, American Psychiatric Association, 1980

Katz JL, Kuperberg A, Pollack CP, et al: Is there a relationship between eating disorder and affective disorder? New evidence from sleep recordings. Am J Psychiatry 141:753-758, 1984

Sitaram N, Kaye WH, Nurnberger JL, et al: Cholinergic REM sleep induction—a trait marker of affective illness, in Biological Markers in Psychiatry and Neurology. Edited by Hanin I, Usdin E. New York, Pergamon Press, 1981